COOKING
The New Way to Success

Published 1985 by
Hamlyn Publishing,
a division of The Hamlyn Publishing Group Ltd,
Bridge House, London Road, Twickenham, Middlesex, England

This edition published by The Leisure Circle Limited
under license from the Hamlyn Publishing Group Limited

Printed and bound in West Germany by
Mohndruck Graphische Betriebe GmbH,
Gütersloh

Arnold Zabert

COOKING
The New Way to Success

The basic principle
of fine cooking
is simplicity.

Johann George Hesekiel, 1872

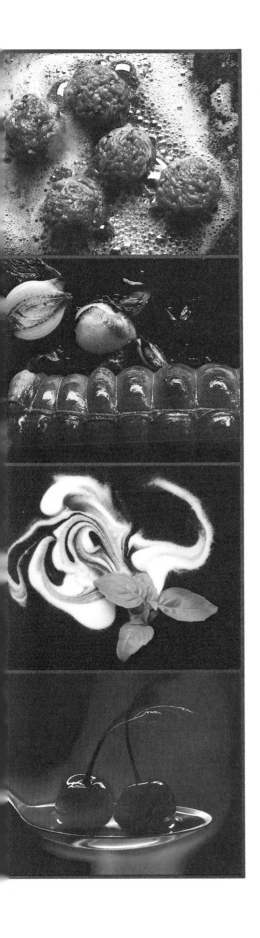

Contents

Where this book will lead you

A great revolution has taken place in cooking in recent years. It has come upon us so unobtrusively that many are only now becoming aware of it. We have adopted radically new attitudes to food and drink. Increasing affluence, foreign travel, a new awareness of our bodies with a concern for fitness and slimming, a zest for life – all have contributed to a new school of cooking.

The 'nouvelle cuisine' much-prized by gourmets may seem avant-garde, but we have long since adopted its basic principles of fresh foods, quickly cooked and attractively served. Growing supermarket sales of wine, refined frozen foods and exotic fruit together with the growing popularity of hamburgers, crepes, pizzas and other 'fast foods', all point to a change in tastes. But there is one more aspect to be considered. What has long formed part of the French and Italian culture, namely cooking for guests and dining with friends, is probably the main improvement to the quality of life that this gentle revolution has brought with it.

A new style of cooking calls for a new cook book. What was right and fitting for our mothers and grandmothers, today seems old-fashioned. *Cooking – the new way to success* is intended as a handbook for a new generation of housewives, cooking enthusiasts, hostesses, single people and gourmets.

Why this book was written

Any 'new' cookery book worthy of its name must start at the beginning. It should encourage beginners, interest experienced cooks and convert the followers of old-style cooking.

This is our new concept – an illustrated book with over a thousand new colour photographs which is also a precise text book with ideas for over two thousand new recipes. The aim is to help you learn to cook systematically but enjoyably.

This is our new teaching method – each chapter, from soups to desserts, begins with a basic recipe. From this we build up in gradual stages. Every important process is illustrated by photographs, every variation is explained. And best of all, you are cooking at each stage! That is systematic cooking. Here is also our building-block technique – within each chapter you can introduce recipes from other sections, giving thousands of different dishes. This is creative cookery.

In addition there are tips on shopping, hints on preparation, advice on drinks and table settings. You will be advised on how to equip a new kitchen. You will learn all you need to know about cooking techniques and how to compile a menu (see pages 50–61). Nevertheless our aim is not to cram you with information but to awaken your appetite to one of the world's greatest pleasures.

Buying:
the first stage
made easy

Compared to fifty, or even ten, years ago the modern shopper has a vast selection of foods to choose from. Not only are there markets and supermarkets, there are also specialist shops selling cheeses or wholefoods, or delicatessens with a wide range of esoteric goods. To our great-grandmothers shopping as we know it would have seemed like a fairy tale and the supermarket a paradise. There is practically nothing that you can't buy. Asparagus at any time of the year? Strawberries in winter? All things are now possible. Exotic spices and fruits, fish from every possible sea, and wine from every possible country – everything is there. In this land of milk and honey the skill lies in buying the best available at the cheapest price, so that cooking becomes a pleasure without the expenditure becoming a burden.

An adventure before you cook

Shopping for a meal can be an exciting adventure, but it needs care if you are to avoid a culinary disaster. If your idea of shopping is to grab anything that takes your fancy, you may find it difficult to turn your purchases into a meal. And not only that, impulse buying can often require a bottomless purse.

The ten golden rules of shopping

1. First check your store cupboard.
2. Make a comprehensive shopping list.
3. Don't attempt to cook game in summer or asparagus in winter.
4. Take advantage of seasonal foods and special offers.
5. Don't be afraid to change your planned menu if you come across a really cheap offer.
6. When foods are cheap buy extra for the store cupboard or freezer.
7. Buy fresh foods wherever possible.
8. Compare prices!
9. Try to save money where possible.
10. Never go shopping when you are hungry!

Food regulations

1. With few exceptions all goods must be marked with the price.
2. The price of packaged goods must be expressed in terms of quantity (per litre or pint, per kilogram or pound) to enable comparison with rival products.
3. The law on unfair competition includes regulations on misleading advertising. Any cheap goods advertised must be available in sufficient quantity and not used merely to attract custom.
4. Food regulations include laws on hygiene, additives and chemicals used in the growing of fruit and vegetables.

Additives

Foodstuffs should contain only permitted additives and these must be included in the list of ingredients on the packet.
1. *Chemical preservatives* make foods keep longer. Permitted preservatives include benzoic acid, formic acid and sorbic acid.
2. *Colourings* must be safe; they are usually added to enhance appearance.
3. *Anti-oxidants* prevent food decaying (becoming rancid) through oxidation.
4. *Artificial flavourings* and other additives are present in many products. There are regulations governing permitted amounts.

Sell-by dates

Food labelling regulations state that packaged, ready-to-eat foods must be clearly marked not only with a list of ingredients used but also with a *sell-by date.*
This date indicates how long foodstuffs will keep if properly stored. This does not mean that foods will be bad after this date, only that the manufacturer will no longer guarantee the quality of the foodstuff.
The date should give the day, month or year preceded by the words 'Best before . . .' or 'Sell by . . .'
Tips:
1. Always obey instructions such as 'Use immediately' or 'Use immediately after thawing'.
2. Don't buy yogurt, curd cheese or cream if the lid bulges outwards.
3. If food is inedible the retailer is obliged to replace it.
4. Products marked 'Will keep for a limited period even when frozen' can be kept in the freezer for a maximum of three months.

Fruit and vegetables

You will be able to tell if these are fresh by looking at them. Official grading gives no indication of the flavour of the contents, but is based on external qualities such as size, weight and length. Fresh fruit and vegetables sold by grade must be completely sound, fresh, free from foreign odours and flavours and with the correct liquid content.

Frozen foods

The range is so wide nowadays that it is possible to make a complete meal entirely from frozen foods. Vegetables, meat, processed foods, fruit – all are readily available in a wide variety of sizes. Unlike canning, freezing preserves most of the nutritious value and flavour of foods.

Tips:
1. Large packets are more economical than small ones.
2. Only buy frozen foods if the packaging is undamaged.
3. Use immediately after purchase.
4. Wrap frozen foods in several layers of newspaper to prevent defrosting during the journey home.
5. Ice crystals in the packet indicate that the food has been defrosted at least once. Do not buy!
6. Remove poultry from the plastic packaging before defrosting and wash thoroughly before use.
7. Do not extend freezing and thawing times unnecessarily. Slow thawing in the refrigerator is best.
8. Use frozen foods immediately after thawing and never refreeze.
9. Date-mark frozen foods and do not exceed storage times.

Cans and jars

Includes fruit, vegetables, meat dishes, soups, sauces, marmalades and jams. Heat-treatment gives a long storage time, but destroys most of the vitamins. The food industry has introduced methods aimed at keeping vitamin loss to a minimum.

Tips:
1. Never buy dented tins.
2. Store in a dry, cool place out of direct sunlight.
3. Never keep food in the can once opened.

Dried fruit

Fruit will keep for a long time if its liquid content is extracted. Apples, pears, plums, apricots, figs, dates and grapes are all suitable for drying.

Tips:
1. Always dry fruit in the air and store in a cool place.
2. Keep an eye on the dried fruit for it is prone to mites.
3. Before use soak in hot water.

Average quantities to serve four people

Soups

Main course	2 litres/4 pints
Starter	1 litre/2 pints

Sauces

As accompaniment	600 ml/1 pint

Meat

On the bone	1 kg/2¼ lb
Boned	900 g/2 lb
Minced meat	450 g/1 lb

Vegetables

Main course	1 kg/2¼ lb
Side dish	900 g/2 lb
For soup	450 g/1 lb

Fish

Whole fish	1 kg/2¼ lb
Filleted	900 g/2 lb

Pasta

Main course	450 g/1 lb
Side dish	350 g/12 oz
For soup	100 g/4 oz

Rice

Main course	450 g/1 lb
Side dish	225 g/8 oz
For soup	100 g/4 oz

Fruit

Stewed	450 g/1 lb

Desserts

Creams	600 ml/1 pint

American measures

In America the 8-fl-oz measuring cup is used. The Imperial pint is 20 fl oz while the American pint is 16 fl oz. The British standard tablespoon holds 17.7 ml while the American holds 14.2 ml. A teaspoon holds approximately 5 ml in all countries.

Solid measures

Metric/Imperial	American
450 g/1 lb butter or margarine	2 cups
450 g/1 lb flour	4 cups
450 g/1 lb sugar	2 cups
450 g/1 lb icing sugar	3 cups
450 g/1 lb rice	2 cups

Liquid measures

Metric/Imperial	American
150 ml/¼ pint	⅔ cup
300 ml/½ pint	1¼ cups
450 ml/¾ pint	2 cups
600 ml/1 pint	2½ cups
900 ml/1½ pints	3¾ cups
1 litre/1¾ pints	4½ cups

Useful facts

Spoon measures: All spoon measures given in this book are level.
Pinch = the amount you can hold between two fingers.
Generous pinch = the amount held on the end of a knife.
When making any of the recipes in this book, follow only one set of measures as they are not interchangeable.

Eating as the source of energy

As long as we live we need energy. Not only for mountaineering, cycling, hiking or spring cleaning, but also for writing, cooking, kissing – even while we are sleeping. If we are to remain fit we must take two things into consideration. First we have to determine the amount of energy we need. Secondly we have to supply our energy requirements with the right combination of foods. Unless we get the first one right we become fat; if the second is wrong we become ill. But there is a third important point to consider – the energy we take in must taste as good as possible.

Carbohydrate

Without plants there would be no life. Plants produce oxygen and provide us with carbohydrate. The process is as follows:
– The plant makes a simple sugar (glucose) which can be immediately absorbed by the blood. Sportsmen take this in the form of fructose.
– From this simple sugar the plant forms dual sugars. These include our domestic sugar (sucrose), lactose and maltose.
– Starches and cellulose are complex sugars.
– In digestion all sugars are broken down into simple sugar.
– Carbohydrate is a prime energy source.
Sources of carbohydrate:
Fruit, vegetables, sugar, milk, potatoes, cereals, dried beans, wholemeal. Carbohydrates are, however, present in every food to a varying degree.
Daily requirement:
Carbohydrate is the main energy source in our diet. 50–65 per cent of the total energy requirement.
– Carbohydrates have a low satiation value. A diet too rich in carbohydrate makes one feel over-full.
– The carbohydrate intake should not fall below 10 per cent of the total energy requirement since they are needed to burn up fats.
– Simple sugar (glucose) is carried by the blood to be stored in the liver in the form of glycogen. It is also stored in the muscles. Excess carbohydrate is turned into fat deposits.

Protein

– All life depends on protein.
– Protein is the main building-block of the human body. All cells contain protein, every enzyme consists of protein. Collagen or gluten is contained in the skin, cartilages and connective tissues.
– Protein is made up of amino acids. The body is unable to produce eight of these amino acids and these must be supplied in the diet. These are the essential amino acids.
– Protein is an irreplaceable building-block for the body.
– The body cannot store protein so it must be taken in regularly.
– In digestion protein is broken down into basic building blocks, amino acids.
– The liver transforms these acids into the body's natural protein and burns off excess protein.
Sources of protein:
Animal protein: Milk and milk products, eggs, offal, fish, meat.
Vegetable protein: Pulses, cereals, potatoes, soya, nuts.
Daily requirement:
The requirement depends on age.
– The growing child needs a lot of protein for cell formation. The old also need a lot of protein to offset cell decay.
Adults:
12–15 per cent of the total energy requirement should come in the form of protein, made up of 50 per cent animal and 50 per cent vegetable protein.

Fats

– Occur in plants through conversion of carbohydrate.
– They may be visible in animal foodstuffs or invisible in vegetable foods (such as nuts).
– Fats produce warmth and are burnt off to provide energy.
– Fats protect sensitive organs such as the kidneys, heart, eyes, intestines.
– Excess fat is stored as fatty deposits.
– In digestion fats are broken down into small droplets and split into their component parts of glycerine and fatty acids, before being used to form body fat or being burnt off.
– Fats are second degree energy producers for they can only be burnt off to provide energy by carbohydrate.
– Fats are the carriers of essential (non-saturated) fatty acids which the body cannot produce for itself but which are essential for life.
– Fats also contain fat-soluble vitamins. The pro-vitamins of vitamin A (carotene) and D (sterin) can only be formed if fat is present.
– *Cholesterol* is one component of animal fat, but is also produced in the body. The intake should not exceed 300 mg per day.
Sources of fat:
Animal fats: Butter, cod-liver oil, meat, lard, sausage.
Vegetable fats: Margarine, nuts, oils (contain large amounts of essential fatty acids).
Daily requirement:
25–30 per cent of total energy requirement, made up of 50 per cent animal fat and 50 per cent vegetable fat.

Water

– The human body consists of around 65 per cent water and can survive for only a few days without water.
– Water is present in every cell and body fluid.
– It dissolves and carries substances to the cells and regulates body temperature (through sweating).
– Water loss: around 1.75 litres/3 pints per day. Water requirement: 2–3 litres/3–5 pints per day (with a large percentage being provided in food).

Roughage

– Substances not used by the body.
– Cellulose is the basis of plant tissue and is a complex sugar which cannot be broken down into simple sugar by digestion.
– Roughage stimulates the peristalsis of the bowel, aids digestion and produces a feeling of fullness by filling the stomach and bowels.
– Eaten in excess, however, it can lead to digestive problems.
Sources of roughage:
Fruit, vegetables, wholemeal products.

Vitamins

Substances essential to life, contained in both animal and vegetable foodstuffs.
– They influence the processes of life and protect from illness. Their importance is self-evident in cases of vitamin deficiency.
– The body is unable to manufacture most vitamins.
– There are fat-soluble vitamins (A, D, E and K) and water-soluble vitamins (B and C).
Sources of vitamins:
Liver, offal, vegetables, fruit.
Requirement/Adults

Vitamin A	0.9 mg/day
Vitamin D	0.0025 mg/day
Vitamin E	12 mg/day
Vitamin B_1	1.6 mg/day
Vitamin B_2	1.6 mg/day
Vitamin C	75 mg/day

Rules for handling vitamins:
1. Vitamins are sensitive to light and oxygen. Cover chopped foods.
2. Vitamins are also extremely sensitive to heat, so keep cooking times as short as possible.
3. Water-soluble vitamins can be lost in washing, soaking or boiling. Always chop fruit and vegetables after washing and always wash in standing water.
4. Don't keep foods hot too long.
5. Vitamins are destroyed by long storage times.
6. Vitamins may be destroyed by metals such as copper.
7. Water-soluble vitamins can be retained by acids. This is why we sprinkle apple or banana with lemon juice.
8. Fat-soluble vitamins need fat to be broken down into pro-vitamins (carotene in vitamin A for instance).

Minerals and trace elements

Substances essential in small quantities which provide no calories.
– They need to be taken daily in food, for they are water-soluble and any excess is expelled from the body.
– Essential building-blocks in the bones, and found in solution in every body fluid.
– The human body cannot produce minerals.
Minerals include:
Calcium (chalk), iron, phosphorus, iodine, salt, potash.
Calcium deficiency damages the teeth, iron deficiency produces anaemia, lack of iodine produces goitres.
Sources of minerals:
Fruit, vegetables, milk, milk products, wholemeal bread, offal.
Requirements: a mixed diet should provide the daily mineral requirement. Precise quantities can be found in the nutrition tables.

All you need to know about energy

Since many of us have weight problems 'calorie' has become a magic word in recent times, yet it is a word that has officially ceased to exist for several years. The international unit for energy, warmth and work is now the 'joule' (kJ). The conversion factor is 1 kcal = 4.1868 kJ. For everyday requirements 4 joules are roughly 1 calorie.

Main energy sources

1 g fat	=	38 joules
1 g alcohol	=	30 joules
1 g protein	=	17 joules
1 g carbohydrate	=	17 joules

How much energy do we need?

For light sedentary occupations the total daily energy requirement is:

Men	10,900 joules (2600 calories)
Women	9200 joules (2200 calories)

Heavy manual work requires correspondingly more energy. A cyclist in the 'Tour de France' for instance needs around 40,000 joules per day! Growing children often need as much energy as a manual worker.

A whole world of flavour

Cooking aside, the history of spices reads like a story from the Arabian Nights. They have started wars, made countries and merchants rich, fed smugglers and customs men. Nor is this confined to the Far East whence these new scents and flavours made their way to Europe. Even in nineteenth-century Austria the salt mines were forbidden territory, accessible only to those with a 'salt pass', so valuable was this white mineral to the Emperor.

Paprika

The pods of the ripe pimiento, dried and ground. There are five different grades of hotness: mild, sweet, semi-sweet, pink and hot.

Juniper berries

They have a bitter, slightly resinous flavour. Juniper berries can be used in salt beef, game dishes, game sauces, goulash and pâtés.

Cinnamon

Sold ground or in sticks. Cinnamon is the dried inner bark of the cinnamon tree and is used in stewed fruit, rice pudding and chicken stock.

Cloves

Used both whole and ground. They are highly flavoured and should be used sparingly. In red cabbage, meat and chicken stock, spiked onion, roast pork or beef, stewed pears.

Ginger

A sweet, hot spice available fresh, in syrup, candied or ground. Fresh or ground ginger is used in chicken soup, minced meat, curry sauce or stewed fruit.

Bay leaf

Bay leaves have a strong, slightly bitter flavour and should be used sparingly. In meat stock, casseroles, salt beef, fish stock and marinades.

Saffron

Saffron is slightly bitter in flavour and is deep yellow in colour. Well-pounded saffron strands or saffron powder should be dissolved in a little hot water for use in risotto, paella, sauces or stocks.

Curry powder

Curry powder is an Indian spice mixture which contains turmeric, cardamom, pepper, ginger, allspice, cinnamon, cloves, nutmeg and coriander. Curry is a popular ingredient for hot exotic dishes and sauces.

Nutmeg

Nutmeg has a strong, rounded flavour, and is strongest when freshly grated. Use in small quantities for cream soups, meat stock, Mornay sauce, spinach and milk custards.

Caraway

Caraway has an acidic aromatic taste and should be used sparingly. Adds extra flavour to white cabbage, goulash, Savoy cabbage, sauerkraut and roast pork.

Pepper

Black: unpeeled, unripe berries, hot and spicy.
White: seed of the ripe berry, finer, hotter flavour.
Green: unripe preserved berries, milder and more aromatic.
Pink: slightly sweet, resinous flavour.

Cayenne

Ground from dried chillies. Very hot and should be used extremely sparingly. In rice dishes, casseroles and sauces.

Eight important tips for spices

1. Store spices in firmly sealed containers.
2. Flavour is lost through long storage. Do not store for longer than twelve months.
3. Where possible buy whole, unground spices.
4. Always freshly grind or grate spices (in a pepper mill, nutmeg grater or mortar).
5. To bring out the full flavour, heat spices in a dry frying pan.
6. Go sparingly with spices – they should never mask the natural flavour of the food. It is better to add more later if necessary.
7. Do not combine too many different spices together. Some go well together but others do not.
8. You can buy made-up seasoning mixtures such as pie seasoning, gingerbread spice or Chinese spice mixture (see also pages 248–9).

Seasoning with wine

Many famous dishes would have remained completely unnoticed were it not for wine. Wine gives a dish a fresh aroma, a pleasant acidic flavour and a beautiful colour. Bear in mind one basic rule: white wine for light sauces, red wine for dark sauces. The French, with their advanced culinary culture, have an additional rule: the wine in the sauce should also be in the glass. Wine should always be reduced to evaporate liquid and alcohol and to allow the flavour of the wine to combine with that of the food. You need not use vintage wine for cooking, but always use a dry wine. Sweet wines can ruin a dish, unless the sauce is meant to be sweet (as in game sauces).

Tips

Any left-over, half-empty bottles of wine or champagne from a party can be kept for cooking. If necessary, for dietary reasons, wine in any recipe can be successfully replaced with water (see also page 234).

Green seasonings from the garden

If you have a nose for it, it is possible to identify certain areas or even certain countries by the smell of their herbs. While elegant Parisian cooking smells of tarragon, Provence is famous for the combined smells of thyme, lavender and garlic. While Roman cooks swear by sage, northern Italy reeks of basil. Bergamot is a native of America. All the scents of the world can be found in your herb garden – or supermarket.

Seasoning with the onion family

The onion is the main seasoning vegetable in cooking. From sauces to casseroles to roasts – from Hungarian goulash to French onion soup. Onions come in various grades of hotness. Experienced cooks will know that the purple Egyptian onion is the strongest of all. When cutting onions try to breathe through your mouth unless you want to dissolve into floods of tears! Green members of the onion family are leeks and chives, but the noblest of the family is the shallot. In French cooking it is used instead of onion in all the best recipes. Shallots are hotter but also have a much better flavour, which goes excellently with wine, butter or cream.

The strongest of the onion family is garlic. Garlic is not only an excellent flavouring, but something of a philosophy of life. Friends and enemies of this highly flavoured bulb remain irreconcilable. The enemy of garlic is much to be pitied for he is missing out on a delightful culinary experience. For all lovers of garlic here are three tips:
Before cutting garlic wet your hands in cold water and afterwards remove the smell with salt and lemon.
Never fry garlic in hot fat or it will burn and become bitter.
Always use fresh, young garlic. The older the bulb the stronger the after-taste.

Chervil
A herb tasting slightly of aniseed. Use the leaves and stems chopped or garnish with sprigs. Used to season scrambled eggs, cream soups and cream sauces.

Rosemary
The needles have a spicy, resinous flavour. Used sparingly rosemary goes with any strongly flavoured food, such as roast pork, leg of lamb or minced meat.

Thyme
A highly flavoured, mild herb which is an essential item in cooking. Used in stews, sauces and roasts.

Tarragon
Important herb in classic cuisine. Its fresh flavour is reminiscent of aniseed and lemon. Use sparingly in Béarnaise sauce, veal, fish and vinaigrette.

Marjoram/Oregano
Strong, spicy flavour. Marjoram is used to season tomato sauce, duck, goose, game and liver. Oregano is wild marjoram and is the staple herb of Italy.

Parsley
The standard seasoning of grandmother's cooking, with a fresh hearty taste. Parsley is especially good with fish, mushrooms and any vegetable.

Dill

A spicy herb which should not be combined with any other. Goes with cucumber, all fish dishes and potatoes.

Lovage

Bitter-sweet flavour very like celery. Always use very sparingly. Suitable for meat stocks, stews and roast beef.

Basil

Its fresh, spicy aroma with a hint of cloves is one that is always associated with Italian cooking. For tomato sauce, pesto, pasta and poultry.

Sage

A sharp, slightly bitter herb which should be used sparingly. For veal schnitzel, poultry stuffings, pasta, liver and minced meat dishes.

Chives

A slightly oniony flavour. Use generously with mushrooms, blanched vegetables, all salads, poached eggs and boiled fish.

Savory

Its spicy, peppery flavour gives a herby taste to stews, red cabbage, scrambled eggs, roast beef, broad and green beans. Can be used generously.

A dozen tips for herbs

1. Fresh, delicately flavoured herbs like chervil, basil and chives should always be added after cooking, for cooking destroys the flavour.
2. Dried herbs need to cook for a time to bring out the flavour.
3. Strongly flavoured herbs such as thyme or rosemary can be cooked as whole stems and removed after cooking.
4. If tied in a muslin bag, herbs can be suspended in a liquid and easily removed when necessary.
5. Use fresh herbs for garnish – and don't always stick to parsley.
6. Fresh herbs can be dried, preserved in vinegar or oil, or frozen.
7. Preserved herbs should be stored in air-tight containers and kept for a maximum of one year.
8. Dried herbs have a more concentrated flavour than fresh ones so you can decrease the amount given in recipes.
9. Dried herbs often differ in flavour from fresh ones.
10. Dried herbs are exellent for flavouring meat on the barbecue. They should be sprinkled onto the charcoal.
11. Ground herbs lose their flavour very quickly, so always buy rubbed herbs.
12. For herbs, as with spices, remember that they should bring out the flavour of the food, not mask it.

The ancient art of preserving

In the so-called 'good old days' cooks of both sexes had to master the art of preserving. There were no refrigerators or freezers, no canning industry to take all the strain out of storing foods. Many old methods are still in use today along with the newer, more modern methods.

Drying
Hang fresh herbs in a well-ventilated place. Once dried rub the herbs and store in airtight containers.

Freezing
Food must be frozen extremely quickly to prevent large ice crystals forming. It is best to spread foods out for fast freezing. Food should always be frozen in an airtight container. You can use special freezer bags or plastic boxes for this.

Potatoes cannot be frozen as this makes them sweet and soft.

Vacuum-packing
Vacuum-packed foods keep well. If properly prepared they will keep in the refrigerator for several days, or longer still in the freezer. You need a special machine for vacuum-packing.

Tins
Many cakes need to be stored for a while to develop their full flavour. If you place a piece of apple peel in a tin of gingerbread this will keep it moist.

Preserving in oil
Certain foods can be preserved in oil in an airtight container. Use neutral-flavoured vegetable oil and store in a cool place. Excellent for: garlic, herbs and meat.

Cling film

Also known as plastic wrap. Delicately flavoured foods should always be tightly wrapped in cling film to prevent them drying out or absorbing foreign smells.

Damp cloth

Delicate vegetables and herbs should be wrapped in a damp cloth and chilled. If the cloth is kept damp they will keep for several days.

Herbs

Where possible buy herbs in pots. In a sunny position they will continue to grow every time they are cut.

Cheese bell

To allow soft cheese to mature, store under a cheese bell in a cool place. When it is fully mature, transfer to the refrigerator.

Aluminium foil

Aluminium foil can be used to wrap or cover any food or type of dish. Always place the matt side in contact with the food for during long storing the shiny side may oxidise.

Spaghetti jar

Long spaghetti stores very well in special jars. A cork makes an airtight seal to keep out moisture.

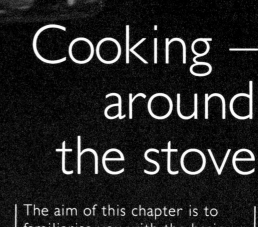

Cooking – around the stove

The aim of this chapter is to familiarise you with the basic techniques of cooking and the initial preparation of food. Experienced cooks can own a large amount of specialist tools but of course not all of these are necessary to be a successful and proficient cook. However, it is useful to know what is available and what can be achieved by use of this equipment. It will be up to you to decide what you need. The basic techniques of cooking – from roasting in the oven to poaching or steaming – are important to learn about because, once mastered, there is no limit as to what you can do.

Equipment for the beginner

Admittedly anyone going into a specialist kitchen shop supplying professional chefs would be amazed at the huge variety of utensils and machines, pots and pans, ladles and knives. But when one remembers how cooking began – with a single pot over an open fire – things take on a different dimension. In fact very little basic equipment is necessary, although these few items should be of top quality. A cheap saucepan can work out expensive if it is too lightweight. The same is true of frying pans that tilt or knives that won't cut.

What you need round the stove:

1. *Frying pans.* Stainless steel pans (preferably copper-bottomed) can be heated to high temperatures without warping. They conduct heat very evenly. Cast-iron pans share these advantages but are more difficult to keep clean as they tend to rust: they should be oiled after use. Stainless steel or iron pans can be cleaned by sprinkling with salt and heating to a high temperature. Plastic-coated pans have not proved as popular as was predicted ten years ago. They are unsuitable for many classic cooking techniques and the plastic coating does not tend to last long. They are, however, good for those on a diet as they can be used without fat.
2. *Pastry brush.* For greasing tins and baking trays.
3. *Palette knife or spatula.* For turning meat and other fried foods, for smoothing mixtures and decorating.
4. *Chopping board.* In wood or plastic. Available in various sizes.
5. *Paring knife.* For easy peeling of fruit and vegetables (see pages 30–1).
6. *Chopping knife.* A knife with a slightly curved blade. Excellent for chopping onions, garlic and herbs, since it cuts with a rocking movement and the knife is always in contact with the board.

7. *Knife with supple blade.* Especially good for cutting and carving meat or filleting fish.
8. *Stainless steel bowl.* For storing, mixing, standing in a bain-marie and also attractive enough for a serving dish. Available in sets of various sizes.
9. *Stewpans.* In various sizes. For boiling vegetables or pasta, for making stock or sauces, for roasting and cooking fish.

10. *Large and small ladles.*
11. *Large and small skimmers.*
12. *Sauté pan.* Excellent for frying vegetables and small pieces of meat or for poaching. The main criteria with a sauté pan is a comfortable grip. With metal-handled pans always use oven-gloves!
13. *Measuring jug or cup.* With both metric and Imperial measures.

14. *Wooden spoons*. Wood is preferable to plastic for cooking spoons. Although they darken in colour after use in hot fat, they won't melt. Long-handled spoons are easiest to use.

15. *Rubber spatula*. For scraping out bowls and pans.

16. *Whisk*. For whipping egg whites, zabaglione, cream, etc. For beating sauces or whisking in butter. A good whisk should have supple blades firmly anchored to the handle. Don't buy too small a whisk as they can only whip a small amount of the mixture at a time and there is more danger of burning.

17. *Sieve*. Use a metal sieve. They have a tendency to rust with time and must be dried carefully after use, but they are extremely strong and won't warp if used for hot liquids. You can get small or larger meshed sieves. Professional cooks use a conical sieve for sauces.

18. *Tea-towels*. For drying dishes and holding hot pans. You should keep a clean tea-towel for straining sauces.

Essential techniques

Much of the work associated with cooking is now a thing of the past. When was the last time you had to descale a carp, pluck a goose or skin a hare? Nowadays, when much of our food arrives hygienically packed in portions, cooking may have lost much of its romance but things are much easier for the modern cook. There are still a number of processes you will have to do for yourself, however, and the main ones are illustrated here.

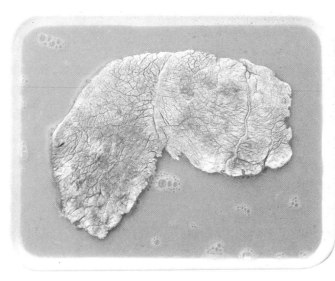

Coating in breadcrumbs

1. Thinly beaten meat is dipped in flour and excess flour shaken off.
2. The meat is dipped in beaten egg.
3. The meat is gently pressed into breadcrumbs and should then be fried immediately over a moderate heat. If you leave the meat to stand for long the crumbs will begin to flake off.

Tying

Using a needle, fish are tied into shape with the head brought round to meet the tail. Asparagus is tied into bundles. Tie a slice of lemon to the base of an artichoke to prevent discoloration.

Peeling tomatoes

1. Cut a cross in the bottom of the tomato and remove the stalk.
2. Plunge the tomato into boiling water for 5–10 seconds.
3. Rinse in cold water.
4. Peel off the skin using a knife and halve the tomato.
5. Spoon out the seeds.
6. On a chopping board cut the tomato into strips or small cubes.

Deseeding cucumber

Halve the cucumber lengthways and scrape out the seeds using a teaspoon.

Crushing garlic

Peel the cloves of garlic, cut up with a wide knife and then chop very finely.

Beating meat

Wrap thin slices of meat in cling film or plastic wrap and beat evenly with the blade of a heavy knife.

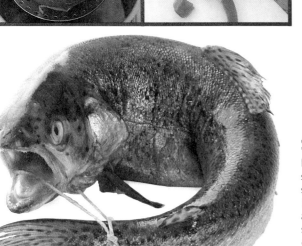

Spiked onion

For seasoning soups or stocks it is very easy to stick a bay leaf and cloves into a peeled onion. They are easy to remove from the stock at the end of the cooking time.

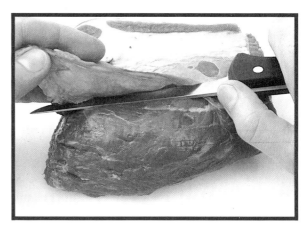

Trimming

Preparation of meat or fish by removing fat, skin and all inedible parts. Use a sharp, pointed knife.

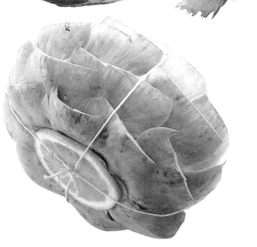

Crushed ice

For chilling drinks or to serve ices or sorbets. Wrap a block of ice or ice cubes in a thick cloth and hit with a hammer.

Straining

Pouring a liquid through a sieve to keep the liquid but not normally the solids.

Anti-curdling

To prevent hot soup curdling tilt the pan and support with a spoon.

Essential tools

A fully automatic kitchen, where everything is controlled by the computer's silicon chip, is still a thing of the future – thank goodness! For it is doubtful if cooking would still be fun under those conditions. As it is there are electrical appliances to make every possible process easier, but we should not forget those good old kitchen tools which have been perfected over the centuries and which do the job just as well.

1. *Truffle slicer* with adjustable blade.
2. *Grater* with three separate functions. Coarse grater for potatoes. Blade to thinly slice cucumber, radishes or carrots. Fine grater for celery, carrots or apples.
3. *Egg-slicer.*
4. *Nut-cracker.*
5. *Garlic press* finely crushes peeled cloves of garlic and retains skin in the press.
6. *Mortar.* One of the earliest implements for crushing foods which retains most of the flavour. Excellent for pesto or nuts.
7. *Pepper mill.* Filled with whole peppercorns. Produces fresh-smelling pepper which is a highly aromatic seasoning.
8. *Cutter* for all types of pastry (zig-zag or plain).
9. *Chopping knife* for quick, easy chopping of herbs and seasonings.
10. *Stoner.* Cherries and plums are placed in the hollow and pressure on the top knob removes the stone.
11. *Lemon squeezer* squeezes the juice of any citrus fruit.
12. *Small sieve* for icing sugar.
13. *Ice cream scoop.* When cutting balls of ice cream dip in hot water after each ball.
14. *Mincer or meat grinder.* For steak tatare, minced meat and stuffings.
15. *Cutter.* For pasta and vegetable slices.
16. *Egg cutter.* Cuts hard-boiled eggs into wedges.
17. *Pastry wheel,* smooth or zig-zagged.
18. *Nutmeg grater* for whole nutmegs.
19. *Kitchen scissors.* For cutting poultry. Also includes bottle and can openers.
20. *Parmesan knife.* For cutting Parmesan cheese into small pieces.

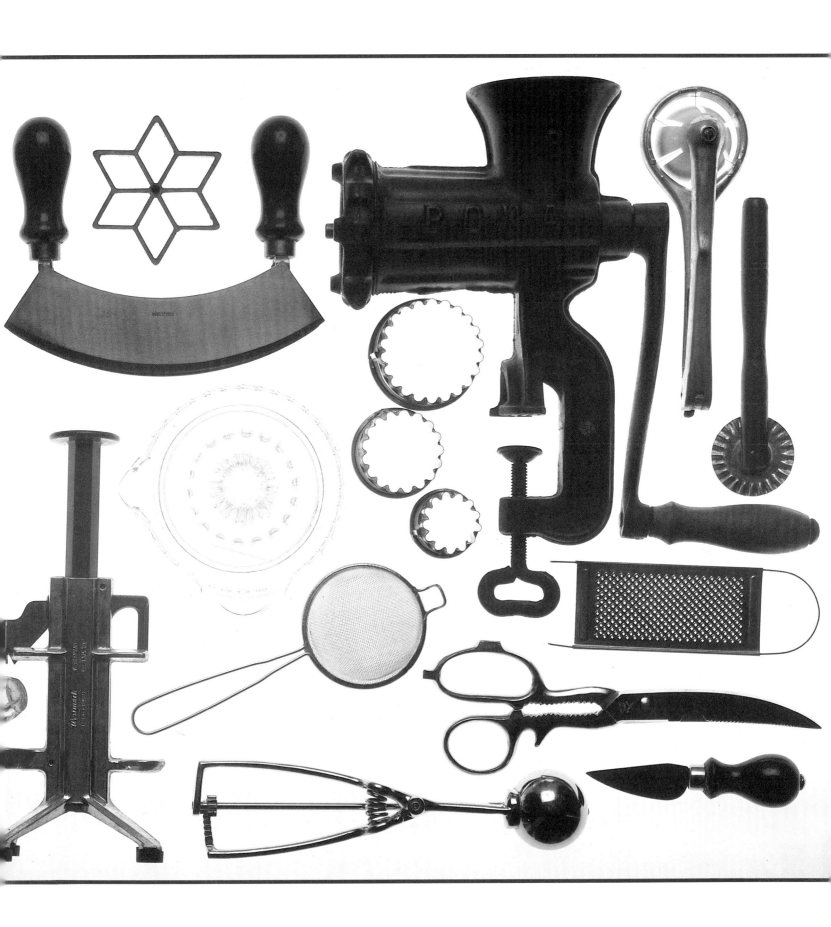

Tools for intricate work

Some of the tools used by professional chefs look as if they might be more at home either in the operating theatre or in a carpenter's tool cupboard. These tools, which are often extremely intriguing in shape, have all been developed to serve a particular purpose. Every indentation, every curve, every hole has its function. There are many ways of cutting food which look as if they must have taken hours of work but which are in fact very easy. Some examples are included in the following pages.

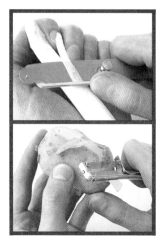

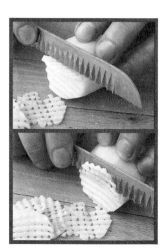

Asparagus peeler. The blade is adjustable to the thickness of the asparagus skin. Holding the peeler at a slight angle, work from the top to the base before chopping off the ends.

Vegetable peeler. For peeling potatoes, carrots, cucumbers and pears. Includes a short blade for digging out eyes or damaged spots.

Kitchen knife. Suitable for cutting onions, garlic, vegetables or fruit. Cut onions in half and slice across towards the root end. Then cut into strips or dice, discarding the remains of the root.

Paring knife with slightly curved blade for cutting up vegetables.

Patterned knife with a thick zig-zag blade is used to cut raw and cooked vegetables. Crinkle-cut chips are very easy. Turn the potato through 90 degrees after each cut (see page 33).

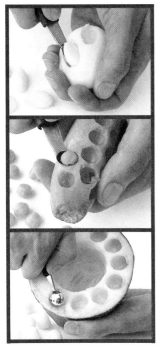

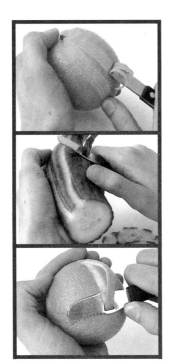

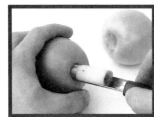

Apple-corer. Pushed through the centre of the apple and then pulled out with the core without damaging the outside shape of the apple so that it can be used whole, either peeled or unpeeled. Can be used for any fruit with a core.

Six tips for intricate work

1. It is essential to buy good-quality sharp tools.
2. Don't cut on metal, stone or ceramic tiles as this blunts knives.
3. Wooden boards are best. Alternatively you can use a plastic board but this will blunt your knives quicker than wood.
4. Place the chopping board on a damp cloth to prevent it slipping as you work.
5. When cutting keep your fingers slightly curved. Keep your thumb behind the other fingers and always work carefully.
6. Keep a few bandaids in the kitchen drawer just in case!

Ball-cutter available in various sizes from small pea-sized balls to oval olive-size. Used for potatoes, carrots, melons and other fruit and vegetables.

Julienne-cutter used to make fine strips of orange or lemon rind which is then blanched and used to garnish.

Orange-peeler is used to peel or decorate cucumber or orange skins.

Adding the restaurant touch

The food set before us by waiters in the best restaurants will usually look extremely attractive. And since appearance is an important aspect of food, you should aim to make the food you serve your guests equally attractive. Take advantage of long-established methods. They are often small things but highly effective – diced vegetables, thinly sliced mushrooms, crinkle-cut potatoes, carrot spindles, celeriac balls, beetroot strips – there are hundreds of possibilities. With the tools we have shown you on the preceding pages you should have no problem in making your food attractive.

Julienne

(sticks, strips)
Cut potatoes into thick slices and then into thick sticks (chips). Cut kohlrabi in the same way. Cut beetroot into matchsticks. Cut leeks into pieces and then halve them. Remove the centre and cut the outside leaves into thin strips. Carrot fingers are cut from lengthways slices.

Chiffonade is lettuce leaves rolled and then cut into fine strips. They can be mixed with other vegetables such as peas.

Brunoise

(cubes or lozenges)
Sticks or julienne can be cut into cubes, lozenges or brunoise (very small cubes). Cut aubergines, courgettes and kohlrabi into large cubes.

Cut beetroot into smaller cubes and potato chips at an angle into lozenges. Brunoise are finely diced vegetables used in soups or as a garnish. The photograph shows brunoise carrots.

Slices

The simplest shape is the slice, and this forms the basis of almost every other shape. Halve and deseed cucumber and then cut into very thin or wide slices. Cut potatoes, either raw or cooked, into thin or thick slices. Cut uncooked mushrooms into very thin slices. Carrots can be cut across to give round slices, at an angle to produce ovals or lengthways into long slices. Large aubergines or courgettes should be halved or quartered before slicing.

Paring

An attractive way of giving vegetables an even shape. You can use this method for cauliflower or broccoli stalks. To pare use six cuts to give the vegetable a spindle-like shape. You can either leave the ends pointed or trim them flat. Carrots can be left on the stalk. The photograph shows pared cucumber, carrot, potato, kohlrabi and courgette.

Balls

You can cut almost any vegetable into balls using a ball, olive or pea-cutter. Melons, courgettes, potatoes, carrots or apples are especially suitable. Don't throw away the left-overs but use them to make a puré or soup.

Grating

A very simple and easy method of cutting up fruit and vegetables. Coarsely or finely grated fruit or vegetables can be used as a salad, garnish or side dish. To make Swiss rösti potatoes should be coarsely grated. Carrots or apples (finely grated) and radishes (coarsely grated) are excellent for grating.

Crinkle-cutting

Using a zig-zag knife you can cut very decorative shapes. All the preceding shapes could also be cut with a zig-zag knife.

The photograph shows beetroot slices, potato chips, carrot ovals, cucumber lozenges and potato slices (see page 30).

New simplicity for garnishes

The days have finally gone when lobsters were turned into monuments, soles into mosaics and tomatoes and eggs into toadstools before being brought to the table. Pretentiousness is out and has been replaced by a new simplicity in garnishing which not only looks more hygienic but is in complete harmony with modern attitudes towards 'healthy' eating. Decorations and garnishes in nouvelle cuisine are intended primarily to be eaten; they are part of the dish rather than a piece of frippery to be cleared away with the dishes. Here are illustrated a few simple examples, both old and new.

Peeled, halved and sliced cucumber which is arranged in a rosette to garnish.
Twists of lime for garnishing fish or poultry. Cut lemons or oranges in exactly the same way.
Herb butter piped into a tomato half and garnished with a sprig of parsley. Serve with grilled or fried meat.
Radishes are cut into spirals with a special radish cutter then opened out into garlands.
Onion slices with flowering borage.
Carrot slices cut with a small flower cutter.
Leeks can be cut into rings or slices for garnishing.
Lemon halves with four indentations cut across the centre and decorated with cress.
Lemon half with thin strip of peel tied into a knot.
Tomato rose. Starting at the top thinly peel the tomato as if peeling an apple. Roll up the skin and garnish with a parsley leaf.
Lemon segments cut from slices to garnish fish.
Radish flowers. Wash the radishes and remove larger leaves. Leave small leaves on the radish. Using a sharp knife cut from the outside towards the centre and soak in cold water so that they open out.

Pepper and leek can be cut into diamonds and arranged to make small flowers.

Carrots finely grated and garnished with leaves.

Mint leaves to decorate sweets, sorbets and sweet-hot dishes.

Pink pepper can be used whole or rubbed between the fingers and sprinkled over food.

Carrot slices cut into intricate shapes and arranged on the plate.

Kohlrabi cut with a small ball-cutter. Mix with carrot balls, blanch, garnish with chervil and serve as a side vegetable.

Mashed potato piped onto the plate or into small bowls.

Onion rings to garnish highly flavoured dishes.

Lemon balm can garnish almost anything.

Cold butter shaped into balls between your hands or two boards and then dipped in chopped herbs, paprika or curry powder.

Herb butter piped onto lemon slices and garnished with parsley.

Cucumber slices cut with a ziz-zag cutter and sprinkled with herbs (see also page 31).

Slashed mushrooms. Raw mushrooms are cut outwards from the centre with a small knife, turning the mushroom as you cut. Garnish with chervil.

Lemon wedges to garnish fish and poultry, for finger bowls or squeezing at the table.

Gherkin fans. Slice small gherkins lengthways and fan out.

Cooking in water

The old joke about people who can't even boil water, never mind anything else, contains a grain of truth. It is certainly true that you need to be able to heat liquids properly before you begin preparing meals. You should be familiar with your stove so that you know automatically which setting gives which degree of heat. This may sound easy until you try it!

What cooking does

Most foods obviously have to be boiled, baked or fried before they can be digested and used by the body. But cooking also changes the taste.

All foods contain protein, fat, carbohydrate, vitamins, minerals and water. Animal protein must be broken down, vegetable protein softened. Fats need other foods such as vegetables or bread for the body to digest them. Carbohydrates, the starch in potatoes for instance, are indigestible in their raw state and have to be cooked first.

Heating breaks down foods, bringing out the flavour and producing an appetising aroma.

However, heat can also destroy important substances contained in food such as vitamins.

It is important to keep cooking times as short as possible. Avoid warming up prepared dishes repeatedly and above all choose the right cooking technique for the type of food and its intended purpose.

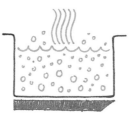

Boiling

Cooking in deep, bubbling liquid in an open or covered pan.

Besides water, foods can also be boiled in milk, stock, wine or broth.
I. *Start in cold water* for lentils, dried fruit, hulled grain.

The water is absorbed, the starches are softened, water-soluble substances are flushed out and the protein is broken down.

To make stock it is best to place bones in cold water to get the full flavour.
2. *Add to boiling water*: pasta, semolina, meat.

This preserves water-soluble vitamins and . minerals.

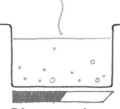

Simmering

Cooking in deep water just below boiling point.

Starches are softened, proteins broken down while water-soluble substances are to a large extent preserved.

For dumplings, rice, egg dishes, fruit.
I. Bring the liquid to the boil.
2. Tip the food into the boiling liquid.
3. Reduce temperature according to type of food – it should not boil from here on.

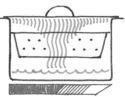

Steaming

Cooking in steam in a perforated container over boiling water in a covered pan.

Steaming is an excellent method of cooking as the steam cannot flush out the nutritious substances in the food. Food retains its shape and more of its natural flavour. For vegetables, potatoes, fish, tender pieces of meat.
I. Place the food to be cooked in the perforated container.
2. Bring the liquid to the boil and place the food above it.
3. Maintain the liquid at simmering point.
4. Season vegetables after steaming.
5. Use the steaming water to make a gravy.

Poaching

Lengthy simmering with the liquid off the boil (eggs).

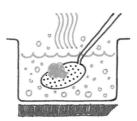

Blanching

Short cooking in boiling liquid. Short boiling de-activates the enzymes which destroy vitamins and minerals. Also used to sterilise vegetables. After blanching plunge immediately into cold water to halt the cooking process. Blanching prevents vegetables discolouring and aids freezing.

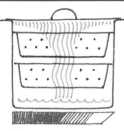  

Pressure-cooking

Cooking in a sealed pan.

Increased pressure produces higher temperature which reduces cooking times. Quick-cooking foods (e.g. vegetables) cook 30–35 per cent faster, while slow-cooking foods (meat, dried beans, poultry) cook 70–75 per cent faster.

With several inside containers you can cook several things simultaneously. Despite the higher temperature, the shorter cooking times preserve the nutritious elements in food better.

When using a pressure cooker always follow the manufacturer's instructions, particularly when opening the cooker. *Never open the pan until you have released the pressure.*

Stewing

Cooking in its own juices with a little additional fat and liquid at simmering point in a covered pan. For delicate vegetables and fruit, fish and tender meats (veal, poultry).

Stewing is the simplest and best method of cooking in water for most of the nutritious value of the food is preserved. Foods with a low-water content should be stewed in a little liquid. Those that contain a lot of water will not need any extra liquid.

Fat improves flavour and separates fat-soluble vitamins from pro-vitamins. Nutritious substances remain in the liquid which makes an excellent gravy base.

Bain-marie or water bath

Gradual warming through in an open container, suspended or standing in hot, but not boiling, water. For delicate vegetables and fruit, fish and tender meats (veal, poultry).

Used for sauces and creams containing butter, eggs or cream which would separate or burn over direct heat.

1. Bring the water to the boil in a large pan.
2. Reduce the heat to moderate.
3. Place the container with the food in the water which should be off the boil. You can buy special double saucepans which hold the water between the two pans.

Steeping

In cold water – for dried foods such as beans, lentils or dried fruit.

Absorption cooking

Cooking over a low heat so that the liquid is absorbed, for example semolina, rice pudding.

Keeping warm

Heating food at a very low temperature, to keep foods warm for a brief period or to soften them.

Reducing

To evaporate off part of a liquid to make it more concentrated. For sauces, soups.

The flavour becomes more concentrated and the aroma intensified.

Glazing

To 'produce a shine' by coating food with beaten egg, or milk, aspic or sugar syrup.

Cooking in fat

Slightly more difficult than cooking in water is the correct use of hot fats. You are cooking at twice the temperature and a single minute can make the difference between success or failure (e.g. steaks). In addition you have to choose the right fat (see page 198). Although butter is the best of all cooking fats, it is entirely unsuitable for frying meats. More difficult still is the technique of combining fats with liquids. There is truth in the statement that anyone who can braise meat can cook anything.

Shallow frying

A quick cooking method in which food is browned in hot fat.
1. Get the frying pan nice and hot otherwise the food will stick to the pan and won't brown.
2. Heat the fat in the frying pan.
3. Never add cold fat during frying as this interrupts the frying process and the food loses moisture.
4. Always use protein- and water-free fats, i.e. fats with a high boiling point.
5. Unless meat is coated in breadcrumbs do not season with salt until it is cooked, for the salt draws out the juice and makes the meat dry.
6. Never prick the meat as it fries or the juice will escape. Use tongs or a spatula to turn it.

Sautéeing

Tossing small pieces of food in a handled pan (sauté pan) in fat that should be hot but not smoking. A mixture of oil and butter is excellent for sautéeing.

Sautéeing is a good method for cooking fish, liver, kidney, strips of steak or pieces of meat.

Always season after cooking! Serve straight from the pan. This means that any vegetables or side dishes should be ready before you begin sautéeing.

The best pans for sautéeing are light copper frying pans or copper-bottomed stainless steel pans. It is important that they conduct the heat well and evenly and that they have a comfortable grip. Cast-iron pans are too heavy for comfortable use.

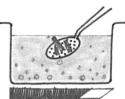

Deep-frying

Frying in plenty of hot fat. Small pieces of meat or fish, potatoes, chips, vegetables in breadcrumbs.
1. The food should be able to float freely in the fat.
2. Always use heat-resistant fats: oil, lard, coconut fat, suet.
3. Don't use the same fat more than two or three times.
4. The fat must remain hot throughout.
5. To test for temperature, dip a wooden skewer or the handle of a wooden spoon into the fat; if bubbles form it is hot enough.
6. Always dry food thoroughly before dropping into the fat.
7. Add the food a little at a time, otherwise you will reduce the temperature and the food won't brown.

You can deep-fry in a saucepan, deep frying pan or deep-fryer.

Meat fondue

Pieces of veal, beef or pork quick-fried in hot fat and served with sauces, salads and white bread.

Chinese hotpot

Pieces of vegetable or white meat quick-cooked in hot stock.

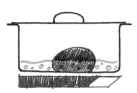  

Braising

Browning in fat and then cooking in a little liquid in a closed pan. A cooking process which combines all the advantages of fat, liquid and steam. Use for inexpensive cuts of meat such as neck, shoulder or flank, meat rolls, goulash, stuffed cabbage.
1. Brown the food to be braised in an open pan.
2. Add hot liquid to come about half-way up the food and continue cooking in the covered pan.

Never add cold liquid or the meat will be tough.

If preferred the hot fat can be poured off before the liquid is added. This will make the dish less greasy.

The fat gives the food a delicious brown crust. The juices can be used for a tasty gravy.

Apart from vitamins, all other nutritious elements are preserved.

In haute cuisine there is also the term white-braising. Here white meat or poultry is sealed in butter without browning before the liquid is added as above.

Flambéing

Quick flaming in alcohol (brandy, rum, Calvados, etc.) to give added flavour. Usually follows shallow-frying. Most of the alcohol burns off to leave only the flavour.

High- percentage-proof alcohols (40 and above) should be used, otherwise you will have to heat it slightly to make sure that it will ignite. Take care when igniting and leave to burn out.

Smoking

A method of cooking and preserving in which protein is broken down by warm or hot smoke.

There are two different ways of smoking. Cold-smoking is a professional method for ham, sausage, smoked salmon etc. For this you need a smoking chamber and a minimum smoking period of around a month. Cold-smoking is one of the oldest methods of preserving food.

There is also the shorter hot-smoking method. The best woods for smoking are beech and juniper. One of the most popular foods for smoking is trout. Warm from the smoke even the relatively tasteless farmed trout are delicious. In recent years it has become quite easy to buy small hot-smoking ovens which can be used on a balcony (following the manufacturer's instructions) without disturbing your neighbours.

Deglazing

Rinsing out a frying pan or saucepan with a liquid such as wine or stock to remove the deposits left after frying meat. The liquid is then boiled to make a gravy.

Glazing

Cooking in hot fat over a low heat so that food cooks without browning (e.g. onions).

Sealing

To cook in hot fat, stirring continuously. Quick cooking without browning (low temperature).

Making a roux

Stir flour into hot butter or margarine until smooth. Dilute with a liquid and cook to thicken (see page 246).

Pot-roasting

Professional cooking method, mid-way between roasting and braising. Meat or poultry is placed on a bed of vegetables and strips of ham, sprinkled with hot butter and roasted in the oven.

Cooking in the oven

In fairy tales the best things always come from the oven. From the technical standpoint this is an enclosed space in which all-round heat radiates onto the food. Large pieces of meat or poultry cook and brown at the same time. With modern technology this excellent basic method can be varied by the use of convection ovens, grills or microwaves.

Grilling

Cooking by browning under an open grill by radiated heat.

This method avoids a hard crust forming. The protein is broken down immediately so no juice is lost. Most of the nutritious value and flavour is preserved. Grilling is excellent for dieters or those on a special diet as it uses no fat.

Grilling is an extremely quick method of cooking used mainly for meat, fish and chicken.

1. Preheat the grill for at least 3 minutes.
2. Place food on the grill tray or spit.
3. Brush lightly with oil if liked, although food grills equally well without fat.

Four tips for grilling

– Season food before grilling but add salt when cooked.
– Brush with fat if food is to brown.
– Place flat food directly under the grill.
– Thicker foods which take longer to cook should be placed lower down under the grill.

Cooking au gratin

To brown dishes (e.g. cheese) by intense heat from above. Professional chefs use a salamander for this, but in the kitchen it is usually done under the grill.

Roasting

Cooking and browning in a little fat at a temperature of 200–240C, 400–475F, gas 6–9. Used for large pieces of meat.

1. Season meat and place in roasting tin.
2. Add a little fat.
3. Surround the meat with vegetables. (e.g. carrots, onion, celery).
4. Roast in a very hot oven (240C, 475F, gas 9) for 15 minutes.
5. Moisten with a little liquid (water or wine).
6. Reduce the heat and continue roasting in a moderately hot oven (200C, 400F, gas 6).
7. Baste the meat repeatedly as it roasts.
8. Use the juices to make a gravy.

Casserole-roasting

Cooking in a closed casserole, possibly with fat, at a temperature of 220C, 425F, gas 7. Before use soak earthenware casseroles in cold water.

Season the meat then roast in the casserole, with or without vegetables, in a hot oven (220C, 425F, gas 7). To brown the meat remove the lid about 20 minutes before the end of the cooking time.

Casseroling

Basically the same technique as braising (see page 38). Professional cooks prefer the latter method because the all-round heat of the oven is better for braising.

Food to be casseroled should, however, first be browned on the hob as this quick browning closes the pores in the meat quicker. When you have added the liquid cover the casserole and cook in a moderate oven (180C, 350F, gas 4).

Baking

Cooking in the closed oven in hot, dry air at a temperature of 120–240C, 250–475F, gas $\frac{1}{2}$–9.

Used for cakes, biscuits, bread, puddings. Most ovens have either top or bottom heat which means that only one shelf can be used. Never place baking tins directly on the bottom of the oven, but always in the middle. Shallow cakes go on the middle shelf, taller ones on the bottom shelf.

The hot air works on the surface of the food and the temperature depends on the type of food being baked. An average temperature is around 200C, 400F, gas 6.

Convection oven

In the back of the oven is a ventilator which sucks in the air, warms it and then returns it to the oven. With these ovens you can use several shelves for baking at the same time as the heat is evenly distributed.

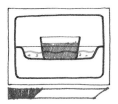

Bain-marie or water bath

Although similar to cooking with a bain-marie on the top of the stove (see page 37), there are important differences between the two methods. Food cooked by the former method (e.g. hollandaise sauce) must be stirred continuously in an open pan. In the oven the food is placed in a covered, buttered baking dish (usually earthenware). The water temperatures are the same in both cases, for which the oven needs to be set at cool (120–150C, 250–300F, gas $\frac{1}{2}$–2).

This is the classic method of cooking terrines.

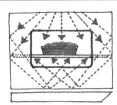

Microwave oven

Microwave ovens cook or warm up food much quicker than the conventional oven.

Microwaves are absorbed by organic matter, i.e. raw, cooked or frozen foods.

The waves penetrate to the inside of the food and heat it, while both the oven and the baking dish remain cold.

Metals reflect microwaves, but the waves pass through porcelain, glass, earthenware, ceramic, cardboard, paper and plastic, so any of the latter can be used in a microwave oven.

The short cooking time means that the food retains most of its goodness and flavour. Foods remain moist and look delicious. Microwaves do not brown but you can buy special browning dishes in ceramic glass which contain a layer of zinc oxide on the bottom. Some ovens include a grill which can be used for browning.

Advantages: makes quick meals very easily, frozen foods are soon ready to eat, many foods can be cooked without fat or water – an advantage for those on special diets.

Barbecuing

Popular for outside cooking. Barbecued food has a smoky flavour and should be seasoned or marinated before cooking.

Never cook over flames but over glowing embers. Do not barbecue very fatty meat for the fat will drip into the charcoal and burn, producing thick smoke.

Roasting in aluminium foil

An easy way of baking in the oven at high temperatures. Food remains moist but does not brown and crisp up. If you want the food to brown you will have to open the foil for the last 20 minutes.

You do not need additional fat for foil-roasting since the juices produced are caught in the foil and cannot evaporate. Use for meat, fish, vegetables.

Using roasting bags

Easy to use: food cooks in its own juice and no fat is necessary.

Roasting bags can be used only for meat or fish, or meat and vegetables. Since the steam does not escape most of the goodness and flavour is retained.

Always follow manufacturer's instructions otherwise the bag may split.

The pleasures of the table

What could be more enjoyable or more friendly than sharing a meal with friends? In ancient cultures eating was something of a ritual. The Chinese court had banquets of a hundred and twenty courses which lasted for three days and three nights; the Romans had mad orgies of eating; and it was at the court of the French Sun King that the pleasures of the table were imbued with strict ceremonial, with more stress placed on etiquette than on the act of eating. Nowadays we are thankfully more relaxed about eating, but we still have our rules and customs which have proved both practical and sensible over the centuries. Many of these customs have been updated and some have become obsolete but the pleasures of the table remain the same. Eating and drinking together is still one of our most enjoyable experiences, and if this is with someone we love, so much the better, for we are all familiar with the saying that the way to a man's heart is through his stomach.

The black elixir

To talk about coffee is to talk about Vienna. This old city on the Danube is as full of legends about coffee as it is with its aroma. The city's association with coffee began three hundred years ago when the fleeing Turks left behind a wagon-load of raw coffee. It ended with the Viennese coffee house becoming a world stage in miniature. Not only in Vienna – in the 'Cafe Odeon' in Zurich James Joyce, Sigmund Freud and a certain Trotsky discussed the ideas that were to change the world.

Those in power have looked on the black bean with some suspicion. On several occasions there has been prohibition of coffee. Frederick the Great sent coffee spies amongst his subjects; and to the church coffee was a hellish brew.

At the beginning of its career coffee was a man's world for it was not until the eighteenth century that it became domesticated. Bach was writing his famous Coffee Cantata and the age of the middle-class coffee shop was just over the horizon. While women were at first merely tolerated in the coffee houses, they have taken them over during the present century.

What was once a pleasure for a small number of the upper classes is today the drink of the people. But if prepared correctly, and with a little imagination, there is still an air of luxury and a touch of the exotic about coffee. The basic recipe is still valid today – hot as hell, black as the devil, pure as an angel, sweet as love. If this is not enough for you, read on.

1. Coffee with whipped cream
Black coffee topped with lightly sweetened whipped cream and sprinkled with cocoa powder

2. Café noisette
Coffee flavoured with a dash of cherry brandy and sugar.

3. Espresso
Made with a dark-roasted coffee in an espresso machine which forces hot steam through the ground coffee. Always serve espresso in small cups.

4. Mocha
A strong, high-quality coffee served in small cups.

5. Café au lait
or 'Cafe latte'. Half strong, hot coffee and half hot milk. Served in a large cup.

6. Iced coffee
Place 1–2 spoons vanilla ice cream in a tall glass and top up with cold, sweetened coffee. Pipe whipped cream onto the top and decorate with a maraschino cherry and grated chocolate.

7. Pharisee
Coffee flavoured with rum.

8. Irish Coffee
Place 2–3 tablespoons whiskey in an Irish coffee-glass and top up with strong, hot coffee. Top with 1 tablespoon whipped cream.

9. Turkish coffee
Made with a special, mild-roasted coffee. The ground coffee is boiled with water and sugar in a special metal jug.

10. Emperor coffee
Beat 1 egg yolk with 2 teaspoons cream and add 1 cup hot coffee. Sweeten with a little sugar and flavour with brandy.

The secret of coffee

The name comes from a region of Ethiopia called Kaffa, where the first coffee trees grew wild in the woods. The stimulative effect of the green beans was first observed in animals feeding from the trees. To be precise, coffee beans are the seed kernel of the coffee tree fruit. They contain 1–2 per cent caffeine together with tannic acid and volatile oils. While the effects of the caffeine are present even in the raw state, the smell and flavour is brought out only by roasting.

Coffee buying – past and present

At one time good specialist coffee shops stocked up to two dozen different varieties, which were distinguished one from the other by: country of origin (Brazil, Costa Rica, Cuba, etc.); bean size; and degree of roasting.

Customers could have their own personal blend made up once they had established what they preferred. This individual style of buying coffee has not proved as popular in the present day, partly on grounds of cost and partly through lack of interest although there are still some specialist shops selling just coffee.

Today large companies produce blends based on market research which contain beans from several countries roasted to an acceptable degree.

Cheap coffees with a bitter after-taste have usually been roasted almost black in an attempt to make cheap beans taste like mocha.

Delicious drinks

A dinner without a drink – that is worse than a dinner without company. You are never alone with the right wine in your glass. On the other hand dining with friends is unimaginable without drinks. Alcohol not only produces a relaxed atmosphere and lively conversation, it is also good for you since it aids digestion – in moderation, of course!

Many people are understandably apprehensive about wine in the face of the wide choice of years, types and countries available. While it is true that for experts wine is a science with a secret language of its own, it is no longer a forbidden area for the layman. Quite the reverse. Equipped with a few basic rules you should not make any serious mistakes. We will tell you here as much as you need to know to get by.

Rules for beginners

As a general rule serve only dry wines with meals – either white or red. Sweet wines do not go well with food and are more indigestible. Dry does not, however, mean sour. Dry German wines usually have yellow tops or are marked 'Trocken' on the label. French, Italian or Swiss wines are usually fairly dry.

If you are serving several wines with a meal work up from the lightest to the heaviest – begin with white and progress to red.

Rosé wines, although very popular at one time, are not good with food, though possibly acceptable with a light hors d'oeuvre. They are better as an aperitif. Always have plenty of mineral water on the table. This is good to drink between different wines, for those who are thirsty or for teetotallers. Do not serve sweet fruit juices with meals.

A wine cooler with ice cubes and iced water is not only decorative, but also useful for keeping opened bottles cool.

Aperitifs

Sherry or gin have long been popular as aperitifs but other drinks rise and fall in popularity as fashions change. Kir is extremely popular at present.

Basic Kir recipe

(illustrated above)

½ teaspoon blackcurrant syrup or crème de cassis topped up with chilled, dry white wine.

Variation: **Kir Royale**

½ teaspoon crème de cassis
I dash cherry brandy

Top up with chilled champagne or dry sparkling white wine.

White wine

A good glass for white wine should be of thin glass and curving in slightly at the rim. This gives you the full aroma of the wine as you drink.

Straightforward table wines can also be drunk from stemless glasses.

The glass should mist over slightly when filled – usually three-quarters full.

Serve chilled.

Drink with: white meat (poultry, veal, fish), egg and pasta dishes, vegetable and potato bakes – providing none of these is too highly seasoned.

Burgundy

A burgundy glass has the classic rounded wine-glass shape which traps the fine aroma of this world-famous red wine. Before drinking swirl the wine gently round the glass and sniff it first. Never fill Burgundy glasses more than one third full.

Beaujolais Primeur. Another wine from Burgundy, but drunk from different glasses, a simple bistro balloon glass or even from small tumblers.

Drink with: red meat (beef, game), smoked fish, highly seasoned stews, casseroles and cheese.

Beer

The traditional beer glass is slightly tulip-shaped, but beer can also be served in tankards, tumblers or tall tapered glasses. Correct care of glasses is more important with beer than other drinks. Never wash glasses with soap or detergent but use clear water if you want the beer to keep a good head of froth.

When serving hold the glass at an angle and pour the beer in slowly.

Don't serve too cold: beer is usually drunk much too cold and loses much of its flavour.
Drink with: pork, hot foreign dishes (e.g. curry or chilli), hamburgers, cheese, herrings.

Clear spirits

Rye whisky, *eau de vie* and vodka should be served in small stemmed glasses or small tumblers with slightly larger glasses for doubles.

Spirits should always be served refrigerated. If glasses are taken from the freezer they frost over in warm air and look particularly attractive.
Drink with: after fatty foods. *Eau de vie* can also be served with oily fish. Serve vodka after Russian dishes or as an aperitif.

Bordeaux

Served in the classically beautiful tulip glass which, according to wine experts, brings out all the qualities of these great wines to the full. Of course these glasses can be used for any red wine. Don't forget to swirl the wine around the glass and sniff the bouquet before drinking (see Burgundy)!

Never fill tulip glasses more than a quarter full.

Like Burgundies, Bordeaux wines should always be opened before you begin the meal to allow the wine to breathe.

Very old wines should be decanted (poured slowly into a carafe) so that any sediment remains in the bottle. Professional wine waiters decant over a candle to illuminate the dark glass.
Drink with: see Burgundy.

Brandy

A brandy glass can of course be used to serve Armagnac, Calvados, fruit brandies, Grappa or other wine-based liqueurs.

Don't fill more than a finger's breadth full.

Serve Cognac and Armagnac at room temperature. To warm brandy hold the bowl of the glass in the palm of your hand and swirl the brandy around the glass.

For fruit brandies and wine-based liqueurs chill glasses with ice before serving room-temperature spirits.

Depending on age, Calvados can be served warm like brandy or cold like fruit brandy. Find out for yourself which you prefer!

Champagne

A narrow, tapering glass, either with or without a stem, is best for champagne or sparkling wine. At one time flat, wide champagne glasses were all the rage even though these did little justice to the fizz of sparkling wines.

Fill champagne glasses almost to the rim – a half-filled glass just isn't the same.

Serve chilled but not frozen. The basic rule is: the better the wine the less cool you should serve it. Never serve thoroughly chilled, for if too cold champagne loses its flavour and bouquet.

Dry champagne (Brut) or sparkling wine (Extra Dry) can be served with any course of the meal and is a popular aperitif at present.

Sweet champagnes go well with desserts.

Beautiful table settings

A rough wooden table in a mountain chalet, bread and butter eaten with a wedge of Cheddar cheese, a glass of fresh milk, can make an unforgettable meal. But to impress guests in your own home you will need to do rather more, although the finest is not always the best. A simple casserole calls for a different type of table setting than a formal dinner. The following basic rules should prove helpful.

Two basic table settings

Simple meals:
Coloured linen tablecloth with matching serviettes and possibly wicker tablemats, earthenware serving dishes and plates, cast-iron casseroles, cutlery with wooden handles, wooden boards, earthenware bowls, simple salt cellar, thick glasses, whisky tumblers, wild flowers, etc.

Formal meal:
White damask tablecloth and serviettes, silver place plate, delicate white (patterned) porcelain, silver cutlery, delicate stemmed wine glasses (at least two per person), cultivated flowers such as roses, etc. These suggestions are intended to point you in the right direction rather than to be followed slavishly.

The art of serving a full menu

With the arrival of nouvelle cuisine it has become more customary to serve dishes directly on the plate. The waiter no longer brings a series of serving dishes to the table where the meat is cut, carved or divided into portions – now food is artistically arranged and garnished on the plate in the kitchen, covered with a silver plate cover and served. This is a method that you can adopt at home (without the silver plate cover). Alternatively you can combine the two methods within one menu, serving starters and entrées on the plate and bringing the main course (leg of lamb or whole fish, for instance) to be served at the table. With the advent of courses served on the plate, the place plate has become fashionable. This is larger than a dinner plate, often in silver or more usually glass. Octagonal plates are very popular. The place plate remains on the table throughout the meal and the plates for each course are placed upon it.

Cutlery for a menu of several courses should always be arranged from the outside inwards with forks on the left and knives on the right and dessertspoons above the plate. Cutlery for the first course should always be on the outside. If this is a soup, the soup spoon should be on the extreme right.

Glasses should always be placed to the right of the place setting, again arranged from the outside inwards, which would normally mean the white-wine glass first and then the glass for red wine. If you want to be absolutely correct the knife for each course should point to the corresponding wine glass.

Aperitifs should be served from a tray and the glasses taken away before you begin eating. For after-dinner drinks do not put glasses on the table until everyone has decided what they are going to drink.

A gala menu

From the feasts of old when everything was placed on the table together and the guests worked their way through it at their own pace, the French developed the classic menu with one course succeeding another. The basic idea behind this was to make food more digestible by making the meal better balanced and to create an almost musical crescendo of taste sensations with the starter and entrée serving as an overture to the high spot of the meal – the main course. Flavour and seasoning should increase as the menu progresses. The taste possibilities of an eight or ten course nouvelle cuisine menu are self-evident.

Menu

Cold starter

Hot starter

Soup

Fish

Sorbet

Poultry

Meat

Dessert

Cheese

Fruit

Coffee/Pastries

Composing your own menus

The most basic set menu consists of three courses and it is difficult to go wrong with this – hot or cold starter or soup – main course of meat or occasionally fish – dessert.

A set menu worthy of the name should have five courses: starter – fish course – meat course – dessert – cheese.

This basic outline provides ample opportunity for variation. For instance: fish soup – vegetable bake – meat course – dessert – cheese. Or: salad – fish – sorbet – meat – cheese. Or as in Italy: hors d'ouevre platter – pasta – vegetable course – meat or fish – dessert.

With coffee or espresso to follow the meal every time.

More than five courses is difficult at home and if this is what you want it is better to try a good restaurant.

Simple menu

page 157	pea soup
pages 190–1	garnished chicken breast
pages 126–7	with braised carrots
page 104	and risotto
page 273	raspberry cream

Filling menu

pages 146–7	beef soup
page 152	with egg custard
page 140	mixed green salad
page 141	with vinaigrette dressing
pages 198–201	fillet steak
page 114	with herb butter
pages 112–13	and foil-baked potato
page 114	with curry curd cheese
page 276	red stewed fruit with sago

Italian menu

Festive menu

Preparing a menu

To impress your guests the main things required are organisation and planning. For a starter choose a cold terrine, smoked salmon, salads – all things that can be bought or prepared in advance. The soup can also be made in advance. The cheese course can be laid out on the board ready to serve (never serve straight from the refrigerator).

The dessert (ice cream, sorbet, fruit, pastries, etc.) should only need decorating.

This will leave you free to concentrate on the fish and meat courses, both of which should come fresh from the stove. If you organise yourself properly you should have only the finishing touches to add once your guests have arrived.

A few tips:

Choose your main courses so that one can be cooked in the oven and the other on the top of the stove to make optimum use of your stove.

Make a time schedule!

Don't worry about gaps between courses once your guests have taken the edge off their hunger. A flustered cook makes everyone feel uncomfortable.

Other points to consider

Plan the seating arrangements in advance.

Have French bread on the table throughout the meal and bring out chilled butter with the aperitif.

Don't fold serviettes intricately (this can be unhygienic).

Warm plates and have a rechaud or plate-warmer ready for use.

Forty-six examples using culinary building blocks

This and the following four double spreads contain forty-six examples of how the building-block system on which this book is based works. You will soon discover how simple it is to combine ideas from different chapters, how quickly you can think up new combinations – and what fun you can have with this new way of planning meals.

We have chosen examples of inexpensive, everyday, festive, dieting and special meals. But you can invent combinations based on different criteria, such as time-saving meals, seasonal foods or even a fish that you have been lucky enough to catch.

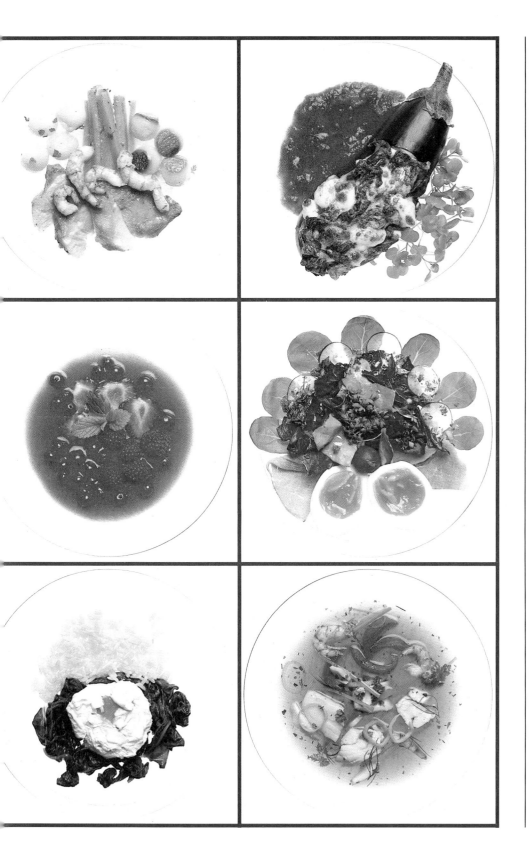

For dieters

Dieting sets automatic constraints on what you can eat. Fats and carbohydrates have to be kept to a minimum, while you need plenty of protein and vitamins. Anyone who has followed a reducing diet will know how monotonous they can be and how difficult to keep to. For dieters the building-block system offers a host of new combinations you can try.

1. Pork medallions (see page 208) with blanched mangetout (see page 130) and carrot balls (see pages 132 and 31).

2. Poached turbot (see pages 166–7) with blanched celery (see page 132) and boiled potatoes (see pages 112–13) in butter.

3. Carrot and potato purée (see page 117) with blanched peas (see page 130).

4. Boned chicken breast (see page 191) with prawns, blanched carrot sticks (see pages 132 and 32), kohlrabi (see page 128) and courgette balls (see pages 138 and 31).

5. Strawberry pureé (see pages 264–5) with redcurrants, raspberries and sliced strawberries.

6. Poached egg (see pages 64–5) on spinach (see page 128) with rice (see page 98).

7. Aubergines (see pages 138 and 225) with spinach and ricotta filling (see page 91).

8. Mixed salad of radicchio, corn salad, lettuce, Iceberg lettuce, radishes and watercress with vinaigrette dressing (see page 141), boiled ham and soft-boiled eggs (see pages 64–5).

9. Fish soup (see page 174) with tomatoes, cod, prawns, leek, carrot strips (see pages 32 and 132), dill and chervil.

Economical meals

When money doesn't come into it, all that is necessary is to know how to cook. But when funds are low – at the end of the month or when you come back from holiday – you will need a few clever tips if you are to have something appetising on your plate. Although this is not easy it is by no means impossible. You'll be amazed how cheaply you can surprise your family – especially if you follow our suggestions!

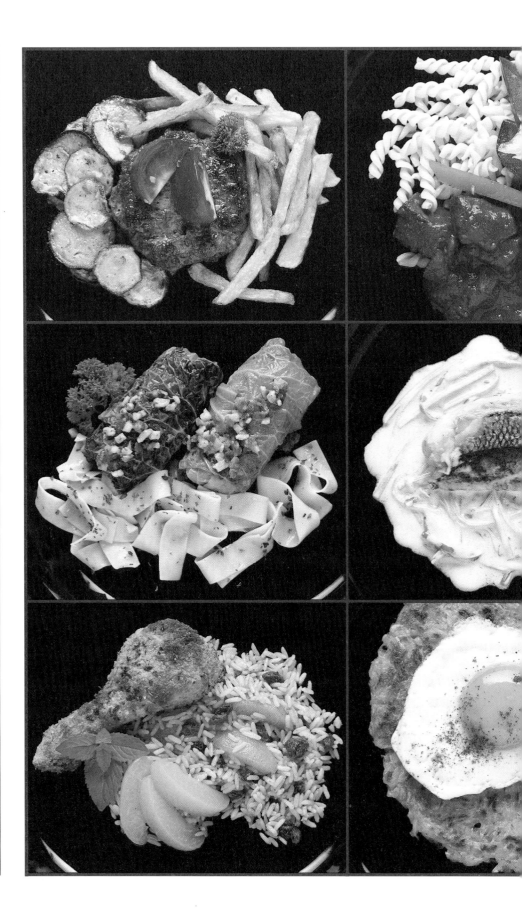

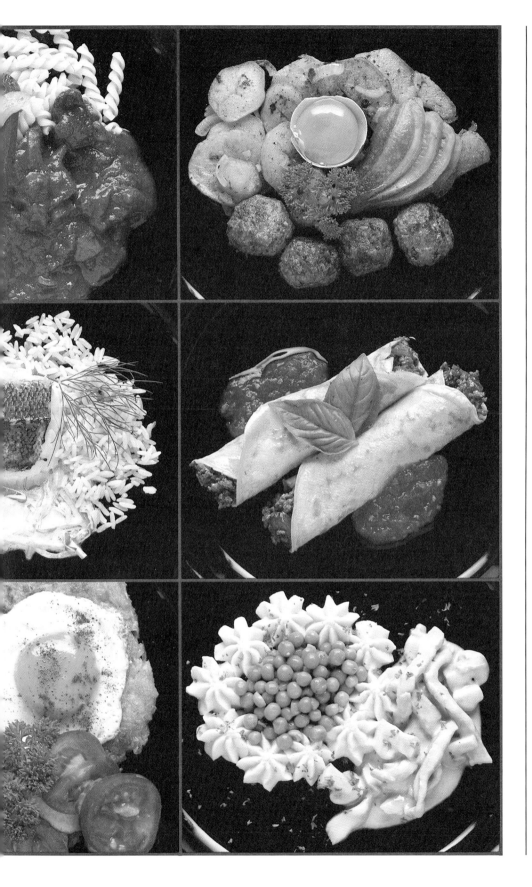

1. Rissoles (see pages 214–15) with fried aubergines and courgettes (see page 138) and chips (see pages 112–13).

2. Stuffed cabbage (see pages 220 and 226) with fried diced bacon and onion, and noodles (see pages 82–3).

3. Coated chicken drumstick (see page 192) with apricot and raisin curried pulao (see page 105).

4. Hungarian goulash (see page 238) with pasta fusili (see page 94) and peppers.

5. Braised fish fillet (see pages 166–7) with rice (see page 98).

6. Rösti (see page 121) with fried eggs and tomato and cucumber slices.

7. Fried potatoes (see pages 112–13) with meat balls (see pages 220 and 214), pickled cucumber, egg yolks and parsley. The egg yolk is stirred into the fried potatoes at the table.

8. Pancakes (see pages 64–5) with minced meat filling (see pages 74–5) and tomato sauce (see pagc 84).

9. Potato purée (see page 116) with peas (see page 130) and Zurich-style veal stew (see page 209).

Appetising everyday meals

Anyone who cooks every day knows how difficult it is to enjoy cooking all of the time and how easy it seems to make the same dishes week after week. But routine never made a good cook! Try something different every now and again. We have given some examples of interesting combinations and with a little imagination you can think up others of your own. Remember – variation not repetition.

I. Rolled veal (see page 241) with potatoes Anna (see page 122) and blanched kohlrabi with cream and chives (see page 128).

2. Lentil hot-pot (see page 160).

3. Poached cod cutlet (see pages 166–7) with tomato rice (see page 102), cucumber in butter, and chive sauce (see page 257) and dill.

4. Stuffed pepper baked with tomatoes (see page 225) and creamed potatoes (see page 120).

5. Green and white noodles (see pages 82–3 and 89) with butter, herbs (see page 87) and grated cheese.

6. Cream of tomato soup (see page 155) with rice.

7. Chicken curry (see page 195) with rice mould (see page 100), butter-fried apricots, coconut-banana (see page 191), garnished with cocktail cherries.

8. Meatball kebab (see page 220) and hot tomato sauce (see page 84) with pulao rice (see page 105).

9. Roast pork (see page 233) with potato purée (see page 116) and sauerkraut (see page 142).

Speciality meals

First it was foreign holidays, then the unfamiliar scents wafting from more and more restaurants, with cooks from France, India, Italy and China familiarising us with the flavours of foreign cuisine. It was inevitable that home cooking would eventually be affected by these foreign influences. With supermarkets and specialist food shops now stocking a host of foreign foods there is no limit to the exotic combinations that can be achieved.

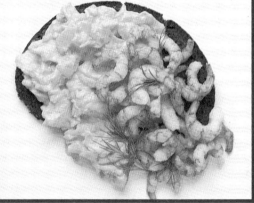

1. Tortellini (see page 90)
with broccoli (see page 128),
cheese sauce (see page 256) and grated
Parmesan cheese.

2. Boiled prawns (see page 173) on
risi e bisi (see page 108).

3. Scaloppine al Marsala sauce (see
page 210), noodles (see pages 82–3) and
celery (see page 132).

4. T-bone steak (see pages 207 and
198–9) with baked potatoes (see
pages 112–13), fried tomato, herb butter
(see page 114) and cress.

5. Pork schnitzel (see page 208) with
fried chanterelles and mushrooms (see
page 139) and croquette potatoes (see
page 118).

6. Beef roll (see page 240)
with Brussels sprouts (see page 129)
and boiled potatoes (see pages 112–13) in
butter.

7. Wun-tun (see page 92) with rice (see
page 98), sweet and sour sauce (see
page 194) and fried bean sprouts (see
page 138).

8. Rhenish marinated beef (see page 236)
with baked potatoes (see pages 112–13),
red cabbage (see page 135) and
breadcrumb butter (see page 252).

9. Curly kale (see page 135) with ham,
shoulder of pork and caramelised
potatoes (see page 120).

10. Brown bread with scrambled egg (see
pages 64–5) and buttered prawns (see
page 173).

Entertaining

Strangely enough it is in the area of entertaining that housewives often feel most limited – probably because they are not called on to produce formal dinner menus very often. On the other hand it is always nice to be able to serve something special when you have friends or relatives to dinner. Here the building-block system of this book can work minor miracles. With a little experience of trying different combinations your traditional roast will become unrecognisable.

1. Pork fillet (see page 208) with herb and wine butter (see page 252), broccoli (see page 128) and green noodles (see pages 82–3 and 89).

2. Larded pot-roasted beef (see page 233) with blanched celeriac, carrot and leek spindles (see page 33).

3. Breast of duck (see page 183) with beurre rouge (see page 251), potatoes au gratin (see page 122) and Savoy cabbage (see page 134).

4. Fillet of beef (see pages 198–9) with Béarnaise sauce (see page 255), mangetout (see page 130), carrots (see pages 126–7) and chanterelles (see page 139).

5. Chocolate mousse (see pages 264–5), redcurrant sorbet (see pages 264–5 and 271), cranberry ice cream (see page 277), kiwi purée (see page 268), sliced strawberries and nectarines and raspberries.

6. Rabbit with prunes (see page 236), spätzle (see page 83) and mushrooms (see page 139).

7. Turkey breast (see chicken breast, page 191) with rice parcels (see page 101), with leek and carrot strips (see pages 32 and 132–3) and beurre blanc (see pages 246–7).

8. Almond trout (see page 179) with boiled potatoes (see pages 112–13) and cucumber salad with vinaigrette dressing (see page 141).

9. Venison medallions (see page 208) with grapes, cranberries, duchess potatoes (see page 119) and cream sauce (see page 246).

Eggs: a miracle of white and gold

The egg is one of the most versatile of foods – perfectly formed, universally useful and pre-packaged. Since man first began to forage for food eggs have been part of his diet. The egg has always been regarded as the beginning of life – if you disregard the old chicken-and-egg dilemma – and as such has been universally celebrated as a symbol of springtime and fertility. In the kitchen it is an indispensable product which has always been highly prized indeed – every great name in the world of cookery has created at least one great egg dish.

Five traditional methods of cooking eggs

While it is true that eggs can be eaten raw or even addled and left to go bad as the Chinese do, neither would be to the taste of most egg-lovers. So here are the five most common methods of cooking eggs, as well as a tip for fried eggs – do not have the pan too hot or the white will brown before the yolk is cooked. If the pan is too cool the white will not solidify and the yolk will become solid. Plenty of butter, a moderate heat and a little patience – and you will have perfect fried eggs!

Testing for freshness

To test whether an egg is fresh break it into a cup or onto a plate. In a fresh egg the white should be firm and the yolk domed and firm. As the egg ages the white becomes thinner and the yolk will easily break. Older egg whites will not whisk as well as fresh ones. It is also possible for the white and the yolk to run into one another or be difficult to separate.

For gourmets

Gull, plover or quail's eggs are available from delicatessen shops, usually tinned or bottled.

Boiling eggs

1. Prick the egg at the flat end using an egg-piercer or needle.

2. Lower the egg into boiling water and leave to boil.

Poaching eggs

1. Bring salted water to the boil in a saucepan. Add 1 tablespoon vinegar.

2. Break the egg into a cup.

Scrambled eggs

 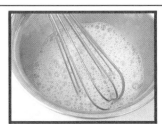

1. Break the eggs into a bowl.

2. Whisk thoroughly then season with salt and pepper.

Omelette

To make 1 omelette:

3–4 eggs
pinch of salt
2 tablespoons butter

(see also pages 70–1)

1. In a bowl lightly whisk the eggs and season with salt.

2. Heat the butter in a frying pan over a moderate heat. Pour in the eggs.

Pancakes

Makes 12

300 ml/½ pint milk
2 eggs
7 tablespoons flour
2 tablespoons sugar
pinch of salt
fat for frying

(see pages 72–5)

1. Break the eggs into the milk, whisk and season with salt.

2. Whisk in the flour and sugar 1 tablespoon at a time (avoiding lumps).

3. Plunge the egg into cold water after boiling.

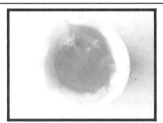

4. A 4-minute egg: the egg is soft and waxy.

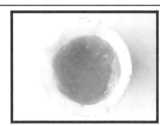

5. A 6-minute egg: the yolk is soft, the white firm.

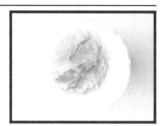

6. An 8-minute egg: both white and yolk are hard.

3. Carefully slide the egg into the water which should now be off the boil.

4. Use a spoon to hold the egg in shape.

5. Cook very gently for 4 minutes.

6. Remove the egg from the pan on a skimmer.

3. Melt butter or margarine in a frying pan over a moderate heat.

4. Pour in the whisked eggs.

5. When the eggs begin to set stir with a spoon.

6. Scrambled eggs should be light, soft and large-grained.

3. Stir the mixture immediately to mix the egg that is setting with the runny egg.

4. When a firm layer of egg has formed carefully roll up the omelette.

5. Tip the pan and slide the omelette to the edge.

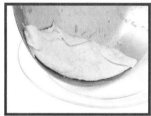

6. Slide the rolled omelette onto a plate.

3. Heat a little fat in a frying pan over a moderate heat.

4. When you add the batter tip the pan until the base is evenly covered.

5. Turn the pancake using a palette knife or spatula.

6. Fry until the pancake is golden brown on both sides.

Eggs transformed

The variations on a simple hen's egg almost borders on witchcraft, but variation is by no means its only attribute. Eggs are both good for you and highly decorative, and have long been one of the cook's main aids. Pale sauces can be coloured with egg yolk, thin sauces thickened, liquid butter transformed into delicious Hollandaise sauce, olive oil into mayonnaise. Whisked egg white makes creams and cake mixtures light, and makes the soufflé possible. Egg white clarifies cloudy meat stocks and is also the ideal adhesive for foodstuffs.

Eggs in a glass

(illustrated top left)
Place hard-boiled, shelled eggs in a glass, sprinkle with finely chopped herbs (optional), serve with butter, Worcestershire sauce and crushed peppercorns.

Cutting eggs

(illustrated bottom left)
Eggs for garnishing can be cut into even slices or wedges using an egg-slicer or cutter.

Easter eggs

(illustrated centre top)
Hard-boiled eggs are stained or painted.

Raw egg yolk

(illustrated centre)
Serve each portion of steak tatare with 1 egg yolk in the centre.

Stuffed eggs

(illustrated centre)
Halve boiled eggs lengthways. Carefully scoop out the yolks and beat with cream, crème fraîche, soured cream or mayonnaise, or soft butter, herbs and seasoning. Pipe the yolks back into the egg whites in rosettes. Garnish with caviar, anchovies, herbs, tomatoes or strips of salmon.

Pickled eggs

(illustrated top right)
Take the shells off hard-boiled eggs. Bring water and a good pinch of salt to the boil with herbs and seasonings (bay leaves, peppercorns, rosemary, caraway, cloves, red wine). Leave to cool and add the eggs. They are ready to eat in one to two days.

To serve:
Shell the eggs and halve across or lengthways. Remove the yolks and fill the hollows with oil, vinegar, mustard or hot spices according to taste. Top with the yolks, rounded side upwards.

Sunshine toast

(illustrated bottom right)
Garnish the rim of a buttered slice of toast with whisked egg white. Slide the raw egg yolk into the centre and brown in a hot oven (220C, 425F, gas 7) for 4–5 minutes.

Sieved egg yolk

(illustrated in the small spoon)
Pass hard-boiled egg yolk through a sieve. Excellent sprinkled on salads, smoked fish, asparagus.

Diced egg white

(illustrated in the large spoon)
Cut hard-boiled egg white into small cubes and use to garnish salads and other dishes.

Egg custard

(see soup chapter, page 152)
For adding to soups.

Egg noodles

(see soup chapter, page 152)

Meringue

Whisk egg whites with a little sugar until stiff. Used to lighten puddings and creams and to garnish fruit soups.

Egg snow

Whisk egg whites with sugar until firm and poach a spoonful at a time in milk. Serve with fruit purées or custard.

Twenty-four ways to serve scrambled eggs

One of the strange things about cooking is that even great chefs had a weakness for scrambled eggs. Perhaps this was due simply to the challenge of turning the most everyday food into something really unusual, so that truffles and caviar came to be associated with scrambled eggs. Gourmet appetisers like these were served in the shell. Although this looks very attractive it is rather fiddly for home cooking (the shells are sunk into a bed of salt). You can serve our suggestions in the normal way as did the great chef Escoffier when he served his famous scrambled egg to his friend, the actress Sarah Bernhardt. His recipe was extremely simple – to stir the egg in the frying pan he used a knife with a peeled clove of garlic stuck on the end. You should try it some time!

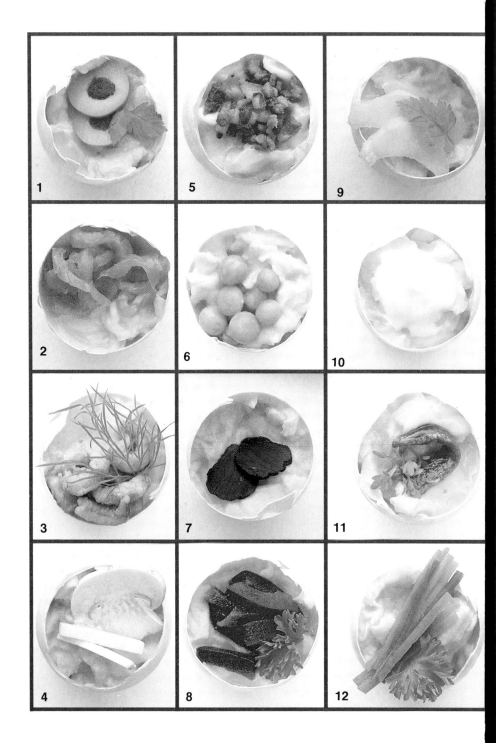

1. Stir sliced olives and parsley into the egg mixture.
2. Garnish with strips of smoked salmon.
3. Cook peeled prawns with the egg and garnish with dill.
4. Fry mushrooms and stir into the scrambled egg.
5. Fry diced bacon until crisp and cook the egg in the same pan.
6. Serve scrambled egg with braised peas.
7. Garnish with sliced truffle.
8. Cook the eggs with strips of pepper and garnish with parsley.
9. Mix artichoke hearts with the egg and garnish with chervil.
10. Serve with soured cream.
11. Stir in anchovy fillets and garnish with cress.
12. Stir in strips of braised carrot and leek, and garnish with parsley.
13. Mix with chopped cress.
14. Fry strips of garlic sausage and cook the eggs in the same pan.
15. Garnish with gherkins.
16. Whisk chives into the egg before cooking.
17. Stir grated cheese into the scrambled egg.
18. Cook with green peppercorns.
19. Mix with caviar or serve separately.
20. Crumble blue cheese into the egg before cooking.
21. Mix the scrambled egg with chopped, blanched spinach.
22. Stir in smoked fish and dill.
23. Mix with strips of tomato and garnish with fresh oregano.
24. Mix with sweet corn and stir in parsley.

A light luxury snack

Omelettes count amongst the most basic culinary dishes, but you need sensitive fingers, a lot of feeling and even more practice before what slides out of the frying pan onto a plate will deserve the name of omelette. But once you have mastered the art there will be no looking back. Omelettes have always had an air of luxury and this feeling can be heightened by a thoughtful choice of filling.

Tips for making omelettes

Experienced cooks use a special cast-iron pan with a rounded edge which makes it easier to slide the omelette out of the pan. The important thing is for the base of the pan to be smooth and non-stick. For this reason omelette pans should never be washed but merely wiped out with kitchen paper.

To make an omelette you need the same ingredients as for scrambled egg; only the method is different. Scrambled eggs are cooked over a low heat and stirred with a spatula or fork as they cook.

When cooking an omelette you want a firm layer of egg over the base of the pan while the top remains semi-liquid. So you need a higher temperature for omelettes than for scrambled eggs.

As a basic rule the omelette should not cook for longer than 1 minute.

Omelette fillings

Because omelettes are delicate in flavour they can be combined with a host of garnishes.

Make the omelette using the basic recipe (see pages 64–5), serve on a plate smooth side uppermost and cut down the centre. Arrange the filling in the slit.

Herb omelette

(Serves 1)
To make a herb omelette, stir 2 tablespoons chopped mixed herbs (e.g. basil, sage, parsley) into the egg mixture. Then cook as in the basic recipe and finally garnish with herbs.

Asparagus filling

(Serves 1)
Cut 100 g/4 oz boiled asparagus into short lengths, coat in 1 tablespoon butter and season with salt and pepper. Arrange the filling in the omelette and garnish with chopped chervil.

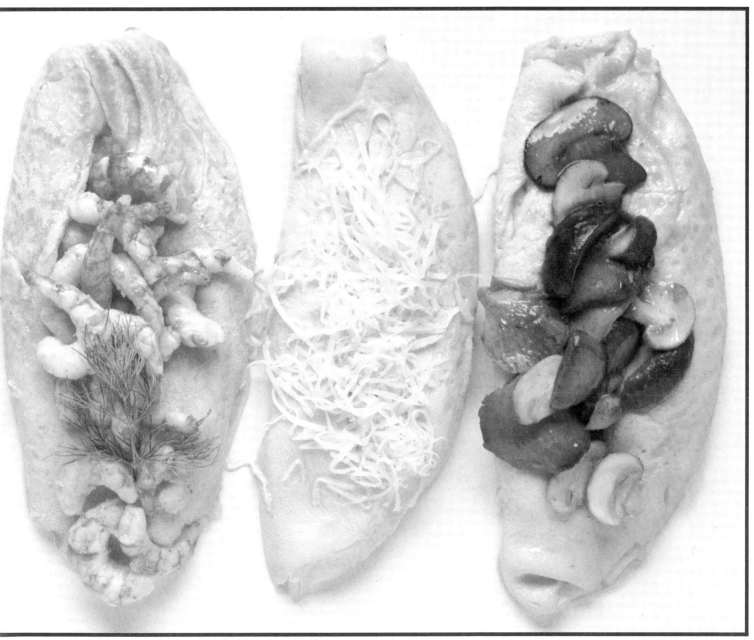

Prawn filling

(Serves 1)
Heat 50 g/2 oz peeled
prawns in 1 tablespoon
melted butter, arrange in
the omelette and garnish
with dill.

Cheese filling

(Serves 1)
Fill the slit in the omelette
with 2 tablespoons grated
Gruyère or Emmental
cheese.

Mushroom filling

(Serves 1)
Fry 100 g/4 oz mushrooms in
1 tablespoon butter, season
to taste and arrange in the
omelette.

Tip: When choosing fillings
for omelettes try some of
those suggested in the
scrambled egg section (see
pages 68–9). All recipes are
interchangeable.

If you prefer a sweet
filling, try one of the
pancake suggestions (see
pages 72–5). Be guided by
your own tastes in food.

Gourmet snacks from France

It is not only the Italian pizza and the American hamburger which have conquered the world, French crepes have also been part of the fast-food scene for some time. These gourmet pancakes are served as quick snacks in creperies, but you can also serve them at home in a variety of ways.

Tips for crepes

The batter should always be runny and if it becomes thick should be thinned down by adding milk and eggs. If you use cream instead of milk your crepes will be lighter.

If you add a little liquid butter to the batter the crepes take on a marvellous colour. Always leave the batter to stand for 30 minutes before use to allow the flour to dissolve.

For savoury fillings omit the sugar.

The basic batter can also be made with 2 tablespoons finely chopped herbs. Crepes are excellent for adding to soup when cut into thin strips.

For the experienced cook kitchen shops sell special crepe pans.

The five basic shapes

1. Twisted into cones (large photograph) crepes are extremely attractive when served with a filling.

2. For flambéing crepes should be folded into triangles.

3. Rolled crepes are easy to fill. Unfilled rolls can be cut into strips to use in soups.

4. Crepe towers have several layers of pancakes with filling between. It can be cut like a cake for serving, in which case choose a thin filling such as jam.

5. Crepe parcels. After filling first fold opposite sides into the centre and then fold over the remaining sides.

Twelve ways to serve sweet crepes

1. Icing sugar
2. Crystallised sugar
3. Brown sugar
4. Grated coconut
5. Chopped or flaked almonds
6. Chopped pine nuts or peanuts
7. Grated chocolate
8. Chocolate vermicelli
9. Maple syrup
10. Honey
11. Peanut butter
12. Sprinkled with liqueur

A dozen suggestions for advanced cooks

Crepes are ideal to experiment with as any adventurous filling that suggests itself will be suitable. These range from the fabulous and proverbial Crepes Suzette (grated orange peel, curaçao, sugar, melted butter) to recipes known only to the real afficionados and passed on by word of mouth (cranberry sauce with crushed black pepper). We suggest a dozen original fillings in the hopes that they will inspire you to create your first truly original recipe.

Savoury crepes

1. Crepes with *chicken fricassee* (see page 194) garnished with lemon wedges and chervil.
2. Crepes filled with cubes of fried *chicken livers* and chopped herbs, garnished with basil.
3. Crepes with strips of fried *ham* and onion rings, garnished with parsley.
4. Crepes filled with flaked *tuna* and garnished with onion rings and dill.
5. Crepes filled with *mixed vegetables* and garnished with watercress.
6. Crepes filled with fried *minced meat*, pepper and onion and garnished with pepper and parsley.

Sweet crepes

1. Crepes filled with *apple slices* fried in butter and sultanas, sprinkled with Calvados and flaked almonds.
2. Crepes spread with *orange jam* and sprinkled with orange liqueur, blanched grated orange rind and icing sugar.
3. Crepes spread with *nut and nougat cream* and sprinkled with grated chocolate.
4. Crepes filled with *raspberry compote* (see pages 264–5) and vanilla ice cream and sprinkled with praline.
5. Crepes filled with *banana* slices fried in butter and sprinkled with grated coconut.
6. Crepes sprinkled with *lemon juice* and chopped pistachios and decorated with a slice of lemon.

Pancakes: the crepe's country cousin

Language describes these two things most admirably. Crepes – the very word has a breath of France about it. Pancake – this sound solid, substantial and crisp and aptly describes a dish that is as easy to make as it is to eat. It is immaterial if one pancake turns out thicker, or misshapen, or browner than the rest. This is all part of its image. If you want, you can alter the quantity of flour and egg to suit your own taste. And if one day you come across your own special pancake batter, you will have joined the experts!

Tip: Pancake batter can be made with buttermilk or oatmeal. If using buttermilk, reduce the amount of milk. If including oatmeal, reduce the amount of flour.

The batter will be lighter if you whisk the egg whites, for which you will have to separate the eggs and beat in the yolks and whites separately.

For frying, cast-iron or copper pans are ideal.

Basic recipe for cherry pancakes

6 eggs
pinch of salt
2–3 tablespoons sugar
600 ml/1 pint milk
225 g/8 oz flour
3 tablespoons butter for frying
450 lb/1 lb sweet or morello cherries, stoned
sugar to sprinkle

1. Beat the eggs with the salt, sugar and milk. Stir in the flour a spoonful at a time to avoid lumps. Strain the batter if necessary.
2. Heat a little of the butter in a frying pan over a moderate heat. Pour in a quarter of the batter and spread with a quarter of the cherries. Keep an eye on the pancake for the batter burns easily. Reduce the heat if necessary. Fry until the bottom of the pancake is golden brown.
3. Use a plate or saucepan lid the same size as the frying pan to help you turn the pancake over. Place the upper side of the plate on the pancake, hold firmly in position and turn both pan and plate over together. The pancake is now on the plate cooked side uppermost.
4. Add more butter to the pan. Slide the pancake off the plate into the pan and fry the other side. Check that the pan is not too hot or the fruit will burn.
5. Before serving sprinkle with sugar. Repeat with the rest of the batter and the cherries so that four pancakes are produced.

Bilberry pancakes

Wash 450 g/1 lb bilberries, remove leaves and stalks, drain thoroughly and cook as in the basic recipe. Blueberries can be used instead of bilberries if the latter are unobtainable.

Bacon pancakes

Fry 150 g/5 oz bacon and 2–3 onions cut into rings in butter for 3 minutes. Spread over the batter in the pan as for Cherry pancake.

Plum pancakes

Stone and halve 675 g/1½ lb plums and cook as in the basic recipe.

Apple pancakes

Peel, core and slice 675 g/1½ lb apples and cook as in the basic recipe. Before serving sprinkle with sugar and cinnamon.

Crespelle with meat filling

From Italy, crespelle are savoury stuffed crepes in a cheese sauce.

I. *For the filling:*

1 tablespoon butter

1 onion, diced

1 clove garlic, crushed

225 g/8 oz each veal tongue, veal and chicken breast, finely chopped

2 tablespoons flour

600 ml/1 pint dry white wine

300 ml/½ pint single cream

juice of ½ lemon

100 g/4 oz mushrooms, coarsely chopped

salt and pepper

2. *For the crepes:*

300 ml/½ pint milk

2 eggs

7 tablespoons flour

2 tablespoons sugar

pinch of salt

fat for frying

3. *For the cheese sauce:*

40 g/1½ oz butter

40 g/1½ oz flour

600 ml/1 pint milk

2 egg yolks

2 tablespoons grated Parmesan cheese

4. *For baking:*

3 tablespoons grated Parmesan cheese

I. To make the filling: melt the butter in a saucepan over a moderate heat and gently fry the onion and garlic until transparent. Add the meat, sprinkle with the flour and stir in the white wine. Simmer gently over a moderate heat for 1 hour.

2. Stir in the cream and lemon juice. Stir in the chopped mushrooms and warm through. Season to taste.

3. Prepare the crepes as described on pages 64–5 and fill with the meat mixture. Arrange the crepes in a buttered ovenproof dish.

4. Cover with the cheese sauce made up as instructed on page 256. Sprinkle with Parmesan cheese and bake in a moderately hot oven (200C, 400F, gas 6) for 15–20 minutes.

Palatschinken with plum filling

'Palatschinken' is an Austrian word for stuffed crepes

Fry 12 crepes (see pages 64–5).

For the filling:

2–3 tablespoons plum brandy

450 g/1 lb plum purée

100 g/4 oz butter, melted

50 g/2 oz icing sugar

I. Stir the plum brandy into the purée and spread over the crepes.

2. Roll the crepes and arrange side by side in a buttered ovenproof dish.

3. Brush with the melted butter.

4. Put the dish in a hot oven (220C, 425F, gas 7).

5. Bake for about 10 minutes.

6. Sprinkle with sifted icing sugar.

Salzburg nockerln

This desert from Salzburg i a light, airy egg mixture.

6 eggs, separated

50 g/2 oz sugar

1 vanilla pod

40 g/1½ oz flour

1 tablespoon butter

2 tablespoons icing sugar

I. Beat the egg yolks with half the sugar for about 5 minutes until thick and creamy.

2. Slit the vanilla pod lengthways, scrape out the pith and stir this into the egg yolk mixture.

3. Whisk the egg whites with the remaining sugar until very stiff, adding the sugar after the whites are firm.

4. Stir a third of the egg whites into the egg yolk mixture with the flour.

5. Gently fold in the remaining egg whites.

6. Grease a large ovenproo dish with the butter.

7. Using a spatula, arrange the mixture in pyramids to fill the dish.

8. Bake in a moderately ho oven (200C, 400F, gas 6) fo 15 minutes, until golden brown.

9. Sprinkle with sifted icing sugar.

Kaiserschmarrn

Pancakes in bite-sized pieces which are cooked twice.

75 g / 3 oz flour
300 ml / ½ pint milk
2 eggs, separated
1 tablespoon sugar
3 tablespoons raisins
2 tablespoons butter
1 tablespoon icing sugar

1. Beat together the flour, milk, egg yolks, sugar and raisins to make a smooth batter.
2. Whisk the egg whites until stiff and fold into the batter.
3. In a frying pan heat 1 tablespoon butter over a moderate heat. Pour in the batter.
4. Fry until golden brown on both sides.
5. Using two forks, break the pancake into bite-sized pieces.
6. Add 1 tablespoon butter and fry for a further 3 minutes.
7. Sprinkle with the icing sugar.

Blinis

Small buckwheat pancakes from Russia.

150 g / 5 oz buckwheat flour
100 g / 4 oz flour
1½ teaspoons dried yeast
150 ml / ¼ pint lukewarm milk
2 eggs, separated
300 ml / ½ pint whipped cream
4 tablespoons butter for frying

1. Sift together the buckwheat and flour.
2. Sprinkle the dried yeast, over the milk and leave for 10 minutes or until frothy.
3. Work the egg yolks, cream and dissolved yeast mixture into the flour.
4. Leave the batter to rise in a warm place for about 1 hour.
5. Whisk the egg whites until stiff and stir into the batter.
6. If the batter is too thick dilute with a little more milk.
7. Heat the butter in a frying pan over a moderate heat and fry small pancakes.
8. Authentic blinis are served with caviar and soured cream.

Orange soufflé

Orange soufflé is a famous dessert from the great tradition of French cuisine.

175 ml / 6 fl oz milk
40 g / 1½ oz flour
40 g / 1½ oz butter, softened
3 eggs, separated
3 tablespoons orange liqueur
grated rind of 1 orange
50 g / 2 oz sugar
1 tablespoon icing sugar for dusting

1. Bring the milk to the boil.
2. Work the flour into the soft butter, stir into the hot milk and bring back to the boil.
3. Stir in the egg yolks one at a time.
4. Add the orange liqueur and rind.
5. Whisk the egg whites until stiff then slowly whisk in the sugar.
6. Stir a third of the whisked egg whites into the soufflé mixture.
7. Carefully fold in the remaining whites.
8. Lightly butter a soufflé dish and sprinkle with flour.
9. Pour the mixture into the dish and place on the middle shelf of the oven.
10. Bake in a moderate oven (180C, 350F, gas 4) for 30 minutes.
11. It is essential that you do not open the oven door while the soufflé is cooking or it will fall.
12. Sprinkle with sifted icing sugar and serve immediately.

Pasta: flour plus imagination

Even the French, who usually claim to have invented anything worth eating, have to admit that in the case of pasta the Italians are the unchallenged world champions. Indeed, it is quite fascinating to consider the whole range of pastas that have been concocted out of flour, eggs, salt and oil. It is only the real expert who knows the name of every type and variety and who can distinguish one from the other. Both the holiday-maker and the owners of Italian restaurants throughout the world rejoice in the fact that with a little dexterity and imagination they can achieve excellent results in their own kitchens.

Home-made pasta

Despite the amazing range of imported pasta on the supermarket shelves, as well as excellent manufactured pastas, there is nothing to beat home-made pasta. Once you have tasted it you will defend it with your rolling pin against all-comers! It is easier to make than you think. You don't necessarily need a pasta-maker although this does make the job easier.

Tips for pasta

Pasta can be served as a starter or light entrée, with a main course, in soup and also, with other ingredients added, as a main course in its own right.

The finishing touch for most pasta dishes is grated cheese, preferably fresh Parmesan. Cheese is sprinkled over the pasta just before serving or at the table.

Small pasta is eaten with a fork, spaghetti with a spoon and a fork. And here is how it's done: Spear a little spaghetti on your fork, place the point of the fork against your spoon and twist the fork. The spaghetti wraps round the prongs of the fork in manageable lengths. Italians have perfected the art with just a fork.

Basic pasta recipe

5 eggs
$\frac{1}{2}$ teaspoon salt
1–2 tablespoons oil
450 g/ 1 lb strong flour

For method see step-by-step photographs on the right.

Tip: If you make pasta with egg yolks rather than whole eggs, it will be beautifully light and a delicous golden-yellow in colour. For 450 g/ 1 lb flour use about 9 egg yolks. Work in a little water if necessary.

1. Get utensils and ingredients ready.

2. Break the eggs into a bowl.

3. Add the salt and oil.

4. Thoroughly beat the eggs, oil and salt.

5. Add 5 tablespoons flour.

6. Beat to give a smooth batter.

7. Pour the batter onto the remaining flour.

8. Work the flour thoroughly into the batter.

9. Knead the dough until smooth and glossy.

10. Wrap the dough in a damp tea-towel.

11. Leave for 30 minutes.

12. Press the dough flat and pass through the pasta-maker.

13. Join the two ends of the pasta.

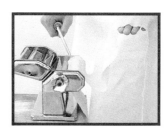

14. Turn the machine to the thinnest setting and pass the dough through once more.

15. Cut into thin strips.

Cooking perfect pasta

Pasta needs a lot of liquid (use 1–2 litres/2–4 pints salted water per 100 g/4 oz pasta). The water must be fast boiling when you add the pasta. The addition of 1 tablespoon oil will prevent the pan boiling over, while the occasional stir will prevent the pasta sticking together.

The cooking time is important. Italians cook pasta 'al dente', so that it still has some bite to it.

The best way is to scoop a piece out of the pan and try it when you think the pasta is almost cooked. In time you will find the precise cooking time for the degree of cooking you prefer.

Overcooked pasta becomes soft and soggy and loses both its attractive appearance and its flavour.

Basic rule: thin pasta (vermicelli and noodles) should be cooked for 3–4 minutes, thicker pasta (macaroni, spaghetti, shells) for 6–10 minutes.

As shown in the step-by-step photographs, the cooked pasta can be plunged into ice-cold water and then warmed through in plenty of butter or olive oil. Or serve Italian-fashion, straight from the pan to the table.

1. Heat 3–4 litres/6–8 pints water in a large pan and add 1 tablespoon salt.

2. Add 1 tablespoon oil.

3. Drop the pasta into the boiling water.

4. Stir well to prevent the pasta sticking together.

5. Turn the heat to moderate.

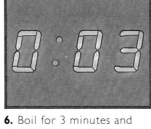

6. Boil for 3 minutes and then test to see if the pasta is cooked.

7. Pour the pasta into a sieve and drain thoroughly.

8. Rinse under cold water.

9. Melt butter in a pan.

10. Warm the pasta through in the butter.

Pasta without a machine

Make the pasta as shown in the step-by-step photographs up to step 11. Then on a floured worktop roll out the dough thinly and evenly with a rolling pin, lightly sprinkling the dough with flour from time to time as you work. Spread the sheets of dough on tea-towels to dry. When the dough is no longer tacky cut it into strips of the required width using a kitchen knife. It is also possible to make other shapes yourself (see pages 90–1).

Spätzle

350 g/12 oz flour
pinch of salt
4 eggs
150 ml/¼ pint stock or water
75 g/3 oz butter
pinch of freshly grated nutmeg

1. Beat the flour, salt, eggs and stock (or water) together and continue beating until the paste is light and airy.
2. Transfer 4 tablespoons paste on to a narrow wooden board and smooth flat with a wet, wide-bladed knife. Using the knife, scrape the dough into the water over the edge of the board into a saucepan of boiling water.
3. Cook for about 2 minutes, drain in a sieve and rinse in cold water.
4. Melt the butter and coat the thoroughly drained spätzle. Season to taste with nutmeg.

Traditional accompaniments

Pasta without a sauce can be a culinary delight, served with grated white truffles for instance, but for everyday pasta dishes – and for special occasions too – a good sauce is usually essential. The numerous sauces made famous by Italian pasta cooks are all variations on three basic recipes – cream sauce, tomato sauce or a green sauce. Three points of departure for your imagination.

Carbonara

(illustrated top right)

450 g/ 1 lb ribbon noodles
4 egg yolks
4 tablespoons double cream
50 g/ 2 oz Parmesan cheese, grated
salt and pepper
100 g/ 4 oz gammon or bacon
1 tablespoon oil

1. Make the pasta using the basic recipe (see pages 82–3) and cook.
2. Beat the egg yolks with the cream and gradually beat in half the Parmesan cheese. Season to taste.
3. Cut the gammon or bacon into strips. Fry in the hot oil for 3–4 minutes, add the noodles and warm through.
4. Turn off the heat. Stir the egg, cream and cheese mixture thoroughly into the noodles and sprinkle with the remaining Parmesan cheese.

Basic cream-sauce recipe

1 onion
1–2 cloves garlic, crushed
2 tablespoons olive oil
600 ml/ 1 pint double cream
40 g/ 1½ oz Parmesan cheese, grated
salt and pepper
pinch of freshly grated nutmeg

1. Finely chop the onion and fry with the garlic in the olive oil until transparent.
2. Add the cream and, over a moderate heat, reduce by half.
3. Remove the pan from the heat and stir in the Parmesan cheese.
4. Season with the salt, pepper and nutmeg.

Mushroom and cream sauce

(illustrated centre bottom)
Make as for the basic cream sauce.
  In addition: warm through 100 g/ 4 oz sliced mushrooms in the cream sauce.

(illustrated centre)
Make as for the basic cream sauce.
  In addition: warm through 2 tablespoons finely chopped herbs (basil, thyme, oregano, parsley) in the cream sauce.

Pesto

(illustrated left)
For ingredients and method see page 149.

Basic tomato sauce recipe

2 tablespoons oil or butter
1 onion, finely chopped
1 clove garlic, crushed
800 g/ 1¾ lb fresh tomatoes
1 tablespoon basil, finely chopped
½ teaspoon salt
pinch of sugar

1. Heat the oil or butter.
2. Add the onion and garlic and fry for about 2 minutes over a moderate heat.
3. Plunge the tomatoes into boiling water and peel, then chop coarsely and add to the pan.
4. Reduce over a high heat for about 15–20 minutes until the sauce is quite thick.
5. Season with the basil, salt and sugar.

Hot tomato sauce

(illustrated bottom right)
Make as for the basic tomato sauce recipe.

Additional ingredients:
100 g/ 4 oz bacon
1–3 chillies
50 g/ 2 oz Parmesan cheese, grated

Finely dice the bacon and fry with the onion and garlic. Add the chillies with the tomatoes. Stir the cheese into the tomato sauce just before serving.

Bolognese sauce

(illustrated top left)
See page 226.

The thirty tastiest combinations

Potatoes are excellent for dressing up, rice is even better, but best of all is pasta, for the variety of shapes means it will go with almost anything. The range of combinations goes from shellfish to left-over cheese. With pasta it is easy for beginners to develop their own ideas at the stove and to try out new combinations.

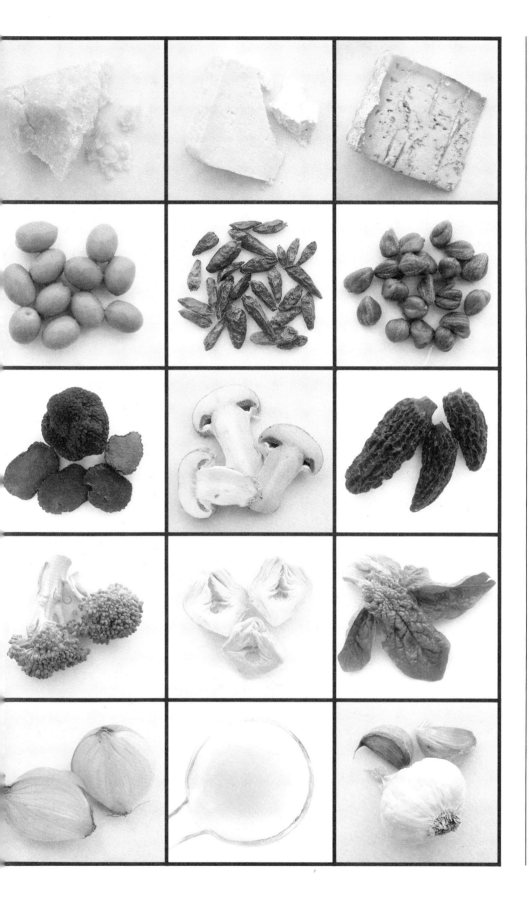

Mussels cooked in white wine and shelled.
Fresh cooked prawns stirred in.
Squid pieces cooked for 3 minutes in white wine.
Parmesan cheese, grated and sprinkled over.
Ricotta cheese, finely crumbled and stirred in.
Gorgonzola, finely crumbled and mixed with hot pasta shells.

Salami strips mixed in.
Parma ham, added to pasta diced or sliced.
Bacon, diced, fried and added to pasta.
Olives, added finely chopped.
Chillies, added finely chopped.
Finely chopped capers added.

Egg yolk stirred into hot pasta.
Melted butter to coat cooked pasta.
Cream stirred in.
Truffles, peeled, chopped and sprinkled over pasta.
Mushrooms, added chopped or sliced.
Morels warmed through in hot pasta.

Tomato purée, stirred with wine and mixed in.
Peperoni, coarsely chopped and stirred in.
Tomatoes, peeled, quartered and deseeded.
Broccoli, quick-boiled and added with a little butter.
Artichoke hearts, quartered and warmed through in pasta.
Blanched spinach, coarsely chopped and stirred in.

Basil, finely chopped and stirred in.
Rosemary, finely chopped and stirred in.
Oregano, finely chopped and stirred in.
Onion, finely chopped, fried in olive oil and stirred in.
Olive oil, heated and stirred in.
Garlic, crushed, fried in olive oil and stirred in.

The art of pasta colouring

The Italians would not be true to their artistic nature if they limited themselves to inventing new shapes for pasta – quite early on they discovered natural methods of colouring their national dish. The time involved is hardly worth mentioning – but the effects are beautiful! Coloured pasta can make a simple dish look stunning, especially if you mix pasta of various colours. You can surprise your guests with contrasting colours – red pasta with broccoli – or go for pleasant toning colours – yellow pasta with egg dishes. This should give you something to think about!

Make pasta using the basic recipe (see page 82) with the following additions.

Herby pasta

Add about 2 tablespoons very finely chopped herbs to the eggs and work with the flour to give a smooth dough.

Tomato pasta

Beat 2–3 teaspoons concentrated tomato purée into the eggs before adding to the flour.

Saffron pasta

Dissolve $\frac{1}{2}$ level teaspoon saffron powder or ground saffron strands in 1 tablespoon hot water and work into the dough.

Beetroot pasta

To make a stronger colouring, reduce 3 tablespoons beetroot juice by half, beat into the eggs and add to the flour.

Variations:

There are no limits to what you can come up with here. The colour of the basic pasta recipe can, for example, be varied by adding the following ingredients: carrot juice, paprika, puréed spinach.

Making your own shapes

Once you can make and colour your own pasta it won't be long before you want to try making the classic shapes yourself. This will give your pasta a personality all of its own, something which guests still appreciate, even today. Next time you have guests for dinner you should try it and see. Nothing can go wrong if you follow one essential rule in making the pasta. Do not allow the pasta to dry out or it will become crumbly and impossible to work. It is best to cover it with a damp cloth before you start to shape it.

The following shapes are simple to make without a pasta-maker from the basic recipe (see page 82).

Lasagne

(illustrated bottom left) Cut the pasta into rectangles 10 × 15 cm/ 4 × 6 in. Arrange in layers in a buttered ovenproof dish with a Bolognese sauce (see page 226) and béchamel sauce (see page 226), sprinkle with cheese and bake in a moderately hot oven (200 C, 400 F, gas 6) for about 30 minutes.

Cannelloni

(illustrated above left) Cut pasta rectangles of about 10 × 15 cm/4 × 6 in and roll up with the filling (see page 92).

Tortellini

(illustrated top left) Roll out the dough until thin on a floured board. Cut into 5-cm/2-in squares and cover with a little filling (see recipe on opposite page). Fold the squares over into triangles – it is not essential for the points to meet exactly. Press the edges gently together. Turn the two outer corners in towards the centre and press together.

Ravioli

(illustrated above centre)
Using a pastry wheel or zig-zag cutter, cut the pasta into 5-cm/2-in rounds. Top with the filling (recipe on the right), moisten the edges and fold over.

Ricotta and spinach filling

for tortellini and ravioli
(illustrated above)

450 g/ 1 lb spinach
225 g/ 8 oz ricotta cheese
2 eggs
100 g/ 4 oz Parmesan cheese, grated
salt and pepper

1. Boil the spinach for 2–3 minutes, squeeze out excess moisture and coarsely chop.
2. In a basin crumble the ricotta cheese and mix with the spinach, eggs and Parmesan.
3. Season to taste.

Can be used to fill any type of sealed pasta.
There are more fillings on the following pages.

Meat filling

for ravioli and tortellini
(illustrated above)

1 tablespoon butter
100 g/ 4 oz turkey breast, finely diced
75 g/ 3 oz garlic sausage, finely chopped
75 g/ 3 oz uncooked ham, in strips
1 egg
100 g/ 4 oz Parmesan cheese, grated
pinch of nutmeg
salt and pepper

Melt the butter in a frying pan over a moderate heat. Fry the turkey breast for 5 minutes. Transfer to a basin and mix thoroughly with all the remaining ingredients.

Noodles

(illustrated bottom right)
Noodles can be made either with a pasta maker (see page 82) or by hand.

Sprinkle the rolled-out dough liberally with flour and roll up. Using a knife, cut the roll into slices of the required width and unroll. For wavy-edged noodles cut strips from a flat sheet of dough using a zig-zag patterned knife or pastry wheel (illustrated above right).

Hidden goodness

All credit to the Italians for inventing pasta, but when we come to fillings cooks in other countries have also come up with a few good things. You should familiarise yourself with these fillings before you begin to experiment with your own.

Maultaschen

(illustrated top left)

For the filling:
75 g/3 oz bacon, diced
4 tablespoons butter
225 g/8 oz minced meat
(½ beef, ½ pork)
1 onion, diced
1 teaspoon fresh or
½ teaspoon dried thyme
225 g/8 oz spinach, blanched
and coarsely chopped
1 tablespoon breadcrumbs
salt and pepper
600 ml/1 pint stock

1. Make the pasta using the basic recipe (see page 82).
2. In a frying pan fry the bacon over a moderate heat until crisp.
3. Add 1 tablespoon butter and fry the minced meat and onion.
4. Stir in the thyme, spinach and breadcrumbs and remove the pan from the heat.
5. Season to taste and leave to cool.
6. Roll out the pasta dough very thinly and cut into 5 × 13-cm/2 × 5-in rectangles.
7. Top each rectangle with filling, brush the edges with water, fold over and press firmly together to prevent the filling escaping during cooking.
8. In a large pan bring the stock to the boil and drop in the maultaschen. Reduce the heat and cook for 15 minutes (do not boil vigorously or the maultaschen may split).
9. Remove the maultaschen from the pan, drain thoroughly and sprinkle with hot butter.

Maultaschen can either be served with grated cheese or with onion braised in butter.

Cannelloni

(illustrated bottom left)

For the filling:
1 tablespoon olive oil
350 g/12 oz minced beef
40 g/1½ oz bacon, finely chopped
1–2 onions, finely chopped
1–2 cloves garlic, crushed
1 tablespoon flour
4 tablespoons concentrated tomato purée
½ cup red wine
1 teaspoon fresh or
½ teaspoon dried thyme
salt and pepper
300 ml/½ pint béchamel sauce (page 256)
Parmesan or Gruyère cheese, grated
15 g/½ oz butter

1. Heat the oil in a frying pan and fry the beef and bacon. Add the onion and garlic and fry for a further 2 minutes. Add the flour and stir continuously for 1 minute.
2. Stir in the tomato purée, add the red wine, season with the thyme, salt and pepper. Simmer until the liquid has evaporated, then remove the pan from the heat and keep warm.
3. Roll out the pasta dough and cut into 10 × 15-cm/4 × 6-in rectangles. In a large pan bring salted water to the boil. Drop 3–4 pieces of pasta into the pan at a time. Remove after a few seconds and lay out on a damp tea-towel.
4. Grease an ovenproof dish with butter. Cover each piece of pasta with 2 tablespoons filling and roll up. Arrange the cannelloni side by side in the dish, cover with béchamel sauce and sprinkle with grated cheese. Dot with butter.
5. Place the dish in a moderately hot oven (190C, 375 F, gas 5) and bake for 15–20 minutes.

Wun-tun

or Won-ton (illustrated right)

For the filling:
350 g/12 oz shoulder of pork, finely chopped
50 g/2 oz mushrooms, finely chopped
2 teaspoons soy sauce
2 teaspoons dry sherry
1 teaspoon sesame oil
1 egg
pinch each of salt and pepper
sugar

1. Make the pasta using the basic recipe (see page 82).
2. Mix all the ingredients together to make the filling.
3. Roll out the pasta until very thin and cut into 5-cm/2-in squares.
4. Place ½ teaspoon filling in the centre of each square, brush the edges with water and bring the edges up (see the photograph on the right).
5. Steam the wun-tuns in a sieve in a covered pan for about 30 minutes.
6. Instead of a sieve you can use the original Chinese steamer which is made of plywood (see photograph).

An astonishing choice

Though you may be familiar with spaghetti and macaroni, noodles and vermicelli, twists and shells, you still have much to learn about pasta. Any Italian housewife can reel off at least two dozen types of pasta – without ever having come across Chinese glass noodles. Here is a summary of the commonest sorts of pasta available in the shops in both words and pictures.

Ready-bought pasta

(illustrated from left to right)
1. Shells
2. Ditalini (small pieces of macaroni)
3. Gramigna
4. Penne ('pen-nibs', short, pointed, hollow pasta)
5. Pitaloni (pieces of macaroni)
6. Fusili (spirals)
7. Tempesta (soup pasta)
8. Plaits
9. Spaghetti
10. Farfalle (bows)
11. Chinese glass noodles

Cooking times vary considerably according to type. Basic rule: cook initially for the shortest cooking time given on the package and then try it. If the pasta still tastes floury cook for a little longer.

Try it again after 1 minute and then every minute until it is as you like it.

Rice: the grain from the Far East

The Ancient Greeks were much too conservative to appreciate these white grains which Alexander the Great brought back from his campaigns. The Romans were much more adventurous in their eating habits. They were so delighted with the rice imported from India that they were soon planting it themselves in the Po valley. Rice thus became incorporated into classic Italian cuisine. This hardly compares with Japan and China, admittedly, where their style of cooking was built around rice. Far Eastern gourmets have seven thousand (!) types to choose from, compared with the nine which we are familiar with. The average Japanese eats 90 kilos or 200 pounds of rice a year, compared with 2 kilos or 5 pounds for those in the West. This is not for want of good recipes . . .

Cooking and types of rice

Could it be a fear of lumps, stickiness or sogginess which puts a lot of housewives and amateur cooks off rice? Nothing can go wrong if you stick rigidly to the basic rules. To my mind it is much easier to boil rice than to fry potatoes. For those who are still apprehensive there is always cook-in-the-bag rice. To get the best results you do, however, need to know the different types and how they differ.

Why is rice good for us?

As well as essential roughage, rice also contains vitamins and minerals such as iron and calcium. The same is true of rice as of all other foods: the less it is treated, the healthier it is.

Cooking rice

Of the various ways of cooking rice, steeping in hot water is best as it preserves most of the natural goodness of the rice.

This method is shown in the step-by-step photographs alongside. Quantities serve two.

Boiled rice

With this method the rice is cooked in a larger volume of water (100 g/4 oz to 2 litres/4 pints water) for 15–20 minutes. It is then drained in a sieve and rinsed under cold water to wash out the starch. The rice is then quickly warmed through in butter.

Cook-in-the-bag rice

The easiest way of cooking rice. Cook cook-in-the-bag rice in boiling water according to the instructions on the package.

Storing cooked rice

Rice can be cooked in advance and will keep for several days. To do this drain the cooked rice thoroughly, tip onto kitchen paper and pat dry. It will keep for up to three days in the refrigerator.

Storing uncooked rice

Rice is an ideal food for the store cupboard. It will keep for several years in a dry place.

1. Measure 1 cup rice and 2 cups cold water.

2. Tip the rice and water into a pan and leave to soak for a few minutes.

3. Add $\frac{1}{2}$ teaspoon salt.

4. With the heat turned on full, bring the rice to the boil and boil for about 2 minutes.

5. Turn off the heat and cover the pan.

6. Leave the rice to steep for 10–15 minutes until it has absorbed all the water.

7. Fluff up the rice and stir in 1 tablespoon butter for extra flavour.

Cook cook-in-the-bag rice in plenty of salted water according to the instructions on the package.

The different types

There are two basic types of rice:

Long-grain rice, also known as Patna rice, has long, thin grains and is white and fluffy after boiling. Serve with meat, fish and vegetable dishes or, with various ingredients added, as a main course in its own right.

Round-grain rice, also known as pudding rice, has small, thick, round grains and becomes quite soft during cooking.

When harvested rice grains are enclosed in a hard shell. Underneath this are several layers of skin. This protects the rice kernel and contains most of the vitamins, minerals, protein and fat.

Depending on the way rice is treated, one can distinguish between four types.

Brown rice
Unpolished brown rice is also sold as 'organic rice'. It still retains its layers of skin. Because of its high fat content it should not be stored for long.

White rice
Polished white rice, with its smooth, shiny surface, will keep for years in a dry place.

Pre-cooked or converted rice
Pre-cooked rice is pressure-steamed in the husk using a method developed in the United States. Vitamins and minerals are forced towards the centre of the kernel and so are not lost. The rice is then polished. Pre-cooked rice, also known as American rice, is yellowish in colour, but after cooking is white, light and fluffy.

Quick-cook rice
(5-minute rice)
Quick-cook rice is a specially treated white rice. It is pre-cooked by the manufacturer and then dried. This pre-cooking makes for a very short cooking times at home.

Round-grain rice

Brown rice

White rice

Pre-cooked rice

Quick-cook rice

Long-grain rice

Brown rice

White rice

Pre-cooked rice

Quick-cook rice

Wild rice

Decorative rice moulds

People who tend to think of rice as a heap of white grains, will usually be highly impressed if you serve them rice moulds – and may even be won over to the delights of rice. Try it some time! The possibilities are as varied as the range of glasses and containers in your kitchen cupboards. You can't fail to come up with a few ideas on how to garnish your moulds.

Basic recipe

To serve as a mould, the hot cooked rice is transferred to a container or mould which has been rinsed in cold water. Press the rice firmly down using a spoon then turn it out onto a plate. It is best to use steep-cooked rice for moulds as this cooking method preserves more of the starch than, say, boiled rice, and it is the starch which holds the shape together.

Rice ring

(illustrated top left)
To make the rice ring use a ring mould of the required size. Dishes cooked in sauce, such as fricassee (see page 195), stew or goulash (see page 238) can be served in rice rings.

Rice parcels

(illustrated bottom left)
You can buy the rice paper to make the parcels in specialist shops. This extremely thin paper tears easily and must be handled very carefully. To make the parcels lay each piece of rice paper out on a damp cloth for about 15 minutes until it becomes pliable. Cover each sheet with a mixture of cooked rice, vegetable pieces and seasoning. Dot with butter and then wrap in the paper. Steam the parcels in a covered pan for about 5 minutes.

Rice bowls

(illustrated centre top)
In the Far East rice is served in small bowls. The rice bowls are first half-filled with rice and then topped with seasoned meat, sauce and braised vegetables. The mild flavour of the rice contrasts well with the hot, spicy meat. It should, of course, be eaten with chopsticks.

Rice timbales

(illustrated top right and bottom centre)
Small, individual rice moulds are especially attractive. As moulds use cups, small glass dishes, deep plates or shallow glasses.

Bed of rice

(illustrated bottom right)
Meat kebabs, or other grilled or fried meat, look good served on a bed of rice.

Twenty-four favourite variations

The idea that rice is rather monotonous, boring and dull, is one that could only occur to those living in the West who are used to the potato as their staple food. The twenty-four variations suggested here – sweet and spicy, brightly coloured and subdued, would bring only a wry smile to the lips of most Japanese cooks, not to mention the reaction of his colleagues in China, the home of thousands of variations on rice. What's the betting you'll be able to come up with dozens of your own variations without really trying?

Herbs, freshly chopped and stirred in.
Tomato, peeled, deseeded, chopped and stirred in.
Saffron strands, cooked with the rice, or saffron powder stirred in.
Curry powder, cooked with the rice, or stirred in afterwards.

Bacon, finely diced, fried and stirred in.
Flaked almonds, coated in butter and stirred in.
Raisins, stirred in.
Root ginger, peeled, finely chopped and cooked with the rice.

Cheese, freshly grated and stirred in.
Prawns, warmed through in the rice for 5 minutes.
Asparagus, cut up, warmed through and stirred into the rice.
Peas, stirred into the cooked rice.

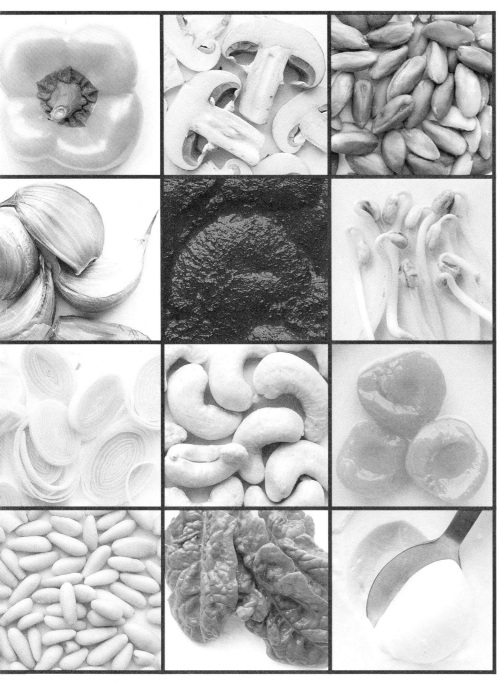

Peppers, chopped, blanched and stirred in.
Garlic, finely chopped or crushed, fried in butter and stirred in.
Leek slices, fried in butter and folded in.
Pine nuts, finely chopped and stirred in.

Mushroom slices, fried in butter and folded in.
Tomato purée, stirred into the rice.
Cashew nuts, chopped and stirred in.
Spinach, coarsely chopped, quick-boiled and stirred into the rice.

Pistachio nuts, finely chopped and mixed in.
Bean sprouts, warmed through in the rice for about 4 minutes.
Apricots, stoned, peeled, chopped and stirred into the rice.
Soured cream, stirred into the rice.

The two most famous rice dishes

Like potatoes and pasta, rice has also inspired two simple dishes which are not only economical, but which smell and taste heavenly. These dishes have formed the backbone of regional cooking for generations, without losing any of their popularity. The two superstars of the genre are risotto and pulao.

Risotto

One of the most delicious inventions of Italian cooking, although one of the best variations comes from the Swiss canton of Tessin. There cooks have mastered the art of cooking round-grain rice until it is thick and creamy but still with some bite to the individual grains.

Basic risotto recipe

1 onion, diced
1 clove garlic, crushed
100 g / 4 oz butter
450 g / 1 lb round-grain rice
150 ml / ¼ pint dry white wine
1 litre / 2 pints meat stock
100 g / 4 oz Parmesan cheese, grated

Risotto can include any type of vegetable, meat, fish or poultry and can be served as a main course. There is one particular risotto, much loved by gourmets. Every autumn its enticing smell floats from the farm kitchens of Tessin. This is cèpe risotto. If cèpes are too expensive, try using flat or button mushrooms. For further variations see photographs on the right.

1. Fry the onion and garlic in 25 g / 1 oz butter.

2. Add the rice and fry for 2 minutes until transparent.

3. Add the wine and bring, stirring, to the boil.

4. Gradually add the stock.

5. Boil for 2 minutes and then reduce the heat.

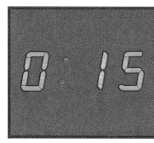
6. Steep-cook for 15–20 minutes.

7. Stir the rice from time to time.

8. Stir in the remaining butter and the cheese.

Variation: add prawns, mushrooms and spinach.

1. Wash the rice in cold water.

2. Drain in a sieve.

3. Fry the onion and garlic in 25 g/1 oz butter.

4. Add the rice and fry for about 2 minutes.

5. Add the stock, season and bring to the boil.

6. Cover the pan and reduce the heat to very low.

7. Steep-cook the rice for about 15 minutes.

8. Stir the remaining butter into the rice.

Variation: add apricots, raisins and curry powder.

Pulao

In Pakistan it is known as pilau, in India pulau, in Iran polo, but each is just another name for the oriental pulao, albeit with regional variations. Pulao is a meat and rice dish always made with long-grain rice.

Basic pulao recipe

350 g/12 oz long-grain rice
1 onion, diced
1 clove garlic, crushed
100 g/4 oz butter
600 ml/1 pint meat stock
generous pinch of salt

In the East pulao rice includes such ingredients as lamb or mutton, vegetables, nuts, star aniseed or fennel seeds, and is served as a main course.

An excellent Central European variation, which has the added advantage of not being very fattening, is pulao with chicken or turkey. This chicken pulao can be served hot (with paprika and peperoni) or mild.

For our suggested variation see photographs on the left.

Ingredients

Serves 4–6

450 g / 1 lb mussels

2 small smoked sausages

225 g / 8 oz lean pork

1 (1-kg / 2¼-lb) oven-ready chicken or chicken portions

2 onions

2–3 cloves garlic

1 red pepper

3 tomatoes

salt and pepper

8 tablespoons olive oil

4 artichoke hearts

225 g / 8 oz long-grain rice

300 ml / ½ pint meat stock

150 ml / ¼ pint dry white wine

¼ teaspoon saffron powder or pounded saffron strands

150 g / 5 oz peas

4 scampi

lemon slices to garnish

The Spanish speciality

Spanish cooks have not made a great contribution to international cuisine, but even if they had produced only this one dish their reputation would be assured. Paella (=pan) is more than a dish for simple peasants and fishermen – it can form the basis for a fantastic culinary work of art which tastes of the sun and the Mediterranean, and whose colour alone is a delight for anyone to whom it is served.

Method:

1. Wash and scrub the mussels and scrape off the beards. Discard any open mussels.

2. Slice the sausage, cut up the pork and chop the chicken into individual portions.

3. Peel and dice the onions and garlic. Wash and deseed the red pepper and cut into strips.

4. Peel, quarter and deseed the tomatoes.

5. Heat 4 tablespoons oil in a large pan. Season the chicken lightly with salt and brown for about 10 minutes. Add the pork, fry for about 5 minutes and season with a little salt.

6. Add the diced onion and garlic, the red pepper and tomato and the drained artichoke hearts and cook for a further 5 minutes.

7. Add the mussels and sausage and cook for 2 minutes.

8. Heat the remaining oil in a paella pan or large frying pan until very hot.

9. Add the rice, stock and white wine and stir in the saffron.

10. Add the meat, vegetables, mussels, peas and scampi and bring to the boil.

11. Transfer the paella pan to a moderate oven (180C, 350F, gas 4) and cook for about 15–20 minutes.

12. When the rice has absorbed the liquid, season with salt and pepper, garnish with lemon slices and serve.

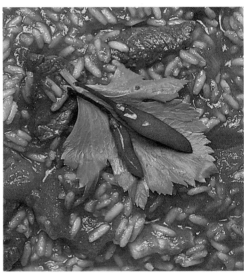

Risi e bisi

from Italy
Serves 6

350 g / 12 oz round-grain rice
100 g / 4 oz butter
1–2 cloves garlic, crushed
1 onion, finely chopped
150 ml / ¼ pint dry white wine
1 litre / 2 pints meat stock
225 g / 8 oz peas
150 g / 5 oz boiled ham
75–100 g / 3–4 oz Parmesan cheese, grated
pinch of salt

1. Make a risotto using the rice, 25 g / 1 oz butter, garlic and onion, white wine and stock (see basic recipe on page 104).
2. 10 minutes before the end of the cooking time add the peas and the ham cut into strips.
3. Continue cooking until the rice is swollen and tender.
4. Stir in the Parmesan cheese and the remaining butter and season with salt.

Serbian meat rice

from the Balkans

450 g / 1 lb boned pork
3 onions
1 clove garlic, crushed
4 tablespoons oil
2 tablespoons concentrated tomato purée
600 ml / 1 pint meat stock
2 teaspoons rubbed thyme
1 tablespoon paprika
salt and pepper
225 g / 8 oz long-grain rice
2 red peppers
1 chilli
3 tomatoes
1 tablespoon chopped parsley to garnish

1. Cut the meat into pieces, wash and pat dry. Dice the onions and add the garlic.
2. Thoroughly heat the oil and brown the meat.
3. Reduce the heat to moderate, and fry the onion and garlic with the meat.
4. Add the tomato purée and stock.
5. Season with the thyme, paprika, salt and pepper and cook for about 30 minutes.
6. Wash and drain the rice. Wash and finely dice the red peppers and chilli. Peel, quarter and deseed the tomatoes.
7. Stir these ingredients into the meat.
8. Cook for about 30 minutes until the rice has absorbed the liquid. Season to taste and serve sprinkled with chopped parsley.

Nasi goreng

from Malaysia

350 g / 12 oz leg or shoulder of pork
3 tablespoons oil
1–2 cloves garlic
1 onion
350 g / 12 oz cooked rice
150 g / 5 oz peeled prawns
1 tablespoon curry powder
5 tablespoons soy sauce
1 tablespoon raisins
salt and pepper
2 eggs
a little butter for frying
1 tablespoon finely chopped parsley to garnish
To serve:
croûtons
lettuce leaves
sambal oelek
Tabasco sauce
soy sauce

1. Clean the meat, trim off any excess fat and cut into bite-sized pieces.
2. Heat the oil in a frying pan and brown the meat then continue frying over a moderate heat until the pork is thoroughly cooked.
3. Finely dice the garlic and onion, add to the pan and fry for about 1 minute.
4. Add the rice and cook for 3–4 minutes.
5. Add the prawns, curry powder, soy sauce and raisins then season to taste.
6. Remove the pan from the heat and keep warm.
7. Beat the eggs with a little salt. Melt the butter in a frying pan and cook the egg for about 2 minutes until set.
8. Remove the egg from the pan and cut into strips.
9. Arrange the rice and meat mixture on a flat dish and garnish with parsley and strips of egg.
10. Serve the croûtons, lettuce, sambal oelek, Tabasco and soy sauce separately in small bowls.

Fried rice

from the Far East

450g / 1 lb lean beef or pork
3 tablespoons oil
4 slices thick-cut bacon
350g / 12oz cooked rice
3 spring onions
225g / 8oz peeled prawns
3 eggs
salt and pepper
For the marinade:
1–2 cloves garlic
4 tablespoons soy sauce
2 tablespoons oil

1. To make the marinade, crush the garlic and stir into the soy sauce and oil.
2. Wash the meat, pat dry, cut into strips and marinate for about 1 hour, turning it after 30 minutes.
3. Heat the oil in a frying pan.
4. Cut the bacon into strips and fry in the oil.
5. Dry the marinated meat and fry in the bacon fat.
6. Add the rice and cook for a few minutes.
7. Cut the spring onions into rings and add to the pan with the prawns and a little of the marinade. Cook for a further 5 minutes.
8. Beat the eggs, add to the pan, stir in and cook for a further 2 minutes until the eggs have set. Season to taste.

Rice pudding with stewed fruit

225g / 8oz round-grain rice
600ml / 1 pint milk
50g / 2oz white sugar
pinch of salt
½ cinnamon stick
1 vanilla pod
For the stewed fruit:
225g / 8oz mixed dried fruit
2 tablespoons sugar
600ml / 1 pint white wine

1. Steep the dried fruit in warm water for 1 hour.
2. In a saucepan stir together the rice, milk, sugar, salt and the cinnamon stick.
3. Bring slowly to the boil and then reduce the heat.
4. Break open the vanilla pod, scrape out the pith and add to the pan with the pod.
5. Steep-cook the rice for about 20 minutes, stirring frequently to prevent it burning.
6. Meanwhile drain the steeping fruit, bring to the boil with the sugar and white wine and boil for about 5 minutes.
7. Remove the vanilla pod and cinnamon stick from the rice and then serve with the fruit.

Shireen polo

from Iran

350g / 12oz long-grain rice
3–4 litres / 6–8 pints salted water
2 oranges
100g / 4oz pistachio nuts
3 carrots
1 (1-kg / 2¼-lb) oven-ready chicken
1 onion
25g / 1oz butter
100g / 4oz sugar
100g / 4oz blanched almonds, chopped
¼ teaspoon saffron powder
4 tablespoons olive oil
600ml / 1 pint water
½ teaspoon salt

1. Bring the rice to the boil in the salted water, and boil vigorously for about 7 minutes.
2. Drain in a sieve and rinse under cold water.
3. Thinly peel the oranges, cut the peel into thin strips and blanch for about 1 minute. Drain in a sieve.
4. Finely chop the pistachio nuts and thinly slice the carrots.
5. Cut the chicken into four portions, wash and pat dry.
6. Quarter the onion.
7. Melt the butter and braise the carrots for 5 minutes.
8. Add the sugar, orange peel, almonds, pistachio nuts and saffron and stir until the sugar has dissolved.
9. Fry the chicken pieces in oil until golden brown, add the onions and then bring to the boil with the water and salt. Reduce the heat and simmer for about 5 minutes.
10. Arrange the rice and carrots in alternate layers over the chicken, cover the pan and cook for a further 20 minutes over low heat.

Potatoes: the people's truffle

This is the truly democratic root vegetable, within anyone's means. The potato gives the cook complete freedom. It suffers maltreatment in chip-shops without complaint, or graces the menus of three-star restaurants. Matthius Claudius wrote a funny poem about it, while the star of haute cuisine, Duglère, turned it into a frivolous creation. Known to the Incas as 'Papas', the potato made its way to Spain early in the sixteenth century. But it was thanks to the far-travelled Englishmen, Sir Walter Raleigh and Francis Drake, that its fame spread in Europe after 1584. Superstition (it was known as 'the devil's root') and a belief that it was poisonous stood in its way for some time. Frederick the Great had to coerce his Prussians to plant it. It was then the turn of agronomist Antoine-August Parmentier to convert the French, of Escoffier to convert the gourmet and of our grandmothers to convert our grandfathers.

Foil-baked potatoes

Potatoes cooked in the oven, also known as jacket potatoes or simply baked potatoes. Served with steaks and other grilled or fried meat. In summer they can be cooked on the charcoal of the barbecue or on an open fire.

I. Prick the potato all over using a wooden skewer, fork or knife.

2. Wrap each potato firmly in aluminium foil.

3. Bake in a very hot oven (240C, 475F, gas 9) for about I hour.

Boiled jacket potatoes

Since these potatoes are boiled in the skin they retain almost all their goodness. This method is best for new potatoes, especially small ones with thin skins.

I. Sort the potatoes and pick out those of similar size.

2. Wash thoroughly under cold running water.

3. Cover with water and bring to the boil with caraway, herbs and salt.

Fried potatoes

Delicious with aspics, chops or schnitzel, or simply with fried eggs. For good fried potatoes they should first be boiled in the skins.

I. Peel the boiled potatoes.

2. Slice the potatoes, dice the onion or cut into rings.

3. Heat 2 tablespoons oil or fatty bacon in a frying pan.

Boiled potatoes

Boiled potatoes are a popular vegetable with meat and fish dishes cooked in a sauce.

I. Peel the potatoes using a potato peeler or knife and then wash.

2. Cut potatoes into similar-sized pieces.

3. Place the potatoes in a saucepan with water and a little salt.

Chips

As well as being delicious simply with ketchup, chips (also called *pommes frites* or French fries) are ideal with grilled meat without sauce.

I. Peel the potatoes. First cut into slices and then into chips.

2. Wash, wipe thoroughly dry and heat the oil.

3. The temperature is right when a wooden skewer dipped into the oil forms bubbles.

4. Unwrap the foil and cut a cross in the top of the potato.

5. Open out each potato slightly.

6. Fill the potato with a filling of your choice.

Recipes and photographs for six delicious fillings can be found on pages 114–15.

4. Simmer over a moderate heat for 20–25 minutes.

5. Drain and return to the pan for a few minutes to evaporate the steam.

6. Serve peeled or in the skins.

Boiled jacket potatoes can be served stuffed (see pages 114–15), mashed (see pages 116–17), or as croquettes (see page 118). Floury varieties are best for this method.

4. Fry the potatoes over a moderate heat for 8–10 minutes and then turn.

5. Add the onion and continue frying until the onion is golden brown.

6. Season with salt, freshly milled pepper and a little thyme or marjoram.

Fried potatoes also form the basis of the potatoes in cream and the caramelised potatoes and filling country breakfast on pages 120–1.

  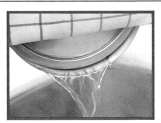

4. Cover the pan and bring to the boil, reduce the heat and simmer for 20 minutes.

5. Prick the potatoes with a fork to check if they are cooked.

6. Drain off the water and evaporate off the steam.

You can reduce the amount of goodness washed out of the potatoes by cooking in as little water as possible (about 600 ml/1 pint water per 1 kg/2 lb).

4. Add the chips in batches and fry for about 3 minutes.

5. Remove from the pan, drain and leave to cool.

6. Return the pre-cooked chips to the oil and fry for about 2 minutes until golden brown.

A number of variations on chips are to be found on page 119.

Six delicious fillings for jacket potatoes

The earthy wholesome smell of potatoes is as delightful as the smell of spring lilac. For those who prefer their food simple a knob of butter and a little salt will be enough. Yet there are no limits to the imaginative fillings which will melt into the hot potato to provide a real treat . . .

Onion and bacon butter

Fry 2 chopped onions and 25 g/1 oz bacon until transparent. When cold work into 4 tablespoons soft butter and season with chives, salt and pepper.

Herb butter

Work 4 tablespoons chopped mixed herbs with lemon juice, cayenne and 1 crushed clove garlic, into 4 tablespoons soft butter. Season to taste.

Curry curd cheese

Crush 1 small banana and mix with 1 teaspoon curry powder. Fold into 4 tablespoons curd cheese or quark and season to taste.

Salmon cream

Cut 2 slices smoked salmon into thin strips and stir with 4 tablespoons soured cream. Add lemon juice. Season to taste.

Dill butter

Work 4 tablespoons butter with 1 tablespoon finely chopped dill. Season with lemon juice and salt and pepper.

Anchovy butter

Finely chop 3 anchovy fillets and work into 4 tablespoons butter with a little lemon juice.

Butter can also be flavoured with horseradish, caviar or caraway. Always add a little lemon juice for improved flavour.

With curd cheese and ham

(illustrated top left)
Stir 4 tablespoons curd cheese or quark with 2 tablespoons chopped herbs (parsley, dill, chives, basil, thyme) and season to taste. Cut a small slice boiled ham into strips. Spoon the curd cheese onto the potato and garnish with ham and herbs.

With prawns and soured cream

(illustrated centre left)
Top the potatoes with 50 g/2 oz peeled prawns and 4 tablespoons soured cream. Garnish with sorrel sprigs.

With remoulade

(illustrated bottom left)
Finely dice 4 gherkins, I teaspoon capers, 2 anchovy fillets, 3 silverskin onions and the white of a hard-boiled egg. Mix with 2 tablespoons mayonnaise, season to taste and spoon onto the potatoes. Sieve the egg yolk and use to garnish together with capers, small gherkins and parsley.

With butter and green peppercorns

(illustrated top right)
Work a little salt into 4 tablespoons soft butter. Spread on the potato and top with bottled green peppercorns.

With blue-cheese cream

(illustrated centre right)
Stir 50 g/2 oz Gorgonzola (or similar blue-vein cheese) with 4 tablespoons soured cream and a little lemon juice. Season to taste, spoon onto the potatoes and garnish with herbs (sage and rosemary).

With tomato and cognac

(illustrated bottom right)
Stir 4 tablespoons mayonnaise with I teaspoon tomato purée or ketchup. Add a little cognac and season to taste. Spoon onto the potatoes and garnish with strips of peeled tomato and chervil sprigs.

Mouth-watering boiled potatoes

Instead of serving boiled potatoes straight from the saucepan, the creative cook may like to turn them into a purée. Simple puréed potatoes are wonderful, but for greater effect they can be coloured, spiced up or sweetened for a change. A treat for the eye as well as the palate.

From mashed potato to purée

Putting boiled potatoes through a potato press gives mashed potato – the basis for purée, potato croquettes and potato cakes (see page 118). You can add extra flavourings to mashed potato and use it as a side vegetable or garnish as it is excellent for piping.

You should use floury potatoes. The recipes alongside demonstrate the various ways in which you can vary the flavour and appearance of potato purée.

Basic recipe for potato purée

1 kg/2 lb potatoes, peeled
50 g/2 oz butter, softened
300 ml/½ pint milk or cream
salt and pepper
pinch of sugar

1. Boil the potatoes.
2. Pass the hot potatoes through a potato press or mash in the pan using a potato masher.

Alternatively place in a food processor and blend until smooth.
3. Stir in the soft butter in small pieces.
4. Heat the milk or cream, or a mixture of milk and cream, and gradually stir into the mashed potato to give the required consistency.
5. Season with salt, freshly milled pepper and a pinch of sugar.

Pea and potato purée

The method is the same as in the basic potato purée recipe, but only 575 g/1¼ lb potatoes are used here.

Additional ingredients:

350 g/12 oz peas
300 ml/½ pint meat stock
salt and pepper
lemon balm to garnish

Boil the peas in the stock for 5 minutes. Reserve a tablespoon. Purée the remainder, stir into the potato purée and season to taste. Garnish with the reserved peas and lemon balm.

Herb and potato purée

Use the method given in the basic recipe.

Additional ingredients:

1 tablespoon chives
1 tablespoon parsley
1 tablespoon thyme
salt and pepper

Finely chop the herbs and stir into the purée. Season to taste and garnish with a small sprig of herbs.

Further potato purée variations

Apple purée stirred into puréed potatoes is delicious with fried liver. Grated cheese (e.g. stale Gouda, Parmesan or Gruyère) gives a strong flavour.

Fried onions are a popular way of adding extra flavour.

These variations can also be tried with ready-bought potato purée.

Carrot and potato purée

The method is the same as in the basic recipe, but reduce the quantity of potatoes to 575 g/1¼ lb.

Additional ingredients:
350 g/12 oz carrots
300 ml/½ pint meat stock
salt and pepper
chervil to garnish

Slice the carrots and boil in the stock for 10 minutes. Purée in a liquidiser or blender and season to taste. Stir into the potato purée and garnish with carrot slices and chervil.

Tomato and potato purée

The method is the same as in the basic recipe, but reduce the quantity of potatoes to 800 g/1¾ lb.

Additional ingredients:
2–3 beef tomatoes
salt and pepper
sprig of basil to garnish

Scald the tomatoes in boiling water then peel. Remove the seeds and strain the tomato through a sieve. Stir into the potato purée and season to taste. Garnish with 2 tomato wedges and a sprig of basil.

Croquette potatoes

To make small gourmet-style potatoes you need neither the skill of the sculptor nor sophisticated kitchen gadgets. All you need is either peeled, uncooked potatoes or puréed, boiled potatoes and a little know-how.

Basic recipe for croquette potatoes

675 g / 1½ lb boiled potatoes
2 egg yolks
salt to taste
pinch of freshly grated nutmeg
For the coating:
3 tablespoons flour
2 eggs
3 tablespoons fine breadcrumbs
vegetable oil for frying

1. Mash the potatoes while still warm.
2. Work in the egg yolks and season with salt and nutmeg.
3. Shape the mixture into a roll 2.5 cm / 1 in thick and cut into 5-cm/2-in lengths.
4. Dip each croquette first in flour, then in beaten egg yolk and finally in breadcrumbs.
5. Fry in hot, deep fat until golden brown.

If the mixture is too loose the croquettes will split during frying. To be on the safe side coat and fry one croquette initially to check the consistency. If it splits work 1 tablespoon cornflour into the mixture.

Alternative croquette shapes

(illustrated from top to bottom)
The classic croquette shape is a longish roll, but you can also shape the mixture into balls.

Alternative coatings:

Flaked almonds

Dip the croquette balls in flour and then in beaten egg yolk. Coat with flaked almonds and finally with breadcrumbs.

With glass noodles or vermicelli

First dip in flour and egg and then in crumbled glass noodles or vermicelli.

Potato cakes

The method is the same as for the basic croquette potato recipe, but using only 350 g / 12 oz potatoes.

Additional ingredients:
50 g / 2 oz bacon, diced
2 onions, chopped
2 tablespoons chopped parsley
1 egg yolk
fat for frying

Fry the bacon until crisp and in the same pan fry the chopped onion until transparent. Pour off the fat and stir the bacon, onion, parsley and egg yolk into the croquette mixture. Shape the mixture into small flat cakes. Shallow fry over a high heat at first and then over a moderate heat until golden brown.

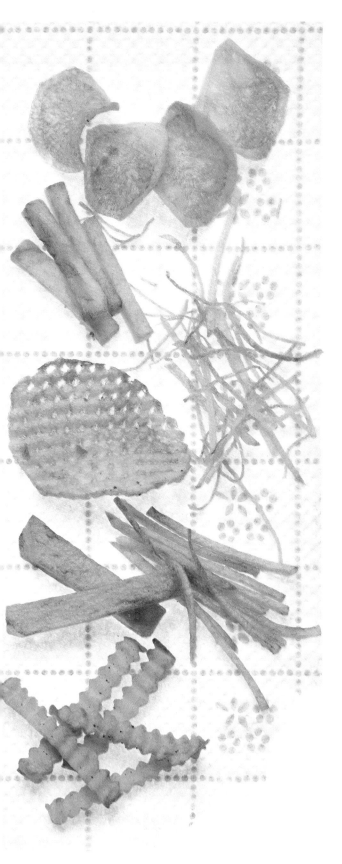

Duchess potatoes

Pommes Duchesse (illustrated bottom left) The method is the same as the basic croquette potato recipe.

Additional ingredients:

2 egg yolks

1 tablespoon soft butter

2 tablespoons melted butter

Work the egg yolks and soft butter into the croquette mixture. Spoon the mixture into a piping bag and pipe onto a baking tray which you have first greased or covered in non-stick baking parchment. Sprinkle with the melted butter. Bake in a moderately hot oven (200C, 400F, gas 6) for 5–10 minutes until golden brown.

Pommes frites and associates

This section shows the variety of shapes you can use for deep-frying raw potatoes. The method for chips is given in detail on pages 114–15.

Top to bottom:

Potato crisps

Pommes chips
Cut the potatoes into extremely thin slices and fry once only.

Mini chips

Pommes mignonettes
Cut the potatoes into sticks about 5 mm/ $\frac{1}{4}$ in thick and 5 cm/2 in. in length. Fry once only.

Potato straws

Pommes pailles
Cut the potatoes into extremely thin strips and fry once only.

Potato waffles

Pommes gaufrettes
Slice the potatoes using a serrated knife and twirl each slice. Fry once only.

Matchstick chips

Pommes allumettes
Cut potatoes to size of matchsticks and fry once only.

Pommes frites

Cut the potatoes into chips about 1 cm/ $\frac{1}{2}$ in thick and 5 cm/2 in. in length. For crinkle chips cut using a patterned knife.

Delicious fried potatoes

There is an old saying that with bacon rind you can catch a mouse, with fried potatoes a man. Nothing has changed much even in these emancipated times except for one thing – any man who masters the art of sautéeing potatoes will impress a woman more than one who serves her caviar.

Creamed potatoes

675 g/ 1½ lb potatoes, boiled in their skins
3 tablespoons vegetable oil
150 ml/¼ pint milk
150 ml/¼ pint double cream
salt and pepper

1. Peel and cut up the potatoes.
2. Heat the oil in a frying pan and fry the potatoes until golden brown.
3. Add the milk and cream and reduce until the milk and cream mixture thickens, stirring frequently.
4. Season generously to taste.
5. Serve with fried poultry or meatloaf.

Caramelised potatoes

2 tablespoons vegetable oil
2 tablespoons sugar
675 g/ 1½ lb small potatoes, boiled in the skins

1. Heat the oil in a frying pan.
2. Sprinkle the sugar evenly over the pan and brown.
3. Peel the potatoes and fry, stirring continuously, until golden brown.
4. Serve with green cabbage or other cabbage and meat dishes.

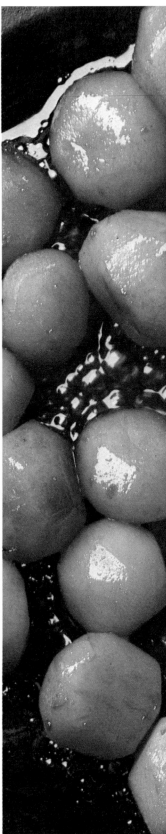

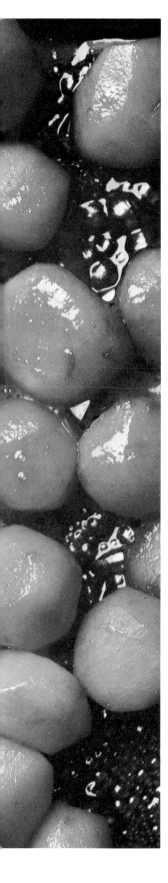

Country breakfast

Serves 1

| 2 medium potatoes, boiled in the skins |
| 2 tablespoons vegetable oil |
| 2 onions |
| 50 g / 2 oz bacon |
| salt and pepper |
| 5 medium mushrooms |
| 2 eggs, beaten |

1. Peel the potatoes then slice or coarsely dice.
2. Heat the oil and fry the potatoes until golden brown.
3. Cut the onions into rings and the bacon into strips then add to the potatoes.
4. Season to taste and fry for about 5 minutes.
5. Trim, wash and finely slice the mushrooms. Stir into the eggs. Add to the pan and cook for about 2 minutes until the eggs have set.
6. Garnish with lettuce, cucumber or tomatoes.

Rösti

(not illustrated)

| 1 kg / 2 lb potatoes, boiled in the skins |
| salt and pepper |
| 4 tablespoons butter |

1. Peel and coarsely grate the potatoes. Season to taste.
2. Heat the butter in a frying pan then add the potatoes.
3. Spread evenly over the base of the pan and press down.
4. Over a moderate heat, cook the rösti until golden brown on both sides. To turn, cover the pan with a saucepan lid or plate of similar size. Turn the pan over then slide the rösti back into the pan.

Luxury potato dishes

Potato gratins are just as much at home in gourmet restaurants or country farmhouses. Thinly sliced potatoes are arranged in layers in a baking dish then covered with butter, cream and cheese and seasoned with garlic, pepper and nutmeg. Ideal to serve with any meat dish without sauce – but delicious enough to eat on their own.

Basic recipe for potato gratin

(illustrated on opposite page)

1 clove garlic
25 g/1 oz butter
450 g/1 lb small potatoes
salt and pepper
300 ml/½ pint double cream
pinch of freshly grated nutmeg

1. Rub the inside of a shallow ovenproof dish with the garlic and grease with 1 teaspoon butter.
2. Thinly slice the peeled potatoes and arrange in overlapping layers in the dish.
3. Season each layer generously with salt and with a little pepper.
4. Pour on the cream so that it stops just short of the top layer of potato.
5. Season with the nutmeg and dot with the remaining butter.
6. Bake in a moderately hot oven (200C, 400F, gas 6) for about 25 minutes, until golden brown.

Cheese and potato gratin

Gratin Dauphinoise (illustrated above left) The method is the same as in the basic recipe.

Additional ingredients:
2 tablespoons grated Gruyère cheese

Sprinkle the top layer of potato with grated Gruyère and flakes of butter. Bake in a moderately hot oven (200C, 400F, gas 6) for about 25 minutes, until golden brown.

Potatoes Anna

Pommes Anna (illustrated left)

100–175 g/4–6 oz butter
4–8 uncooked peeled potatoes
salt and pepper

Grease a shallow, ovenproof dish with a teaspoon of the butter. Thinly slice the potatoes. Heat the butter in a small frying pan until a layer of foam forms on the surface. Scoop off the foam using a spoon. Arrange the potatoes in overlapping layers in the dish, seasoning each layer generously, and then sprinkle with the hot butter. Bake in a moderately hot oven (200C, 400F, gas 6) for about 25 minutes, until golden brown.

Delicious with vegetables

You can invent your own gratins using vegetables. Try filling the dish with layers of carrots and courgettes, turnips and kohlrabi. Season the vegetables with a little lemon juice, salt and pepper.

Vegetables: a rich source of vitamins

No supermarket, however up-to-date its piped music and hygienically packaged products, can ever rival the magic of a local market. The very profusion of vegetables is a delight in itself; the mountains of onions and courgettes, carrots and cabbages, tomatoes and salad ingredients. Then there is the colour contrast, as rich as an abstract painting: aubergines next to lemons; radicchio amongst lettuce; peppers in green, red and yellow. Then there is the smell — spicy, herby, sweet, earthy — in which our senses can wallow. It seems hard to believe that these colourful things are good for you as well, and that they taste as good as they look!

The five professional methods

The widespread vegetable family has so many members that one would expect to have to cope with a complicated range of cooking methods. Nothing is further from reality! When you have mastered the five methods used by professional chefs you will be able to begin inventing your own creations with vegetables.

What you should know about vegetables

Vegetables contain vitamins, minerals, trace elements, vegetable proteins and a little fat and carbohydrate

The cell walls of plants are made of cellulose. Our bodies are unable to digest cellulose so it acts as roughage and helps the digestive process along.

To keep vitamin loss as low as possible, you should follow these rules:

Always use fresh vegetables.
If you have to store vegetables wrap them in paper or a damp cloth and keep in a cool, dark place.

Preparing vegetables for cooking

1. Cleaning
2. Washing
3. Chopping
Vegetables should never be chopped before washing, but always washed whole. This prevents water-soluble vitamins being washed away.

Never leave chopped vegetables exposed to the air, but always cover with a damp cloth.

Essential rules for preserving vitamins can be found on pages 14–15.

Regardless of whether you are blanching, braising, boiling or frying vegetables, always keep the cooking time to the minimum. Vegetables, regardless of type, should always have some bite to them when served.

The following cooking methods are interchangeable and can be used for any type of vegetable. Beans, for example, can also be braised or steamed.

Blanching

Short cooking in boiling water.

450 g/1 lb green beans
2 litres/4 pints water
½ teaspoon salt
1 tablespoon butter

Steaming

Cook by steam in a sieve or steamer inside a covered pan. Retains all the goodness.

Braising

Cooking the vegetables in their own juice in a covered pan, with a little fat if necessary.

450 g/1 lb carrots
1 tablespoon butter
5 tablespoons water (if necessary)

Boiling

Cooking in plenty of boiling water at 100C/200F in a covered pan.

1 cauliflower
2 litres/4 pints water
½ teaspoon salt
1 tablespoon butter

Frying

Browning in fat.

450 g/1 lb courgettes
1 tablespoon butter
salt and pepper

1. Trim and wash the beans.

2. Add the salt and bring the water to the boil on the highest heat.

1. Place 450 g/1 lb washed broccoli in a steamer.

2. Fill a pan with water to a depth of 2.5 cm/1 in.

1. Melt the butter in a pan on a high heat.

2. Add the vegetables and stir.

1. Clean the cauliflower by soaking in cold, salted water for 20 minutes.

2. Place the cauliflower and water in a pan and cover the pan.

1. Peel the courgettes, cut into lengths and then each length into quarters.

2. Melt the butter in a frying pan on a high heat.

3. Drop the beans into the boiling water.

4. Test the beans after 5 minutes and cook for up to 3 minutes more if necessary.

5. Remove the beans from the hot water and plunge into cold water.

6. Coat in butter.

3. Place the steamer inside the pan.

4. Cover the pan.

5. Bring to the boil on a high heat then cook on a medium heat.

6. Check after 8 minutes and continue cooking if necessary.

3. Add a little water.

4. Cover the pan.

5. Reduce the heat to medium.

6. Test after 4 minutes and cook for a few minutes more if necessary.

3. Bring to the boil on a high heat then reduce the heat to medium.

4. Boil for 15 minutes.

5. Lift the cauliflower out of the pan.

6. Serve with the butter.

3. Reduce the heat to medium.

4. Add the courgettes.

5. Fry, turning continuously.

6. After 3 minutes, season the courgettes and serve.

Best-sellers in the market

Nothing could be easier or more expensive than making an unusual meal from exotic ingredients. But a really creative cook can be recognised from the way he or she serves common vegetables. This is an area in which nouvelle cuisine has set new standards which appeal to both the nutritionist and the gourmet. This is achieved by blanching, a quick cooking method which preserves vitamins and flavour. It will help you view your usual vegetables in a new light. Try it and see! You need not adopt it to the exclusion of all else, for braising, boiling and frying also have their advantages.

Kohlrabi

One of the cabbage family with a pale grey or bluish swollen stem.
Availability: Grown under glass for part of the year, outdoor kohlrabi is available in the summer.
Preparation: Thinly peel the bulb. Peel more thickly towards the base. Cut off any woody parts.

Wash the bulb, halve or quarter it, cut into thin slices or sticks.
Cooking: Blanch for 3–6 minutes.

Coat in melted butter and season lightly with salt and grated nutmeg. Sprinkle with parsley or chives or serve with béchamel or cheese sauce (see page 256).

Alternatively kohlrabi can be steamed, braised in cream, or served as a gratin (see page 122).

Spinach

There are two ways of buying spinach: root and leaf spinach. With root spinach the whole plant is cut just below the top of the root. With leaf spinach individual leaves are cut above the root. Spinach is rich in vitamin C and iron.

Spinach is usually available in spring, autumn and winter but not in summer.

Spinach should always be eaten immediately it is cooked!

Preparation: Sort spinach carefully, cut off roots and woody stalks and wash several times. The drained spinach should be left whole or coarsely chopped for cooking.
Cooking: Blanch for about 3 minutes. Then squeeze out excess moisture, toss in butter and stir with a clove of garlic stuck on the end of a fork.
Variations:
1. Warm blanched spinach through with a mixture of fried bacon and onion cubes, or coat in cream.
2. Spinach makes an excellent stuffing, either on its own or mixed with minced meat or cheese. Use in puff pastry pies or with pasta (see page 191).
3. Spinach in a gratin with Gruyère cheese, or mixed with diced boiled ham.
4. The classic way of eating spinach: with boiled potatoes and fried or poached eggs.

Broccoli

Closely related to cauliflower, but dark green in colour. A vegetable originally from Italy with a high vitamin C content.
Availability: Spring and autumn.

Broccoli with a slight yellowish tinge is no longer fresh and is on the point of flowering. It has lost its flavour and you should avoid buying it.
Preparation: Remove the leaves, peel thick stems.
Cooking: Blanch for 3–4 minutes. Toss in butter with toasted flaked almonds, season to taste (see page 252).

Peppers

A member of the *Solanaceae* family whose fruit is eaten as a vegetable, a spice or an extract.

Every sweet pepper begins life as a green pepper. If left to ripen on the plant the peppers turn first red then yellow.
Availability: Throughout the year, but most plentiful in the autumn.
Preparation: Remove stalks, seeds and white pith, and then wash. To peel, fry peppers in hot oil. To cook leave whole, or cut into thin strips or cubes.
Cooking: Blanch for 3–5 minutes.
Variations:
1. Stuff whole peppers with minced meat and rice (see page 225) and braise in a sauce.
2. Cut up to serve in soups.
3. For a side vegetable toss in butter or a mixture of diced, fried bacon, onion and garlic and season with salt, pepper and paprika.
4. Cut peppers into strips or cubes and serve in a salad with sweet corn, tomatoes, spring onions and lettuce with a vinaigrette dressing (see page 141).

Tomatoes

Beef, English, cherry or plum tomatoes vary both in shape and the firmness of the flesh and can be eaten in salads, soups, sauces or just as they come.
Availability: Throughout the year.

Beef tomatoes have firm flesh, few seeds and a fruity flavour.

English tomatoes have a lot of seeds and are juicy, but weak in flavour. They are the best shaped tomato for garnishing.

Plum tomatoes are usually only available tinned.

Cherry tomatoes are strong in flavour and thick skinned.
Preparation: Wash the tomatoes, remove the stalks and cut away any green flesh. Further preparation, see right.

Step-by-step illustrations of how to peel tomatoes can be found on page 27.

When making sauces it is unnecessary to peel tomatoes. Halve the tomatoes, remove the seeds and boil to reduce. The skins roll up separately and are easy to remove.

Brussels sprouts

Brussels sprouts are buds that form at the angle of the stalks and stem. They are roughly the size of a walnut when harvested.

Once the sprouts have been cut they cannot be stored for long. Sprouts become more tender, tastier and easier to digest after exposure to frost.
Availability: From late summer to spring.
Preparation: Remove outer leaves and any damaged inner leaves. Cut off the ends of the stalks and cut a cross in the stalk. Wash several times.
Cooking: Blanch for 7–8 minutes. Toss in a little melted butter and season with salt, pepper and grated nutmeg.
Variations:
1. Sprinkle with grated cheese and flaked butter then brown.
2. Serve in cheese sauce (see page 256).
3. Braise, sprinkle with parsley and serve with diced ham.

Adding extra flavour

Blanched vegetables can be served just as they come, with a pinch of salt of course, although they do taste better if they are tossed in butter or cream and sprinkled with herbs or seasoning before serving.

One step up the scale is to serve vegetables such as celeriac, cauliflower or kohlrabi in a béchamel sauce. Alternatively all these vegetables are delicious browned under the grill in a cheese sauce (for both sauces see page 256).

Better still are the flavoured butters which turn everyday vegetables into a feast. Try hazelnut and almond or, if you prefer something more savoury, garlic butter (see pages 252–3).

The most popular sauce in nouvelle cuisine is undoubtedly beurre blanc. This goes with any vegetable, is slightly sour in flavour and is easy to digest (see page 250).

Five advantages of blanching

1. Vegetables remain crisp and firm.
2. Vitamins and other important trace elements are mostly preserved.
3. The natural flavour of the vegetables is preserved.
4. No colour is lost.
5. It is the easiest of all the cooking methods.

Seeds from the pod

These are considered the classic casserole vegetables, whence comes their reputation of taking hours to cook. This image is a hang-over from the time when most cooking was done with dried vegetables. Nowadays fresh vegetables are available whatever the season, either from the greengrocer or the freezer. Peas and beans both taste much better if you blanch them.

Mangetout

Also known as sugar or snow peas. Pods without the tough inner skin and peas which have just begun to develop. Eaten whole.
Availability: Throughout the summer.
Preparation: Top and tail the mangetout and pull off any side strings. Wash and then cook whole.
Blanching time: 2–3 minutes.

Peas

Garden and marrowfat peas. The sweeter and tenderer marrowfat peas are slightly wrinkled with tough pods. They should be picked and eaten young, for they are hard and bitter when fully mature. Garden peas have large, smooth peas and are slightly floury when fully ripe.
Availability: Throughout the summer.
Preparation: Shell, wash and drain the peas.
Blanching time: 3 minutes.

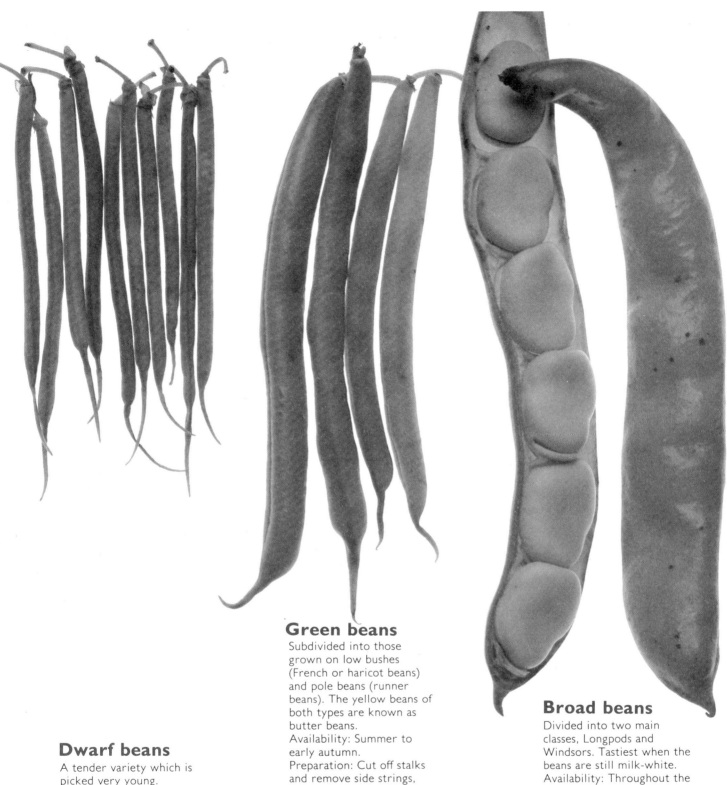

Dwarf beans

A tender variety which is picked very young.
Availability: Throughout the year.
Preparation: Top and tail, wash and drain the beans.
Blanching time: 3–5 minutes.

Green beans

Subdivided into those grown on low bushes (French or haricot beans) and pole beans (runner beans). The yellow beans of both types are known as butter beans.
Availability: Summer to early autumn.
Preparation: Cut off stalks and remove side strings, wash and drain. Cook whole or cut into lengths.
Blanching time: 5–8 minutes. Warm through quickly in a frying pan with bacon and onion.

Broad beans

Divided into two main classes, Longpods and Windsors. Tastiest when the beans are still milk-white.
Availability: Throughout the summer.
Preparation: Open the pods, remove the beans, sort, wash and drain.
Blanching time: 10–15 minutes.

Good things from underground

It is difficult to imagine the differences among the wide range of vegetables which grow below ground. The scale of flavours ranges from the onion to the asparagus, while the range of colours goes through, white, pale mauve, pale green and red. As far as cooking goes, all these vegetables have one thing in common – it is blanching that most successfully brings out their subtle flavours to the full.

Fennel

This dense fleshy bulb can be used both as a vegetable and in salads.
Availability: From autumn to spring.
Preparation: Cut off the leaves and any woody stalks then cut out any damaged portions. Wash the bulb, halve lengthways, then cut into quarters or thin strips.
Cooking: Blanch for 3–4 minutes. Toss the slices of fennel in browned butter, season to taste and sprinkle with chopped fennel leaves or dill.
Variations:
1. Blanch fennel halves and scoop out some of the flesh. Stuff with a mixture of seasoned minced meat, the chopped fennel which you removed and soured cream. Sprinkle with cheese and brown for about 20 minutes.
2. Braise fennel halves for about 8 minutes. Mix in crispy bacon cubes and chopped, peeled tomatoes, then sprinkle with parsley.
3. Use uncooked fennel in mixed salads.

Asparagus

Both green and white asparagus are available. Green asparagus is more strongly flavoured and contains more vitamin C.
Availability: Mainly in springtime.
Preparation: Peel white asparagus thinly from the tip to the base and cut off woody ends. Do not peel green asparagus, simply cut off the woody ends. Wash the asparagus and cook whole, unless used in soups or salads.
Cooking: Blanch for 8–10 minutes. Sprinkle generously with browned butter.
Variation:
Serve with hollandaise sauce (see page 255).

Celery

The crunchy stalks can be used in salads, crudités or vegetable dishes.
Availability: Autumn, winter and early spring.
Preparation: Chop off the base and the leaves. Wash individual sticks and cut into 5-cm/2-in lengths or into slices 1–2 cm/$\frac{1}{2}$–1-in thick.
Cooking: Blanch for 3–5 minutes and toss in melted butter.
Variations:
1. Warm through in cream/soured cream.
2. Sprinkle with salt, pepper, parsley, chives or basil.
3. Warm through in tomato sauce and stir in chopped spring onions.
4. Browned with cheese (see page 143).

Scorzonera

Also known as black salsify. Scorzonera is easy to digest.
Availability: In the winter.
Preparation: Scrub under cold running water, peel and stand for a few minutes in vinegar and water to keep the flesh white. Cook whole or chopped.
Cooking: Blanch for 8–10 minutes. Toss in melted butter.
Variations:
1. Wrap in uncooked ham, sprinkle with cheese and brown for about 15 minutes.
2. Warm through in parsley butter (see page 253).

Carrots

Varieties range in colour from yellow to orange, and long or stumpy in shape. Of all the vegetables carrots have the highest carotene content which is turned into vitamin A with the addition of fat.
Availability: Throughout the year. They store well.
Preparation: Trim, peel and wash the carrots. Cook whole, sliced, diced or in sticks (see page 32).
Cooking: Blanch for 3–5 minutes. Toss in butter or cream, season to taste, sprinkle with parsley, dill, chervil or lemon balm.
Variations:
1. Glaze old carrots in butter and 1 teaspoon sugar. A little sugar complements carrots which can be served sweeter than any other vegetable.
2. Braise carrots for about 10 minutes, see step-by-step photographs pages 126–7, and stir in chervil or chives.

Celeriac

A thick-skinned root vegetable. Used with or without the leaves as a vegetable, in soups or crudités. Celeriac is excellent for storing.
Availability: Autumn and winter.
Preparation: Peel celeriac thickly, wash and stand in water with a little lemon juice to keep the flesh white. Cut into cubes, slices or sticks.
Cooking: Blanch for 5–7 minutes, toss in butter, season with salt, pepper, grated nutmeg and celery salt, sprinkle with parsley and chives.
Variations:
Fill an ovenproof dish with alternate layers of sliced celeriac and bacon, sprinkle with cheese and dot with butter. Brown in a hot oven (220C, 425F, gas 7) for 15 minutes.

Spring onions

Very early onion variety with a mild flavour. Used whole or chopped as a vegetable and uncooked in salads.
Availability: Spring and summer.
Preparation: Cut off the leaves, leaving about 13–15 cm/5–6 in. Cut off roots and peel if necessary. Wash and cut into quarters, or thinly slice.
Cooking: Blanch for 2–3 minutes, then toss in butter and sprinkle with chopped garlic. Alternatively warm through in soured cream or with diced bacon.

Leeks

A relation of the onion with a thickening of the lower third of the stem.
Availability: Throughout the year.
Preparation: Trim off the roots, cut off limp or damaged leaves. Halve the stem lengthways and wash thoroughly. Cut into lengths, slices or sticks.
Cooking: Blanch for 3–5 minutes. Warm through with bacon cubes or cream, season with salt, pepper and grated nutmeg, or simply sprinkle with parsley.
Variation:
Wrap blanched leeks in boiled ham and bake in an ovenproof dish with cheese or cheese sauce (see page 256).

White cabbage

A firm, round, compact cabbage with smooth leaves.
Availability: Summer to end of winter.
Preparation: Remove limp leaves, cut into halves or quarters and cut out the stalk. Cut into thin or wide strips, or simply separate the leaves. Cut out thick ribs.
Cooking: Mix 1 kg/2 lb white cabbage with salt, pepper and ½ teaspoon ground caraway or 100 g/ 4 oz diced bacon, or braise in 1 tablespoon pork dripping over a moderate heat for 30–40 minutes.

Variations:
1. Braise small smoked sausages with the white cabbage.
2. Braise coarsely chopped white cabbage with pork and season with salt, pepper and vinegar.
3. White cabbage is excellent in stews (see page 163).
4. With salt added, chopped white cabbage is fermented to make sauerkraut.
5. Stuffed cabbage (see page 226).

Savoy cabbage

A curly-leafed cabbage, less compact than white cabbage. Light to dark green in colour.
Availability: Throughout the year.
Preparation: Remove limp or damaged leaves, cut into halves or quarters, cut out the stalk and cut into coarse or fine strips.
Cooking: Braise for 20 minutes. Stir 1–2 table-spoons soured cream into 1 kg/2 lb cabbage and serve with strips of fried bacon. Season to taste.
Variations:
1. Braise Savoy cabbage with smoked meat or smoked sausages.
2. Blanch cabbage leaves for 2 minutes, place several leaves one on top of the other and stuff with minced meat (see page 215).
3. Savoy cabbage gives any casserole an excellent flavour (see page 161).

Cabbage, the supreme leaf vegetable

Nowhere in the world is cabbage used as well as in Germany, be it white, green, red or purple cabbage. Germany is definitely the king when it comes to preparing cabbage dishes. Not only do sauerkraut and red cabbage taste delicious, they are also good for you and make fatty foods such as pork or sausage more digestible. And despite all assertions to the contrary, cabbage is an essential part of any calorie controlled diet. Nouvelle cuisine has adopted Savoy cabbage as one of its favourite vegetables.

Red cabbage

Red or purple cabbage.
Round cabbage with
compact dark red or purple
leaves.
Availability: For most of the
year.
Preparation: Like white or
Savoy cabbage, cut into
coarse or fine strips.
Cooking: Fry 2 onions in 1
tablespoon fat or dripping
until transparent. Add 1 kg/
2 lb red cabbage and 150 ml/
¼ pint red wine, 2 allspice, 4
cloves and 1 chopped apple.
Braise for 60 minutes.

Bind with 1 tablespoon
redcurrant jelly or cran-
berry sauce (optional).

Serve red cabbage and
braised apple rings (or pears
in red wine) with game,
beef or poultry.

Chinese cabbage

Also known as Chinese
leaves, Nappa cabbage and
celery cabbage. Chinese
cabbage has longish, dense
heads with coarse, crinkly
leaves and a weak cabbage
flavour.
Availability: Autumn and
winter.
Preparation: Remove limp
leaves, cut off the stalk,
wash and drain the leaves.
Before cooking cut into
coarse or fine strips.
Cooking: Braise for 3–6
minutes. Braise 1 kg/2 lb
cabbage in 2 tablespoons
butter and 150 ml/¼ pint
water. Season with salt,
pepper and lemon juice,
sprinkle with parsley,
chervil or chopped nuts.

Variations:
1. Bake Chinese cabbage
with a cheese sauce (see
page 256).
2. Mix with braised carrots,
peas or asparagus.
3. Chinese cabbage, with its
mild flavour, can be served
in a mixed salad with
radicchio, endive and
Iceberg lettuce in a
vinaigrette dressing (see
page 141).

Curly kale

A cabbage with dark green,
curly leaves. Rich in
vitamins A and C.
Curly kale tastes best
after frost.
Availability: Throughout the
winter.
Preparation: Remove limp,
damaged leaves and thick
ribs, wash several times and
coarsely chop.
Cooking: Season 1 kg/2 lb
curly kale with salt, pepper
and grated nutmeg. Braise
for 1 hour with 100 g/4 oz
bacon cubes or 1 onion. You
can bind the kale with 1–2
tablespoons oatmeal or add
1–2 teaspoons mustard.
Curly kale is really tasty if it
is braised with smoked
sausage, bacon or smoked
meat.

A sextet for specialists

There are half a dozen vegetables of which gourmets are extremely fond. These include cauliflower, which is extremely easy to digest and has therefore come to be thought of as something of an invalid food but which is tasty enough for everyone. More popular still in recent years are sweet corn, exotic okra or old-fashioned turnips. Finally we come to the artichoke which has become a favourite food for lovers, for one can sit over it for hours, pulling off one leaf after another without ever feeling full!

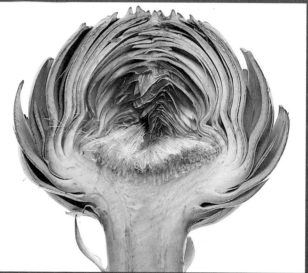

Cauliflower

The head should be white, compact and without blemishes.
Availability: Throughout the year.
Preparation: Cut-off outer green leaves, soak in cold, salted water. Cook whole or in rosettes.
Cooking: see step-by-step photographs (pages 126–7).
Variations:
1. Serve with breadcrumbs browned in butter (see page 252), hollandaise sauce (see page 255) or flaked butter.
2. Bake with cheese.

Sweet corn

Cobs with sweet, tender seeds. Rich in vitamin B1 and calcium. Boil corn cobs in deep salted water for 8–10 minutes. Fry or cook on the barbecue wrapped in foil (1–2 cobs per person).
Stick a fork into each end of the cob and nibble off the corn.
Variations:
1. Remove corn from the cob and quick-fry with cooked kidney beans, bacon and green pepper.
2. Use cold, boiled corn in salads.

Artichokes

The artichoke is a fist-sized flower bud which can only be eaten cooked.
Availability: Autumn to spring.
Preparation: Cut off the stalk, cover the cut with a lemon slice and tie into place (see page 27). Boil in deep water and added lemon juice for 35 minutes. The leaves are pulled off individually, dipped in sauce and then scraped between the teeth. Suitable sauces include vinaigrette (see page 141), hollandaise, Bèarnaise (see page 255). The best part of the vegetable is the artichoke heart which is also used as a garnish.

Okra

Also known as lady's fingers or gumbo. Fleshy, hexagonal pods grow to finger length.
Availability: Throughout the year.
Preparation: Wash, cut off stalks, possibly halve or slice.
Cooking: Boil in deep salted water for 5–10 minutes depending on size.
  Stir in hot butter with fried onion and garlic and serve with lamb (see page 242–3) or fish.
  Mix okra with braised carrots, green peppers, prawns, curry powder and coriander.

Beetroot

A root vegetable with a reddish-brown skin and dark red flesh.
Availability: Summer to end of winter.
Preparation: Cut off leaves to about 2.5 cm/1 in above the root and scrub under cold running water.
Cooking: Boil beetroots, unpeeled, in deep salted water for 60–70 minutes. Plunge into cold water, peel and cut. Serve beetroot as a vegetable, seasoned with salt, pepper and dill, or use in salads.

Turnip

White, globe-shaped turnips or flat-rooted purplish turnips.
Availability: Best in early summer.
Preparation: Cut off roots and leaves, thinly peel and slice, dice or cut into sticks for cooking.
Cooking: Boil 450 g/1 lb turnips in deep salted water for 10–20 minutes depending on size. Serve as a vegetable tossed in 1 tablespoon butter or 2 tablespoons cream with meat, goose or duck.
Tip: Turnips can be seasoned with the following herbs: chervil, dill, chives.

Mushrooms and other vegetables suitable for frying

The smell of cooking in the French countryside is one of woods and meadows – vegetables and mushrooms from the frying pan, highly seasoned with herbs, fried in olive oil or butter: a real feast. As a side vegetable or on its own if you add a few extras such as bacon, ham or cream. The French also invented the method of frying known as sautéeing in which the pan is continuously shaken as food quickly fries in hot fat.

Aubergines

Or egg plants. Little inherent flavour. Their full flavour comes only with cooking.
Preparation: Cut off stalks, wash, slice, possibly sprinkle with salt and leave to stand for a few minutes. This draws the bitterness out of the vegetable and prevents them absorbing too much fat during frying. Finally rinse in cold water.
Cooking:
1. Season 450 g/1 lb aubergines with pepper. Use 2 tablespoons flour to cover lightly and fry for 3–4 minutes in plenty of fat. Season with thyme and serve as a vegetable with meat dishes.
2. Fry aubergines with chopped garlic, mix with diced, peeled tomato and sprinkle with basil.
3. Serve stuffed (see page 225).

Bean sprouts

Tender sprouts of the germinating soya bean. White-yellow to reddish-brown in colour. Highly perishable. Remove from packing as soon as possible. Rich in vegetable protein. One of the basic ingredients of Oriental cooking, which combines well with any vegetable.
Preparation: Wash in cold water and drain.
Cooking: Season with salt, pepper and soy sauce and fry for 3–5 minutes.
Variations:
1. Mix with fried strips of meat, braised peas and strips of leek.
2. Add to fried minced meat and braise together for a few minutes (see page 215).
3. Season with soy sauce, Tabasco and pepper.

Courgettes

Also known as zucchini. A dark-green fruit similar to a small cucumber. Delicate flavour and flesh.
Availability: Summer to mid winter.
Preparation: Peel large courgettes, cook smaller ones with the skin. Wash under cold, running water, halve lengthways, cut into finger-thick slices or cubes.
Cooking: Coat 450 g/1 lb courgettes in 2 tablespoons flour (optional) and fry with chopped onion for about 5 minutes. Sprinkle with sage.
Variations:
1. Layer thin slices in a buttered baking dish and bake with cream and grated cheese for 10–15 minutes.
2. Courgettes are one of the ingredients of ratatouille (see page 142) and can also be served as a vegetable with many meat dishes.
3. Delicious flavoured with herbs such as thyme, oregano or sage.

Cèpes

Also known as ceps or boletus. They are a variety of wild mushroom and have an especially good flavour. They seem quite rare now and are consequently quite expensive.
Availability: Summer to beginning of autumn.
   Cook as in basic mushroom recipe.
Variations:
Quick-fry cèpes in a hot pan without fat and season simply with salt and pepper.

Oyster mushrooms

Usually available as cultivated rather than wild mushrooms. Flesh is white, soft and tender.
Availability: Cultivated throughout the year, in the wild in late autumn.
   Cook as in basic mushroom recipe.

Button mushrooms

Availability: Throughout the year.
   Cook as in basic mushroom recipe.
Variations:
1. Fry with other vegetables such as baby carrots, mangetout or spring onions and season with herbs.
2. Stuff large heads with herby minced steak, sprinkle with cheese and brown.
3. Serve sliced mushrooms as a salad with celery and mixed herbs and a vinaigrette dressing (see page 141), flavoured with mustard or tomato purée.

Chanterelles

Funnel-shaped, yellow-capped mushrooms.
Availability: Summer to late autumn.
   Chanterelles are highly flavoured.
   Cook as in basic mushroom recipe.
Variations:
1. Mix with scampi or serve on braised spinach.
2. Serve chanterelles in cream with pasta (see page 82) and chives.

Mushrooms

are available throughout the year. They are extremely versatile. Since they contain around 80 per cent water they need gentle handling.
Preparation: Only very dirty mushrooms need be washed in water and lemon juice. Scrape off soil particles. Cut off the ends of the stalks and possibly peel. With button mushrooms remove very dark gills. Cook whole, halved, quartered or sliced.

Basic recipe: Fry 450 g/1 lb mushrooms in 2 tablespoons butter with 1 chopped onion, 1 crushed clove garlic or 1 tablespoon chopped herbs. Always salt after cooking. Mushrooms can also be served mixed with 75 g/3 oz fried bacon or ham cubes and 2 tablespoons cream or soured cream. Mushrooms should not be reheated!
   All mushrooms can be added to sauces or soups, or marinated cold in vinaigrette dressing (see page 141).
   Use sliced in salads in combination with lettuce, spring onions, radishes and cress.

The A to Z of salads

One could write a work of several volumes about salads and their dressings without exhausting their limitless possibilities. The choice of dressings begins with the type of oil, ranging from olive to hazelnut oil. The variety continues with special vinegars from sherry vinegar to the Italian aceto balsamico. Then you can choose between sweet, sour or hot dressings. Any dressing can be made quite unique by the addition of unusual seasonings, from roasting juices to champagne mustard. You can do anything with salad. It is a wide field for both beginners and experienced cooks.

All leafy salad vegetables can be combined with one another or with various other vegetables. Almost all salad stuffs are now available throughout the year, but all have their seasons when they are grown in the open rather than under glass and are cheaper and tastier for it.

Ten basic salad rules

1. Always make salads fresh.
2. Trim leaf vegetables and remove limp leaves.
3. Break leaves off the stalk or cut above the roots.
4. Wash leaves whole in cold water. This washes out as few vitamins as possible.
5. Remove leaves from the water and drain thoroughly, preferably shaking in a lettuce basket.
6. Tear leaves into pieces or cut into strips (Iceberg lettuce or chicory).
7. Never crush lettuce or it will turn brown.
8. Always toss leaf salads with the dressing just before serving, otherwise they become limp.
9. Never leave prepared salad to stand or it will lose its vitamins.
10. Salads should never be served swimming in dressing. The dressing should rather cling to the leaves.

Radish

Hot flavour, round or oval in shape. Close relative of the winter radish.
Availability: Throughout the year, by the bunch.

Winter radish

Large round or longish radish with white, reddish or black skin and hot flavour.
Availability: Throughout the year, sold singly.
Sprinkle peeled sliced or grated radish with salt and leave to stand. This makes them milder.

Cucumber

Long, green salad cucumber is a member of the *Cucurbitaceae* family.
Availability: Throughout the year.
Tip: Always peel towards the stalk to avoid spreading the bitter substances in the stalk over the whole cucumber. Season with salt just before serving, otherwise the salt will draw out water and make the dressing thin.

Red onion

Deep red to purple skin and mild, spicy flavour which makes it excellent for salads.
Availability: Summer and autumn.

Cabbage lettuce

Also known as round or butterhead lettuce. Compact lettuce with pale green leaves. If the cut stalk is white the lettuce is fresh.
Availability: Throughout the year.

Curly endive

Known as chicory in America, it has large, pale green, curly leaves and slightly bitter flavour.
Availability: During winter months.

Iceberg lettuce

Also known as crisphead lettuce. A round lettuce with densely packed, light green leaves, curly at the ends. The crisp leaves will not wilt as quickly as cabbage lettuce once tossed. Good flavour.
Availability: Throughout the year.

Radicchio

Originally from the Italian province of Treviso. A small, compact, round leaf vegetable, pale red to purple in colour with a slightly bitter flavour.
Availability: Throughout the year, best from autumn to spring.

Lamb's lettuce

Or corn salad. Usually available only in parts of Europe. A wild plant with small light green or larger dark green, oval leaves on short stalks. Rich in vitamin A.
Availability: Throughout the year, but best in spring and autumn.
Preparation: Cut leaves off above the root and wash thoroughly for it can often be covered in soil.

Watercress

A member of the cress family with dark green, juicy leaves and strong, slightly bitter flavour.
Availability: Throughout the year.

Chicory

Also known as Belgian endive. Contains bitter substances which give it a strong flavour. The long oval heads range from white to yellow and have compact, fleshy leaves.
Availability: Throughout the year, best during winter months.
Preparation: Remove outer damaged leaves and cut out a wedge of the bitter stalk using a sharp knife. Chicory can also be braised and baked (see page 143).

Cress

Sold in small cartons, usually as mustard and cress. The young shoots are snipped off just above the soil with scissors. Slightly hot in flavour. It is easy to grow oneself: sprinkle seeds on damp cottonwool or soil and water thoroughly. You will have cress for cutting in only 3–4 days.
Both cress and watercress are ideal for seasoning soups and sauces and are often used as a garnish.

Basic recipe for cream dressing

300 ml/½ pint single cream
juice of ½ lemon
salt and pepper

Add the cream to the lemon juice which should be seasoned first. This cream dressing can be flavoured to taste with mustard, tomato purée, horseradish and walnuts, mandarine or orange segments, herbs or chopped onion.

Basic recipe for vinaigrette dressing

salt and pepper
2 tablespoons vinegar
8 tablespoons olive oil
3 tablespoons finely chopped mixed herbs
2 tablespoons finely chopped tomatoes (from peeled tomatoes)

1. Beat the salt and pepper into the vinegar.
2. Whisk in the oil. Important: Always add the oil to the vinegar, rather than beating both together, for the oil forms a coating around the seasoning which will not then dissolve.
3. Stir in the herbs and tomato.
   For a salad dressing the ratio of vinegar to oil is 1:2 or 1:3, according to taste.

Basic recipe for Thousand Island dressing

2 egg yolks
2 tablespoons vinegar or lemon juice
salt and pepper
300 ml/½ pint oil
3 tablespoons tomato ketchup
1–2 tablespoons brandy
150 ml/¼ pint double cream, whipped
1 tablespoon finely chopped herbs (parsley, chives)

1. Beat the egg yolks with the vinegar, salt and pepper.
2. Whisk in the oil a few drops at a time. To prevent the mayonnaise separating, all the ingredients should be at room temperature.
3. Stir the ketchup and brandy into the mayonnaise.
4. Fold in the cream.
5. Add the chopped herbs and season to taste.

Ratatouille

3 tablespoons olive oil
3–4 onions, chopped
2 cloves garlic, crushed
1 red pepper
2 green peppers
4 medium tomatoes
1 (350-g/12-oz) aubergine
350 g/12 oz courgettes
salt and pepper
1 tablespoon chopped herbs
(e.g. parsley, basil, thyme)

1. Heat the oil over a
moderate heat.
2. Fry the chopped onion
and garlic.
3. Dice the peppers or cut
into strips. Peel, deseed and
coarsely chop the tomatoes
and add both to the pan.
Braise for about 10 minutes
stirring occasionally.
4. Slice the aubergine and
courgettes and add to the
other vegetables.
5. Season to taste. Braise for
about 10 minutes in the
open pan to evaporate off
the liquid.
6. Stir in the chopped herbs.

   For a more homogenous
ratatouille, braise for a
further 15–20 minutes.

Sauerkraut

2 tablespoons pork dripping
2 onions, chopped
675 g/1½ lb tinned or bottled
sauerkraut, drained
300 ml/½ pint dry white wine
1 large (or 2 small) bay leaf
5–6 juniper berries or
2 cloves
salt and pepper
pinch of sugar
1 uncooked potato, grated

1. Heat the dripping.
2. Fry the onions.
3. Gently separate the
sauerkraut and add to the
pan.
4. Add the white wine.
5. Add the bay leaf and
juniper berries.
6. Braise for 10 minutes.
7. Season with salt, pepper
and sugar then stir in the
grated potato. Cook for a
further 10–15 minutes.

Baked beans

2 cups dried Boston or small
haricot beans
2 large onions, chopped
2 cloves garlic, crushed
3 tablespoons oil
1 bay leaf
750 ml/1¼ pints meat stock
100 g/4 oz concentrated
tomato purée
2 tablespoons prepared
mustard
3 tablespoons red wine
vinegar
3 carrots
3 tablespoons butter
3–4 apples
salt and freshly milled black
pepper

1. Soak the beans overnight
in cold water.
2. Fry the onion and garlic
in the heated oil until
transparent.
3. Drain the beans and add
with the bay leaf.
4. Add the stock, bring to
the boil and simmer for
about 1 hour.
5. Stir in the tomato purée,
mustard and vinegar.
6. Slice the carrots and
braise in the melted butter
for about 5 minutes.
7. Peel, core and cut the
apples into wedges.
8. Add the carrots and
apples to the beans, season
to taste and transfer to an
ovenproof dish.
9. Cover the dish and bake
in a moderate oven (180C,
350F, gas 4) for about 1½
hours.

Baked celery

2 heads celery (about 1 kg/
2 lb)

300 ml/½ pint dry white wine

3 tablespoons chopped
mixed herbs

salt and pepper

4 tablespoons breadcrumbs

4 tablespoons soft butter

1. Cut the sticks of celery
into equal lengths.
2. Blanch for 5 minutes (see
step-by-step photographs on
pages 126–7).
3. Pour the white wine into
an ovenproof dish and
sprinkle with the herbs.
4. Add the celery.
5. Season to taste.
6. Work the breadcrumbs
into the butter and spread
over the celery.
7. Put the dish in a
moderately hot oven (200C,
400F, gas 6) and bake for
20–25 minutes.

Pasta and vegetable bake

225 g/8 oz pasta noodles
(page 82)

150 g/5 oz broccoli

150 g/5 oz mangetout

3 large tomatoes

2 onions

1 clove garlic

1 tablespoon butter, to
grease the dish

salt and pepper

150 g/5 oz soured cream

150 ml/¼ pint double cream

3 eggs, separated

1 tablespoon chopped
parsley

1 tablespoon chopped basil

3 tablespoons grated cheese

1. Boil the pasta in deep
salted water for 3–5
minutes and rinse under
cold water.
2. Blanch the broccoli and
mangetout separately for
3 minutes each (see pages
16–7).
3. Peel and chop the
tomatoes.
4. Finely chop the onions
and garlic.
5. Arrange the pasta and
vegetables in alternate
layers in a well-buttered
ovenproof dish, seasoning
each layer.
6. Beat together the soured
cream, double cream and
egg yolks, and season to
taste.
7. Whisk the egg whites
until stiff and fold into the
cream mixture with the
herbs.
8. Pour this mixture over
the ingredients in the dish
and sprinkle with the
cheese.
9. Bake in a moderately hot
oven (190C, 375F, gas 5) for
45 minutes.

Baked chicory

8 heads chicory

2 tablespoons butter

150 ml/¼ pint dry white
wine

8 slices boiled ham

a little butter to grease the
dish

8 slices Emmental or
Gruyère cheese

salt and pepper

1. Trim and wash the
chicory and cut out the
bitter stalk in a wedge.
2. Fry the chicory in 2
tablespoons butter over a
moderate heat for 2–3
minutes.
3. Add the wine, cover
the pan and braise for 15
minutes.
4. Remove the chicory from
the pan and wrap each head
in a slice of ham.
5. Arrange in a well-
buttered dish.
6. Cover each head with a
slice of cheese.
7. Season to taste.
8. Bake in a moderately hot
oven (200C, 400F, gas 6) for
10–15 minutes.

Soups: deliciously warming

With the great reliance nowadays upon canned and packet soups, soup is gradually losing its appeal as a great treat. Its image has become somewhat tarnished in recent years. Yet there is no other course on the menu which offers such variety of colour and flavour. Soups range in scale from the thin broths of the poor to Bocuse's famous truffle soup with its topping of puff pastry – from goulash soups to what has become the Austrian national dish, beef soup with Tafelspitz. Gone are the days of the delicious broths of old Vienna and the refined 'potages' of Escoffier's Paris. Soups are nevertheless capable of bringing back delightful memories – grandmother's Scotch broth, a minestrone in Tuscany, French onion soup in Montmartre, bouillabaisse on a mild Mediterranean evening . . . From filling broths to the delicate creations of nouvelle cuisine, there is a soup to suit everyone and every occasion.

Queen of the stew pan

Whether we refer to it as vegetable soup, beef stew or broth, all these refer to the classic beef soup which the French call 'pot au feu'. Do not skimp on either the beef, vegetables or stock – fill the biggest pan you have. Eat some of the soup when you make it and freeze the rest to use as meat stock (see page 148) or as a base for other soups.

Basic recipe for beef soup

675 g–1 kg| 1½–2 lb stewing beef, on the bone (shin, middle or top rib)

2 marrow bones

1 onion

1 bunch soup vegetables (carrot, leek and celeriac)

3 litres| 6 pints water

1 bunch flat-leaved parsley

½ teaspoon salt

black pepper

I. Wash the meat and marrow bones in cold water.

3. Place all the ingredients in the pan. Add the cold water to cover.

2. Peel the onion and cut crossways in half. Brown the cut side of both halves in a frying pan without fat. This is easiest in a non-stick pan.

4. Heat gently on a medium heat without allowing the water to boil.

5. Skim off the scum as it rises to the surface, and repeat until scum stops forming. This will prevent the soup being cloudy.

6. Bring to the boil and reduce the heat. Simmer very gently for 2 hours. The surface of the stock should just move slightly.

7. Lift out the beef and vegetables using a serrated spoon.

8. Lift out the marrow bones. Cut up the vegetables. Season the soup to taste with salt. Reheat the meat and vegetables in the broth. Season with freshly ground black pepper.

Giving the soup extra flavour

Cook an onion in the soup. Initial frying of the onion gives a much better flavour. In addition include: whole stems of herbs, left-over vegetables, small pieces of chicken. The longer the soup is left to simmer, the better the flavour. You can leave it on the stove for hours, or even the whole day. Cooking in an open pan intensifies the flavour even more. In a *pressure cooker* beef soup takes about 20 minutes. Add chopped vegetables 5–10 minutes before the end of the cooking time. Go sparingly with the salt at first, for the stock reduces as it cooks and can become salty.

Chicken soup

This is made by the same method as the basic beef soup recipe. Use the same amount of liquid and vegetables but replace the beef with chicken pieces. If you prefer to use a whole chicken you will need slightly more water, and you can omit the marrow bones. Cooking time: with roasting chicken about 1 hour, with a boiling fowl about $2\frac{1}{2}$ hours. If you like add a little ground cinnamon.

Bolliti misti

Mixed meat broth
This Italian speciality is made with ox tongue, sausage, stewing beef, leg of veal and chicken. Using the same method as the basic beef soup recipe, but omitting the marrow bones, all the ingredients are cooked one after the other in a large pan.

Start with the tongue which has to cook for 3 hours. Add the boiling fowl 30 minutes later which takes $2\frac{1}{2}$ hours to cook. After another 30 minutes add the beef which takes 2 hours to cook, and so on.

In Italy the beef is cut into slices and served with a green sauce called 'pesto' (see page 149), but there is no reason why you can't serve bolitti misti as a filling soup.

The secret of bouillon

Beef soup forms the basis for meat stock (bouillon), consommé, meat essence and meat jelly.

Strained and defatted, the stock can be used as it comes or reduced as the basis for other soups. In concentrated form, as an essence, it makes delicious sauces.

Simple meat stock

'Bouillon'
is strained, defatted beef soup, which can be served with a variety of added ingredients (see pages 150–1).

Consommé

is made by gently simmering the bouillon with its meat and vegetables for a further 1 hour, and then defatting. The stock is now golden yellow in colour and with a strong flavour.

Concentrated consommé

'Consommé double'
is made in the same way as consommé, but with twice the quantity of meat (e.g. chopped beef). This is golden brown in colour. Concentrated consommé is the ideal starter for a classic menu.

Meat essence

is concentrated consommé further reduced. It can be served in small cups as a starter, but is mainly used as a base for fine sauces or added to casseroles to give extra flavour.

Meat jelly or Aspic

is made from consommé or concentrated consommé, gelatine, wine, sherry or madeira (450 ml/¾ pint stock, 1 sachet gelatine, about 150 ml/¼ pint wine, sherry or madeira). Meat jelly/aspic is used for topping up meat pies or coating pâtés, or diced as a garnish.

The basic beef soup recipe (see page 146) produces meat stock when all the solid ingredients are removed and the liquid strained through a sieve lined with kitchen paper or muslin.

To defat, draw a piece of kitchen paper or a paper serviette over the surface of the hot stock. Alternatively leave the stock until cold and lift off the coagulated layer of fat using a skimmer.

Useful tip:
Defatted stock will freeze for up to six months.

Adding extra flavour to meat stock

1. Season the cooked stock with salt, pepper or a little cayenne.
2. Season with a little sambal oelek (made from chillies).
3. Add 1–2 teaspoons soy sauce per portion.
4. Season with saffron powder (a generous pinch per 1 litre/2 pints stock).
5. Stir in a little ground cinnamon.
6. Season with grated nutmeg (a generous pinch per 1 litre/2 pints stock).
7. Simmer a garlic clove in the hot stock for a short time.
8. Add 1 tablespoon *herbes de Provence* (in a muslin bag) to the hot stock for about 5 minutes.
9. Stir in concentrated tomato purée just before serving (1 teaspoon per 1 litre/2 pints stock).
10. Flavour by adding finely chopped wild mushrooms about 1 hour before the end of the cooking time and finely strain the stock.
11. Just before serving, stir a little port, sherry or brandy into the stock.

A sauce for the soup

In France and Italy soups and broths are often served with an oil-based sauce or highly seasoned mayonnaise. From France comes aioli, which gives flavour to vegetable soups and which can also be spread on bread. Pesto is an Italian speciality which also serves as a pasta sauce.

Aioli

1 tablespoon breadcrumbs
2 tablespoons lemon juice
2 cloves garlic, crushed
2 egg yolks
$\frac{1}{2}$ cup olive oil
$\frac{1}{2}$ teaspoon salt
pepper

In a basin stir the breadcrumbs with the lemon juice and garlic to give a smooth paste. Beat in the egg yolks. Whisk in the olive oil a few drops at a time and season to taste.

Pesto

1$\frac{1}{2}$ cups fresh basil leaves
1 clove garlic
1 tablespoon pine nuts
2 tablespoons Parmesan cheese, grated
2–3 tablespoons olive oil

Strip the basil leaves from the stalks and finely chop the stalks. Slice the garlic. Pound the basil (leaves and stalks) with the garlic and pine nuts in a mortar to give a smooth paste. Work in the Parmesan and olive oil.

Thirty quick variations

You can serve a clear soup as a starter for a special menu, as a hot starter for a cold supper or as the main course of a slimming meal. It is just a matter of finding imaginative variations on the basic recipe. You will find thirty variations here, but you should be able to come up with plenty more of your own.

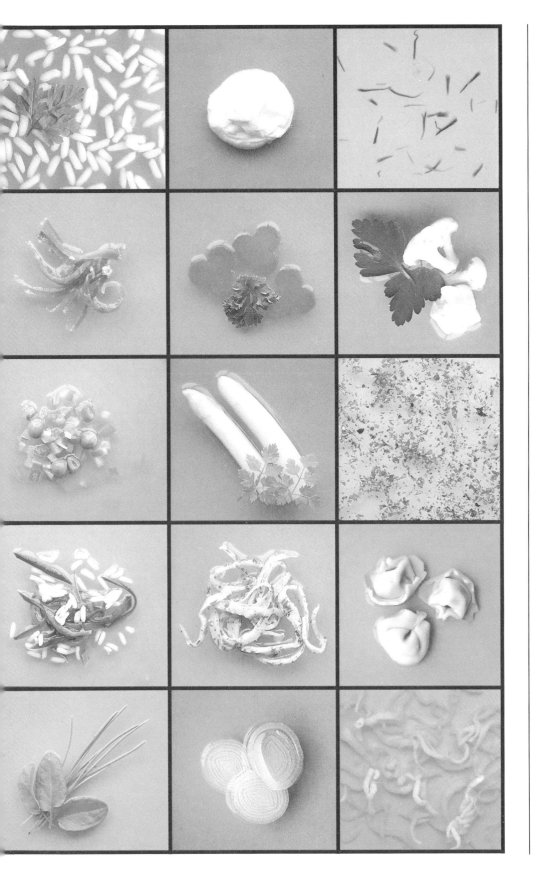

(Illustrations from left to right)

Beef marrow, sliced, warmed through in the soup for 5 minutes.

Celeriac, in thin sticks, cooked in the soup for 5 minutes.

Beetroot, chopped, cooked for 2 minutes and sprinkled on the soup.

Rice, add 1 tablespoon boiled rice per person to the soup.

Cream, top each portion of soup with 1 tablespoon whipped cream.

Saffron strands, sprinkled into the soup and simmered for 10 minutes.

Lettuce, shredded, sprinkled onto the soup just before serving.

Tomatoes, peeled, deseeded and thinly sliced, cooked for 15 minutes.

Mushroom slices and chopped chives warmed through in the soup.

Ham, in strips, sprinkled on just before serving.

Carrot slices, cooked in the soup for 5 minutes, garnish with parsley.

Cauliflower rosettes, cooked, served in the soup with celery leaves.

Vermicelli, cooked in the hot soup for 15 minutes.

Celery and leek strips, braised and served in the soup with chervil leaves.

Star pasta cooked in the soup.

Carrot, celeriac and other diced vegetables cooked in the soup.

Asparagus tips, boiled and warmed through in the soup for 5 minutes.

Herbs, freshly chopped, added to the hot soup.

Tomato cubes with basil leaves, warmed through in the soup.

Smoked sausage slices and *red cabbage* warmed in the soup.

Peas, asparagus and carrots, quick blanched and added to the soup.

Pepper strips and *rice*, cooked and added to the soup.

Pancakes, cut into fine strips and added.

Tortellini cooked in the soup for 15 minutes.

Mushroom slices, pieces of *apple and tomato* with *pasta*, added to the soup.

Peas, shelled, cooked in the soup for 20 minutes.

Gruyère cheese, grated, sprinkled on the soup just before serving.

Sorrel and *chives*, simmered in the soup for 2 minutes.

Leek slices cooked in the soup for 10 minutes.

Egg vermicelli (see page 152) added to the hot soup.

Five favourite additions

You can turn any soup or broth into something special, even a ready-bought soup. Canned game or oxtail soup can be turned into a delicious starter. The best known additions for soup are egg custard, veal or marrow dumplings and croûtons.

Egg custard

2 eggs
½ cup milk
salt

1. Beat the eggs until frothy. Heat the milk.
2. Whisk the hot milk into the beaten eggs and season with salt.
3. Pour into a bain-marie full of hot water (or suspend the basin in a pan of hot water without allowing it to stand on the base of the pan).
4. Cook for 30–40 minutes over a moderate heat until firm. Do not uncover the pan during this time.
5. Loosen from the basin using a knife.
6. Cut first into slices and then into pieces.
Variations:
Egg custard or dumplings will be even better if you mix into them:
– chopped spinach
– chopped pistachio nuts
– chopped herbs
– chopped truffles
– chopped almonds
– paprika or curry powder
– saffron powder

Egg vermicelli

1 egg
2 tablespoons flour
salt
freshly grated nutmeg

1. Beat the egg.
2. Whisk in the flour.
3. Season the mixture with salt and nutmeg to taste and strain to remove any lumps.
4. Press the mixture through a skimmer, spätzle press or fine sieve into the hot soup.

Marrow dumplings

(illustrated left)

½ cup beef marrow

1 tablespoon chopped parsley

½ cup white breadcrumbs

½ cup beaten eggs

salt and pepper

a little flour

1. Remove the beef marrow from the bones.
2. Mix the parsley into the breadcrumbs and add the eggs. Mix thoroughly.
3. Knead the finely chopped marrow into the mixture and season to taste. If the mixture is too loose work in a little flour.
4. Sprinkle a worktop with flour. Shape the mixture into a thin roll, cut into slices and shape into balls.
5. Cook in broth (or in salted water) for 15 minutes until cooked.

Veal dumplings

(illustrated left)

100 g / 4 oz lean veal

4–6 tablespoons double cream

salt and pepper

1. Finely slice the veal. Stir in 2 tablespoons cream and season to taste.
2. Blend in a food processor or blender.
3. Beat in the remaining cream until light.
4. Shape teaspoons of the mixture into dumplings.
5. Poach in salted water for 15 minutes.

Fried bread cubes

'Croûtons'

3 slices white bread

1 tablespoon butter

salt

1. Cut the crusts off the bread and cut the bread into small cubes.
2. Quick-fry in a frying pan without fat, then add the butter.
3. Stir until the cubes are golden brown.
4. Season with salt to taste.

Grilled toppings

For 4 cups soup, beat 4 tablespoons whipped cream with 1 egg yolk. Pour the soup into heatproof bowls and top each with 1 spoon cream. Place under a preheated grill and cook until the tops are golden brown. Soups can also be browned under the grill with freshly grated or thinly sliced cheese.

Soup with puff-pastry topping

Roll out the puff pastry and cut four rounds, slightly larger than the top of the soup bowls. Pour the soup into heatproof bowls. Brush the rims with egg yolk, cover each with puff pastry and press into position. Brush the pastry with the remaining egg yolk. Place the bowls in a hot oven (230C, 450F, gas 8) and bake until the pastry is golden brown.

The three-star method

Escoffier, the old-master of haute cuisine, made his own contribution to the world of soups, creating the ultimate version of cream soup. These also include the 'veloutés', which translates as 'velvety'. Their creaminess is provided by a light roux (cooked butter and flour). But there are various other tricks . . .

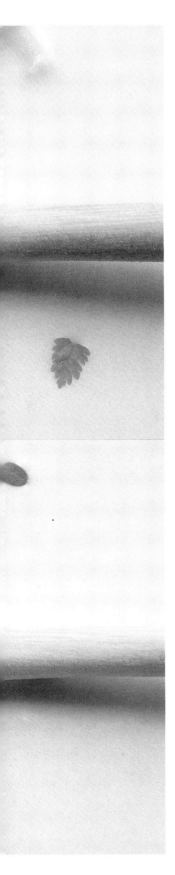

Cream of mushroom soup

(illustrated left below)

100 g/4 oz mushrooms
1 shallot (or 1 onion)
1 tablespoon butter
750 ml/1¼ pints meat stock
150 ml/¼ pint double cream
1 egg yolk
salt and freshly ground
black pepper
thyme to garnish

1. Finely chop the mushrooms and shallot. Keep a few slices of mushroom to garnish.
2. Fry the remaining mushrooms and the shallot in the butter until transparent.
3. Add the stock and boil for 3 minutes.
4. Remove the soup from the heat and thicken by beating together the cream and egg yolk and stirring into the soup.
5. Reheat without allowing the soup to boil and season to taste.
6. Garnish with the reserved mushroom slices and a little fresh thyme.

Cream of cauliflower soup

(illustrated left above)

½ large cauliflower
750 ml/1¼ pints water or
meat stock
3 tablespoons butter
2 tablespoons flour
300 ml/½ pint double cream
1–2 egg yolks
salt and freshly ground
black pepper
chervil to garnish

1. Separate the cauliflower into rosettes, and finely chop, keeping a few rosettes to one side for the garnish. Boil in the stock for 5 minutes then purée in a food processor or blender.

2. Heat the butter, add the flour and immediatly pour on the stock.
3. Whisk the mixture then simmer for 2–3 minutes.
4. Remove the pan from the heat. Beat together the cream and egg yolks and stir into the stock.
5. Reheat without allowing the soup to boil and season to taste.
6. Garnish with the reserved cauliflower rosettes and a little fresh chervil.

Cream of asparagus soup is made in the same way. Cook 350 g/12 oz asparagus for 10 minutes first and garnish with asparagus tips.

Cream of tomato soup

1 spring onion or leek
1 carrot
1 onion
3 beef tomatoes
2 tablespoons butter
1½ teaspoons flour
750 ml/1¼ pints meat stock
3 tablespoons double cream
salt and black pepper
sugar

1. Chop the spring onion or leek (use only the white of the leek).
2. Slice the carrot.
3. Peel and dice the onion.
4. Halve and chop the tomatoes.
5. Fry the vegetables in the butter, sprinkle with the flour and pour on the stock. Simmer for about 20 minutes.
6. Strain the soup.
7. Stir in the cream, reheat and season to taste.
8. For a special meal top each portion with 1 teaspoon whipped cream or serve the cream of tomato soup with a few prawns added.

The principle of binding

Binding soups means making them thicker and tastier with cream and egg yolks. To bind 1 litre/2 pints soup, beat about 300 ml/½ pint double cream with 1 egg yolk. Remove the hot soup from the stove and stir in the cream and egg mixture. Reheat the soup, but do not boil otherwise the egg yolk will separate.

The trick with flour and butter

Any soup or sauce can be thickened with a mixture of flour and butter – beurre manié. It is advisable to make this mixture in advance. For example, work 100 g/4 oz flour into 100 g/4 oz soft butter, shape into balls and keep in the freezer (keeps for at least four months). When needed stir the flaked flour and butter mixture into the hot soup and boil for a few minutes.

Improving ready-bought soups

All instant or canned soups can be improved by adding cream, flour and butter, flaked butter, sherry, wine or madeira to them.

For instance a ready-bought chicken soup can be thickened or improved by adding sherry; a clear oxtail soup can be served with cream and madeira; the flavour of lobster or crab soups improves with a knob of butter added.

The nouvelle cuisine trick

Now we turn to a range of thick soups, guaranteed to be non-fattening, as their basic ingredients are no more than puréed vegetables and stock. Nouvelle cuisine has brought these soups back into favour. Of course you can add cream as this improves the flavour, but it is by no means essential.

Basic recipe for puréed vegetable soup

450 g| I lb vegetables

600 ml| I pint meat stock

salt and pepper

I. Chop the vegetables.
2. Bring to the boil with 150 ml/¼ pint stock and simmer for 10–15 minutes, depending on the choice of vegetables.
3. Strain through a sieve or purée in a liquidiser or blender.

4. Warm the purée through with the remaining stock and season to taste.

Improving vegetable soups: Stir in freshly chopped herbs, double or soured cream, or flaked butter.

All kinds of fruit

can be used in the same way as vegetables to make puréed fruit soups.

Replace the vegetables with the same quantity of fruit. Replace the stock with water – or water and wine – and add a little sugar. The cooking time will depend on the type of fruit. Simmer gently without boiling for 4–8 minutes. Strain the cooked fruit through a sieve or purée in a liquidiser or blender and then thin with milk. Sweeten to taste and serve hot or cold.

Improving fruit soups: Instead of milk use cream to thin the soup.

Illustrated above

Pale green: puréed fresh peas cooked with mint to add interest to the flavour.
White: puréed cauliflower seasoned with a little grated nutmeg to bring out the flavour.
Red: puréed beetroot with a little lemon juice to take off some of the sweetness.
Orange: puréed carrots and oranges give this soup its bright colour.

Dark green: puréed broccoli and herbs – good for you and rich in vitamins.
Pink: raspberries puréed uncooked, strained and mixed with milk and double cream.

The pride of Italian cooking

There is no country in the world that does not have some type of vegetable soup, but none can rival the Italian minestrone. This inventive mixture of dried beans, fresh vegetables, herbs and bacon, breaks the basic rules of cooking, for it is unusual for dried and fresh ingredients to be used in combination, for crunchy vegetables to be cooked this long and for basil and parsley to cook with the soup throughout.

Minestrone
Italian vegetable soup
Serves 6

100 g/4 oz dried kidney beans, white or red
225 g/8 oz bacon
2 onions
1 clove garlic
1 leek
2 carrots
1 stick celery
2 potatoes
2 courgettes
100 g/4 oz Savoy cabbage
100 g/4 oz peas
100 g/4 oz green beans
4 beef tomatoes
bunch of parsley
bunch of basil
2 tablespoons butter
1.5 litre/2¾ pints meat stock
100 g/4 oz round-grain rice
salt and black pepper
50 g/2 oz Parmesan cheese, grated

1. Soak the dried beans overnight.

2. Chop the bacon, vegetables and herbs.

3. Melt the butter in a large pan.

4. Fry the bacon until crisp, add the diced onion and garlic and fry for a few minutes.

5. Add the vegetables and herbs.

6. Fry for about 10 minutes, stirring from time to time.

7. Top up with the stock and simmer for about 1 hour over a low heat.

8. Sprinkle in the rice and cook for a further 15 minutes. Season to taste and serve sprinkled with Parmesan cheese.

Delicious hot-pots

The more filling a soup, the more popular it tends to be, and most filling of all are the hot pots. Eating a hot-pot can be either a frightful or a wonderful experience – it all depends on how it is made and how the various ingredients are combined and seasoned. Every hot-pot should be a satisfying meal in itself, but whether it makes an enjoyable meal depends on you. Here you will find four well-known recipes to inspire you to experiment.

Whatever you have in the kitchen . . .

. . . can be used in hot-pots, for they are an ideal method of using up left-overs. Basically any hot-pot can be made with left-over meat and vegetables, and even canned vegetables (added at the last minute to prevent over-cooking). Smoked bacon adds an excellent flavour. Cooked chicken or roast meat can also be included. Here are a few suggestions:

Basic recipe for hot-pot

450g/1 lb stewing meat

vegetable oil for frying

1–2 bunches soup vegetables (carrot, leek and celeriac)

450g/1 lb mixed vegetables

butter for frying

bunch of mixed fresh herbs

salt and pepper

1. First fry the chopped meat in the hot oil.
2. Cook the meat and soup vegetables for 1½ hours as shown in the basic beef soup recipe (see pages 146–7).
3. Meanwhile fry the vegetables separately in butter.
4. Depending on the length of time each takes to cook, gradually add the vegetables to the meat stock (about 20 minutes before the end of the cooking time).
5. Stir in the freshly chopped herbs and season to taste.

Provençale vegetable hot-pot

450g/1 lb beef or mutton

1 peperoni sausage

1 bunch soup vegetables (carrot, leek and celeriac)

1 clove garlic

1 onion

1 courgette

1 red pepper

1 aubergine

2 tomatoes

3 tablespoons vegetable oil

1 teaspoon concentrated tomato purée

salt and pepper

fresh thyme, rosemary and basil to taste

1. Cook the meat and soup vegetables for about 1½ hours as given in the basic beef soup recipe (see pages 146–7).
2. Coarsely chop the onion, garlic and vegetables, fry in the oil and add to the hot-pot for the last 10 minutes.
3. Stir in the tomato purée, season to taste and stir in the chopped herbs.

Lentil hot-pot

225g/8 oz lentils

450g/1 lb beef

1 bunch soup vegetables (carrot, leek and celeriac)

4 carrots

1 leek

2 onions

2 tablespoons vegetable oil

5 potatoes

salt and pepper

1 tablespoon chopped parsley to garnish

1. Soak the lentils overnight. Cook the beef, soup vegetables and lentils for 1½ hours as given in the basic beef soup recipe (see pages 146–7).
2. Fry the vegetables in the oil and add to the hot-pot

with the peeled, diced potatoes 20 minutes before the end of the cooking time.
3. Season to taste and sprinkle with chopped parsley.
Variations:
Add bacon or left-over smoked ham.

Spring hot-pot

450 g/ 1 lb chicken or veal

1 bunch soup vegetables (carrot, leek and celeriac)

750 ml/ 1¼ pints meat stock

1 kohlrabi

5 carrots

2 tablespoons vegetable oil

1 cauliflower

225 g/8 oz peas

salt and pepper

bunch of chives

bunch of parsley

1. Cook the chicken or veal with the soup vegetables and stock for 1½ hours, as given in the basic beef soup recipe (see pages 146–7).
2. Fry the sliced kohlrabi and carrots in the oil.
3. Add the cauliflower rosettes and peas to the hot-pot 20 minutes before the end of the cooking time.
4. Season to taste and stir in the chopped herbs.

Autumn hot-pot

450 g/ 1 lb smoked pork

750 ml/ 1¼ pints meat stock

¼ Savoy cabbage

¼ white cabbage

150 g/5 oz green beans

450 g/ 1 lb potatoes

2 tablespoons vegetable oil

1 teaspoon caraway seeds

salt and pepper

1. Cook the pork in the stock for about 30 minutes.
2. Shred the cabbages, cut up the beans and dice the potatoes.

3. Fry the cabbage and beans in the oil then add to the hot-pot with the remaining vegetables and caraway seeds about 10 minutes before the end of the cooking time.
4. Season to taste.

Vichyssoise
from France

350 g/12 oz potatoes
1 leek
2 tablespoons butter
1 litre/2 pints meat stock
300 ml/½ pint double cream
salt and black pepper
1 tablespoon chopped chives
to garnish

1. Peel, wash and coarsely chop the potatoes.
2. Trim, halve, wash and slice the leek.
3. Heat the butter in a deep pan and fry the potato and leek for 3 minutes.
4. Top up with the stock.
5. Simmer for 20–30 minutes until the potatoes are very soft.
6. Purée the soup in a blender or food processor and strain through a sieve.
7. Stir in the cream.
8. Season to taste.
9. Chill the soup.
10. Serve sprinkled with chopped chives.

Mulligatawny
from India

1 (1.5–2-kg/3–4½-lb)
boiling fowl
3 tablespoons oil
3 onions, sliced
1 clove garlic, crushed
225 g/8 oz quark (or yogurt)
1 litre/2 pints water
pinch of salt
1 teaspoon chilli powder
½ teaspoon ground ginger
½ teaspoon ground coriander
seeds
generous pinch of ground
star aniseed
3 cloves
75 g/3 oz long-grain rice
juice of ½ lemon

1. Cut up and wash the chicken.
2. Heat the oil in a deep pan.
3. Fry the chicken pieces.
4. Add the onion and garlic and fry for a few minutes.
5. Add the quark and fry until a crust forms on the base of the pan.
6. Add the water, scrape the bottom of the pan, season with a little salt and warm through.
7. In a frying pan without fat, heat the spices over a moderate heat. Sprinkle into the soup.
8. Cook until the chicken comes away from the bones (about 3 hours).
9. Meanwhile boil the rice and keep hot.
10. Remove the chicken from the pan, discard the bones and chop into small pieces, then return to the pan.
11. Reheat and remove the pan from the heat.
12. Add the lemon juice, stir thoroughly, season to taste and serve with the rice spooned on top.

Zuppa pavese
from Italy

750 ml/1¼ pints meat stock
4 slices white bread
1 tablespoon butter
4 egg yolks
4 tablespoons grated
Parmesan cheese

1. Heat the stock.
2. Fry the bread on both sides in the butter.
3. Pour the hot stock into soup plates.
4. Slide 1 raw egg yolk into each plate.
5. Add the fried bread cut into pieces and sprinkle with Parmesan cheese.

Borshch

from Russia

350 g/ 12 oz stewing beef
½ celeriac
1 leek
2 carrots
1 bay leaf
1 clove
salt and pepper
1 oven-ready duck or
chicken
5 tablespoons oil
2 cooked beetroots
1 onion
½ Savoy cabbage
3 tablespoons butter
300 ml/½ pint beetroot juice
1 tablespoon wine vinegar
juice of 1 lemon
225 g/ 8 oz chipolata sausages

1. In a large pan cover the
beef with water and bring
to the boil.
2. Cut a piece 5 cm//2 in
thick from the peeled
celeriac and dice.
3. Trim, wash and chop the
leek and carrots. Add to the
meat with the celeriac, bay
leaf and clove. Season with a
little salt and simmer for
about 2 hours.
4. Cut the peeled beetroots,
onion, cabbage and the
remaining celeriac into
strips.
5. Melt 1 tablespoon butter
and brown the duck or
chicken all over, then
transfer to the stock. Fry
the vegetables in the
remaining butter and stir in
the beetroot juice and
vinegar. Add to the meat
with ½ teaspoon salt.
6. Simmer gently for a
further 30 minutes.
7. Stir in the lemon juice
and season with pepper.
8. Remove the beef from
the pan and cut up into
small pieces.
9. Return the beef to the
pan with the sliced sausages
and warm through.

Gazpacho

from Spain

1 clove garlic
1 onion
2 red peppers
1 small cucumber
1 slice white bread
4 tomatoes
3 tablespoons olive oil
1 tablespoon wine vinegar
300 ml/½ pint iced water
salt and pepper

1. In a large bowl crush the
garlic.
2. Finely chop the onion.
3. Halve, deseed, wash and
finely dice the peppers.
4. Peel the cucumber, scoop
out the seeds with a
teaspoon and finely dice.
5. Keep 2 tablespoons each
of the cucumber and pepper
in reserve.
6. Finely crumble the bread.
7. Add the onion to the
garlic and crush against the
sides of the bowl to make a
paste.
8. Dip the tomatoes in
boiling water for 10
seconds, rinse in cold water
and peel. Halve, deseed and
dice the tomatoes, keeping
2 tablespoons in reserve.
9. Add the oil and vinegar
to the bowl.
10. Stir in the diced
vegetables.
11. Add the iced water and
chill for at least 30 minutes.
12. Just before serving mix
in the bread and season to
taste.
13. Serve the vegetables
kept in reserve separately
with the soup.
For a more homogenous
soup, purée in a blender or
food processor.

Onion soup

from France

3 onions
2 tablespoons butter
600 ml/ 1 pint meat stock
300 ml/½ pint dry white
wine
½ teaspoon ground caraway
seeds
salt and pepper
4 slices white bread, cut to
the size of the bowls
100 g/ 4 oz Gruyère cheese,
grated

1. Slice the onions into
rings.
2. Melt the butter and fry
the onion until transparent.
3. Add the stock and wine,
stir in the caraway and
simmer gently for about 5
minutes.
4. Season to taste.
5. Pour the soup into four
bowls, cover each with a
slice of bread and sprinkle
with the cheese.
6. Heat under a preheated
grill until golden brown.

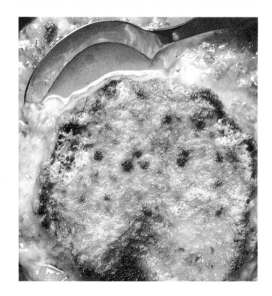

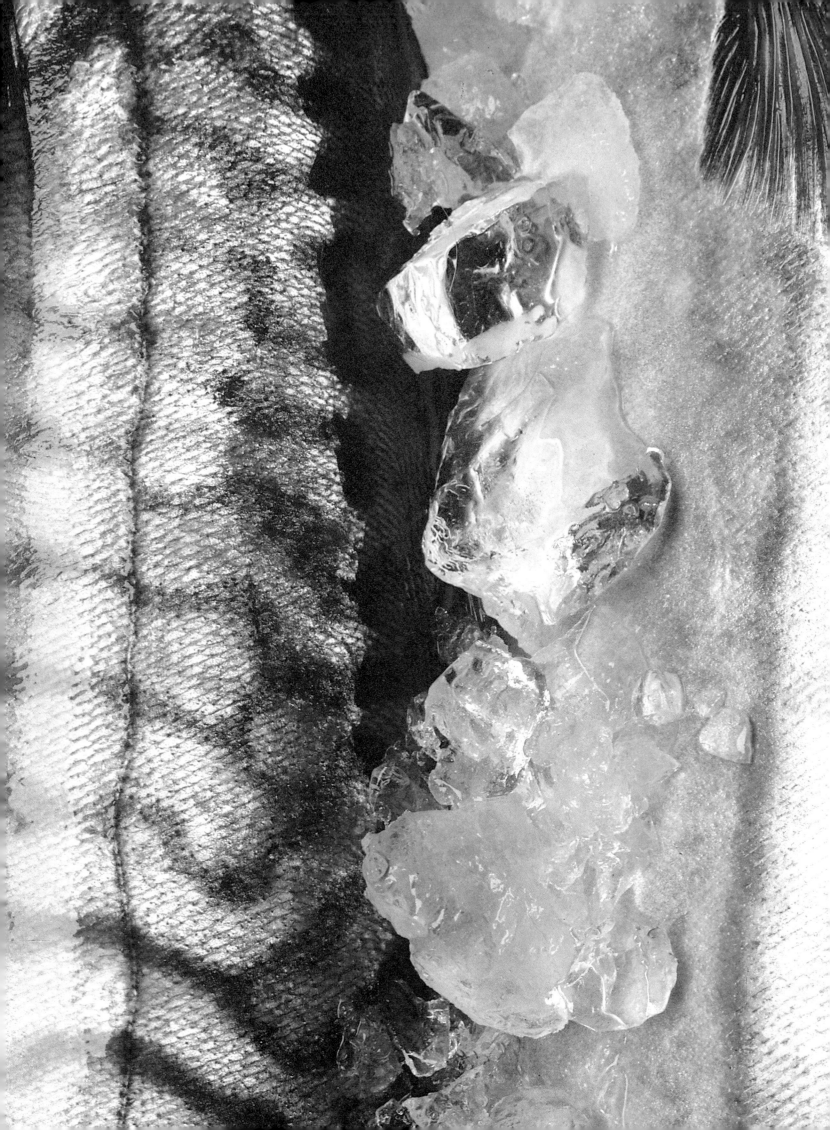

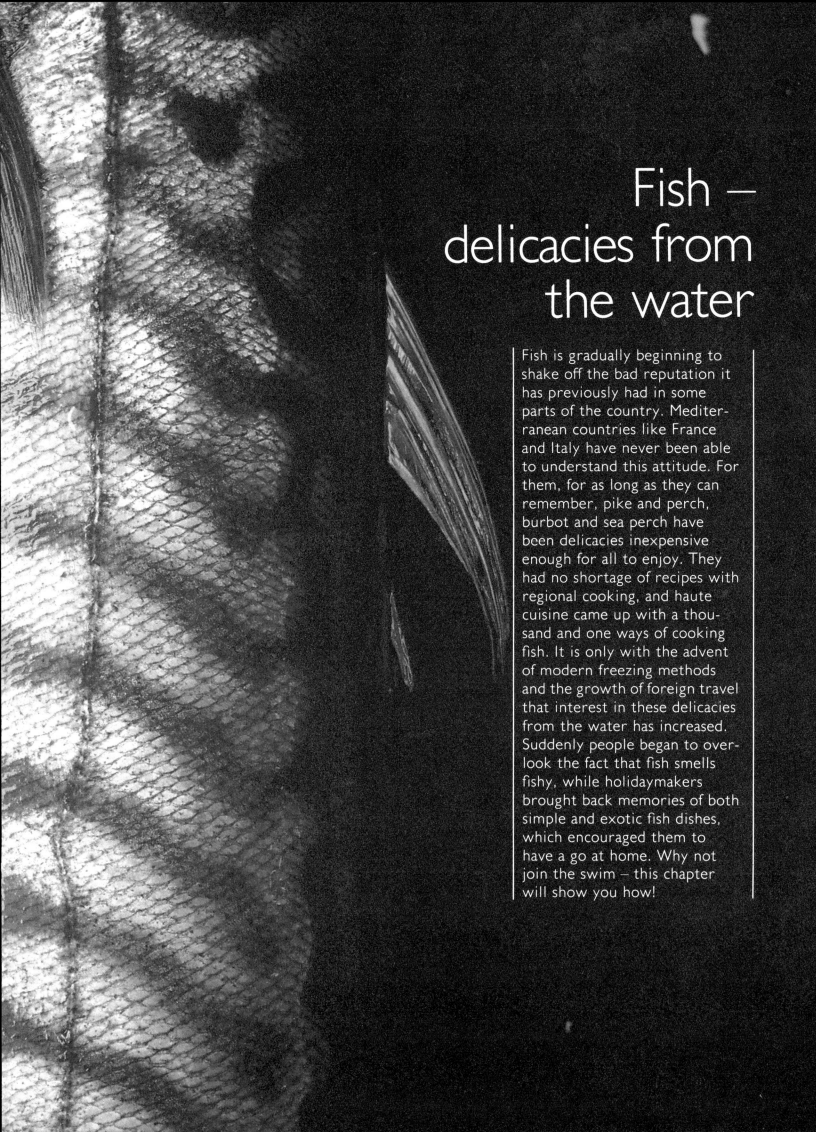

Fish – delicacies from the water

Fish is gradually beginning to shake off the bad reputation it has previously had in some parts of the country. Mediterranean countries like France and Italy have never been able to understand this attitude. For them, for as long as they can remember, pike and perch, burbot and sea perch have been delicacies inexpensive enough for all to enjoy. They had no shortage of recipes with regional cooking, and haute cuisine came up with a thousand and one ways of cooking fish. It is only with the advent of modern freezing methods and the growth of foreign travel that interest in these delicacies from the water has increased. Suddenly people began to overlook the fact that fish smells fishy, while holidaymakers brought back memories of both simple and exotic fish dishes, which encouraged them to have a go at home. Why not join the swim – this chapter will show you how!

Five basic cooking methods

Regardless what cooking method you choose, there is one rule that applies in every case – fish must be fresh! It is a common mistake to think that you can disguise a poor fish by pickling or highly seasoning it. You will never be able to disguise it properly. If your nose doesn't tell you, your stomach will. Freshness is of the essence if you choose a cooking method which brings out the most delicate flavours of the fish. So the first thing is to look for a good fish shop. You can tell a good shop because it won't reek of fish . . .

Buying

How can you tell if fish is fresh? Remember the four following basic rules:
1. The gills should be pink and closed.
2. The eyes should be rounded, bright and shiny.
3. The slimy coating should be smooth and not sticky.
4. The fish should smell of the sea or water: it should not smell fishy.

Every good fish shop will prepare the fish if you tell them how you intend to cook it (gutting, descaling, filleting, boning).

Preparation

Unwrap the fish and wash thoroughly under cold running water. If you are going to poach the fish this is all you need to do – don't soak it in vinegar or salt it. If the fish is to be braised or fried, season with salt and sprinkle with lemon juice *just* before cooking. This will keep the fish firmer. A word of warning – once you have salted the fish never leave it to stand, for the salt draws out the moisture to give a dry, tasteless fish when cooked.

Poaching

Cooking in hot liquid
Ingredients:
juice of 1 lemon, 1 litre/
2 pints boiling water,
½ teaspoon salt.

1. Pour the juice of a lemon into 1 litre/2 pints boiling water.

2. Add ½ teaspoon salt.

Poaching in vegetable stock

Ingredients:
1 carrot, 1 onion, 5 sprigs parsley, 1 small leek, ½ lemon, ½ teaspoon peppercorns, 1 litre/2 pints water.

1. Tip all the ingredients into a saucepan.

2. Boil over a high heat for 1 minute.

Braising on a bed of vegetables

Ingredients:
1 carrot, 1 small leek, 225 g/ 8 oz celery, 300 ml/ ½ pint dry white wine, 1 tablespoon butter, salt and pepper.

1. Coarsely grate the vegetables and arrange in an ovenproof dish.

2. Add the wine.

Steaming

is the easiest way of cooking fish. Use a pan with a steamer (or a fish kettle).

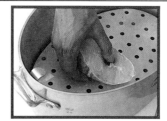

1. Arrange the fish on the steamer.

2. Pour 600 ml/1 pint dry white wine into the pan.

Frying

Ingredients:
salt and pepper, 3 tablespoons flour, 1 tablespoon butter.

1. Season the fish and dip in the flour.

2. Heat the butter in a frying pan.

3. Remove the pan from the heat.

4. Using a skimmer lower the fish into the hot water.

5. Leave the fish in the hot water for 10–15 minutes.

6. Lift the fish out of the water and serve.

3. Remove the pan from the heat and leave to stand for 10 minutes.

4. Lower the fish into the stock.

5. Return the pan to the heat.

6. Cook at the lowest setting for 15 minutes.

3. Dot the vegetables with butter.

4. Place the fish on the vegetables and season.

5. Put the dish in a moderately hot oven (200C, 400F, gas 6).

6. Braise the fish for 20 minutes.

3. Cover the pan firmly.

4. Bring the liquid to the boil.

5. Steam for 20 minutes over a moderate heat.

6. Lift the fish out of the pan and serve.

3. Lower the fish into the hot butter.

4. Fry the fish for 1 minute each side initially.

5. Fry fry for a further 10 minutes, turning frequently.

6. Remove the fish from the pan.

The art of combining

No wonder nouvelle cuisine cooks have chosen fish as one of their favourites. Firstly it is a light dish, and secondly it makes creative cooking easy. This makes cooking easy for the beginner too. You can use practically any cooking method for any fish (see pages 166–7). And any sauce, garnish or side-dish is interchangeable or usable in combination. If you can allow your imagination to play upon this freedom, it won't be long before you swear by fish – and your family and friends too.

The two types of fish.

Regardless of all the differences between individual types of fish, they can be divided into two broad categories:

Sea fish

These include almost all inexpensive, everyday fish (cod, haddock, red mullet, etc.). Like the herring, which has recently become something of a delicacy, all are caught in the North Sea. From both the North Sea and the Atlantic we also get high quality fish such as sole and turbot.

Freshwater fish

These can be caught in our native rivers and lakes but, in the case of trout and carp, are often farmed. They are more delicate and milder in flavour than the more hearty sea fish which live in salt water. Pike and eel, perch and river trout are generally considered the best. Carp and farmed trout are the most popular.

Why is fish so good for us?

Fish are rich in protein. The flesh is light and easily digestible. Fish is satisfying without making one feel over-full.

Fish contains many minerals (calcium, iron and phosphorus), trace elements (iodine and fluorine) and vitamin B.

The fat content varies from fish to fish. Oily fish (herring, eel and salmon) also contain the fat-soluble vitamins H and D which help digestion.

Light fish (e.g. sole and turbot) are excellent for dieters but also for those who love to eat well without gaining weight.

Cooking times

There is no need to go as far as the avant-garde nouvelle cuisine chefs who poach fish so briefly that it is still pink along the bones. But one thing is certainly true: fish should be cooked for as short a time as possible if its flavour and goodness is to be retained. In addition a properly cooked fish should be moist. Overcooked fish will become mushy or become dry and stringy and lose its flavour.

It is not essential to use fresh fish. There is now a wide selection of frozen fish which after slow defrosting (in a refrigerator perhaps) can be cooked just like fresh fish.

White fish will keep for up to eight months in a freezer, oily fish up to four months.

Cod cutlet with mustard sauce and spinach

4 cod cutlets (2.5 cm/1 in thick)

450 g/1 lb spinach

1 tablespoon butter

salt and pepper

lemon slices and dill sprigs to garnish

1. Poach the fish as shown in the step-by-step photographs on pages 166–7.

2. Sort and wash the spinach. Cook in boiling salted water for 1 minute. Finally rinse in cold water and press out excess liquid. Warm the spinach through quickly in melted butter and season to taste.
3. Make the mustard sauce following the recipe on page 256.
4. Garnish the cod with half slices of lemon and sprigs of dill. Serve with dill potatoes (boiled potatoes tossed in hot butter and ½ teaspoon chopped dill).
Variations:
Red mullet, haddock.

Plaice fillet with herb sauce and mushrooms

2–4 plaice fillets per person (depending on size)

450 g/1 lb mushrooms

2 tablespoons butter

salt and pepper

parsley, tarragon and basil to garnish (optional)

1. Poach the plaice fillets for 2–4 minutes depending on size (see pages 166–7).
2. Trim and slice the mushrooms and fry in the butter over a moderate heat for 2–3 minutes. Season to taste.

Garnishing

All fish like a little acidity, so your basic garnish should be slices or wedges of lemon or lime.

Dill, tarragon and chervil are popular herbs which go with almost any type of fish. Use dill sparingly, however.

Always serve with delicately flavoured vegetables to bring out the flavour of the fish rather than swamping it.

Among the best are: spinach, asparagus, mushrooms, carrots, celery and leeks.

To serve with fish, blanch vegetables briefly and then fry in butter until cooked. Pieces of peeled cucumber should be quickly braised in white wine.

The best – and most appropriate – garnish for any fish is shellfish, cooked separately (see page 173).

Side dishes

The most popular accompaniment for fish are potatoes despite their rather coarse flavour. Improve the flavour of boiled potatoes by adding butter and/or finely chopped herbs.

Rice, with its neutral flavour, is ideal with all fish dishes. Rice timbales are particularly attractive (see page 101).

You will find alternative suggestions in the chapter on rice.

From the new school of Italian cooking comes the combination of various coloured pasta tossed in butter (see pages 88–9). See also the chapter on pasta.

Sauces

The simplest and indeed the classic way of serving fish is with freshly melted hot butter.

For gourmets: in a light, delicate wine and cream sauce (see page 259).

Fisherman-style: cook everyday fish like cod in a tasty tomato sauce (see page 84).

Wine

Even though food snobs in the best Paris restaurants are now drinking light red wines as the *dernier cri* with fish, it is better to stick to the old-fashioned rules: With fish drink a light, dry white wine such as Riesling or Muscadet. For special occasions serve a Chablis or champagne!

3. Make the herb sauce from the recipe on page 258.
4. Garnish the plaice with sprigs of herbs. Serve with buttered potatoes or rice.
Variation:
Sole fillets.

Sole rolls with saffron sauce and prawns

2–4 sole fillets per person (depending on size)

225 g / 8 oz peeled cooked prawns

2 tablespoons butter

salt and pepper

chervil leaves to garnish

1. Roll up the sole fillets with the smooth side innermost and secure with a wooden cocktail stick. Poach as shown in the step-by-step photographs on pages 166–7.
Important: Reduce cooking time to 5–7 minutes.
2. Fry the prawns in hot butter for 3 minutes.
3. Make the saffron sauce following the recipe on page 259.
4. Garnish the sole with the prawns and chervil leaves.
5. Serve with rice.

Salmon with butter sauce and vegetable sticks

225 g / 8 oz salmon fillets per person

2–3 carrots

1 leek

1 tablespoon butter

salt and pepper

fresh tarragon to garnish

1. Poach the salmon slices for 3–5 minutes depending on thickness (see step-by-step photographs on pages 166–7).

2. Trim and wash the vegetables and cut into thin sticks. Boil in salted water for 3 minutes. Rinse under cold water. Before serving toss in hot butter and season.
3. Make the butter sauce (beurre blanc) as shown on page 250.
4. Garnish the salmon with the vegetable sticks and tarragon. Serve with buttered potatoes.
Variation:
Salmon can also be served as a cutlet on the bone and in the skin. For a cutlet about 2.5 cm / 1 in thick allow about 2 minutes extra cooking time.

The main attraction

It is admittedly easier to cook fish in fillets, rolls or slices. To cook whole fish you need a long fish kettle with a serrated rack. In addition fish cooked whole needs more preparation – meaning both the dressing-up of the fish and attractive preparation of vegetables. But the final result is worth it. Nothing could impress your guests more!

The basic recipe

In order to cook a fish whole you need a long fish kettle containing a serrated rack which makes it easy to put the fish into the pan and take it out.

Preparation:
Rinse the gutted fish quickly in cold water. To give the fish extra flavour, stuff it with grated vegetables (carrot, leek, spring onion) or an assortment of herbs. Tie up the fish with cooking thread.

Large fish should be slit along the backbone to allow the stock to soak into the whole fish.

The pan should contain enough liquid to just cover the fish, otherwise it won't cook evenly.

Vegetable stock

1–1.5 litres/2–3 pints liquid depending on the size of the pan ($\frac{1}{2}$ water, $\frac{1}{2}$ dry white wine)

2 carrots

1 onion

1 leek

2 sticks celery

2 bay leaves

1 bunch parsley

$\frac{1}{2}$ bunch dill

$\frac{1}{2}$ teaspoon peppercorns

1 teaspoon salt

1 lemon, cut into wedges, to serve

1. Bring all the ingredients to the boil in the liquid.
2. Remove the pan from the heat and leave to steep for 10 minutes.
3. Place the fish on the rack, lower into the pan and pour on the stock with the vegetables.
4. Warm over a low heat for about 30 minutes (do not boil).

5. Reduce the strained stock over a high heat and boil with cream to make a sauce. Flavour with a little brandy and season.
6. Just before serving lightly season the fish to taste. Have a salt cellar, pepper mill and lemon wedges on the table so that guests can season to their taste.

Stock from coconut milk

coconut milk
lemon juice to taste
ground ginger
salt and white pepper

Use fresh or tinned coconut milk, or make it yourself from desiccated coconut by soaking it for 10 minutes in hot water, draining through a sieve and pressing out excess liquid.

Red wine stock

Use red wine instead of white. All other ingredients as for vegetable stock.

Chicken stock

Cook fish simply in chicken stock with no added ingredients.

Stock for shellfish

5 litres/10 pints water

5 teaspoons salt

1 tablespoon caraway seeds

1 bunch dill

1 bunch soup vegetables

(carrot, leek and celeriac)

(optional)

1. Bring all the ingredients to the boil together.
2. Plunge the shellfish head first into the boiling water (for cooking times see below).

Stock for mussels

1 onion

2 carrots

1 small leek

1 small piece celeriac

1 clove garlic, crushed

1 tablespoon butter

600 ml/1 pint dry white wine

salt and pepper

Dice all the vegetables, add the garlic and fry in the butter. Add the wine and season to taste.

The stock is sufficient for about 1 kg/2 lb mussels = 2 servings.
1. Scrub the mussel shells thoroughly under running water.
2. Stand the mussels in cold salted water for about 20 minutes to bring out any sand or impurities.
3. Rinse the mussels again and drain.
4. Drop the shells into the fast boiling stock and cover the pan firmly. The mussels are cooked when they open (5–8 minutes). Any mussels that do not open during cooking will be inedible and should be discarded.

A delicious family

Lobster, crawfish and crabs are to be found amongst the top echelons of haute cuisine. Their reputation even exceeds their flavour – and that is saying something. The delicious deep-sea prawns have long been popular. Nevertheless the confusing varieties of crustaceans is almost a science in itself. Here you will find all the information a beginner needs – and this is more than many self-appointed experts can muster!

In the photograph on the left:
Crawfish or rock lobster (centre top) Cooking time: 20–25 minutes. Eat: tail.

Lobster (top left) Cooking time: 20–25 minutes (depending on size). Eat: tail, claws and legs.

Langoustines, Dublin Bay or king prawns also known as saltwater crayfish in America (centre left) Cooking time: 10 minutes. Serve 5–8 per person. Eat: tail and claws.

Crayfish (bottom left) Cooking time: 8–10 minutes. Serve 15 per person. Eat: tail and claws.

Prawns or Jumbo shrimps (centre bottom) Cooking time: 10–15 minutes. Serve 3 per person.

Pink shrimps (bottom right) are usually pre-cooked and sold either shelled or in the shell.

Brown shrimps (extreme right) are cooked on the boat immediately they are caught. The shell twists easily off.

Mussels (centre right) can be served in deep plates with the stock. Alternatively you can reduce the stock and stir with cream to make a sauce.

Snails (centre right) are cooked like mussels.

Pleasure on a spoon

A pan over the fire, fish and herbs simmering in stock, a bottle of wine and a loaf of bread – this must be one of man's oldest pleasures. Cooks have since turned this simple fisherman's dish into delicious bouillabaisse, and added sauces to make it a real delight. Why not try filling your kitchen with the scent of the Mediterranean, a breath of mythology and garlic – turn an everyday meal into a real holiday.

Basic recipe for fish soup

1 onion
2 carrots
1 leek
1 clove garlic, crushed
1 bay leaf
½ teaspoon thyme
1 tablespoon butter
300 ml/½ pint dry white wine
600 ml/1 pint water or fish stock, if available
salt and pepper
pinch of saffron powder
450 g/1 lb fish, in bite-sized pieces (cod, haddock, red mullet, salmon trout, turbot)

Finely chop the vegetables, add the garlic then fry in the butter, add the liquid and season with salt, pepper and saffron. Add the fish and simmer over a moderate heat for 15 minutes.

Variations:
The following ingredients can be added to the soup (cooking time in brackets).
Prawns (5 minutes).
Mussels (5 minutes).
Beef tomatoes, peeled and diced (5 minutes).
Fennel root, diced (15 minutes).
Green pepper, diced (15 minutes).
Root ginger, thinly sliced (15 minutes).
Chillies, finely chopped (cooked throughout).
Double cream, 2 tablespoons to thicken.

In Mediterranean cooking fish soup is served with aioli or pesto sauce (see page 149) for a special meal. Serve with toasted French bread rubbed with a clove of garlic.

Alternative seasonings:
coriander, parsley, sambal oelek, Tabasco.

How to make fish stock

As with sauces for meat, when making a good fish sauce the main thing you need is a concentrated fish stock. For the stock use fish off-cuts (bones, heads and fins) preferably from quality fish like sole and turbot. (Your fish shop will probably let you have some!)

The main rule is to stick to white fish, never oily fish (like eel or mackerel).

Finely grate soup vegetables (carrot, leek and celeriac) and fry in butter. Add liquid (600 ml/1 pint water, and 600 ml/1 pint dry white wine).

Add the fish off-cuts and simmer over a low heat in an open pan for 30 minutes at the most.
Important:
1. Do not stir the fish stock while it is cooking or it will become cloudy.
2. Do not cook the stock for more than 30 minutes before straining it or the flavour will be affected.

Reduce the strained stock by boiling vigorously. This stock can then be combined with cream, butter, egg yolk or flour and butter (see page 155) to make sauces.

Fish stock will keep in the freezer for several months.

Satisfying flat fish

Be it plaice or flounder, turbot or sole, flat fish will fry as evenly as pancakes. Fried fish makes a satisfying spring meal especially when the first plaice are landed and when it is warm enough to open the kitchen window. A pleasure for which many food-lovers would willingly exchange caviar and champagne!

Basic recipe for plaice

4 plaice
juice of 1 lemon
salt and pepper
6 tablespoons flour
100 g/4 oz butter
1 tablespoon oil

1. Rinse the plaice under cold water and dry on kitchen paper. Sprinkle with lemon juice and season to taste.
2. Make a slit in the darker side of the plaice, as this makes it easier to remove the fish from the bone later. Dip in the flour.
3. Heat the butter and oil until moderately hot in a heavy iron frying pan. Fry the plaice for 3 minutes.
4. Turn the fish using two fish slices and fry for a further 3 minutes. Shake the pan occasionally to prevent the fish sticking.
Tip: Fish for frying must always be dry as water makes the fat spit.

Variations:
1. *Plaice with bacon*
Sprinkle fried bacon cubes over the plaice.
2. *Plaice with prawns and bacon*
Serve with peeled prawns and fried bacon cubes.
3. *Plaice meunière*
Brown butter, chopped parsley and lemon.
4. *English-style plaice*
Rub with Worcestershire sauce before frying.
5. *Almond plaice*
Fried plaice sprinkled with flaked almonds fried in butter.
   Traditionally served with buttered potatoes and cucumber salad with dill or a green salad.

Other fish suitable for frying:
Sole – these should be skinned before frying (ask your fish shop to do this).
Flounder – the dark upper skin should be removed.

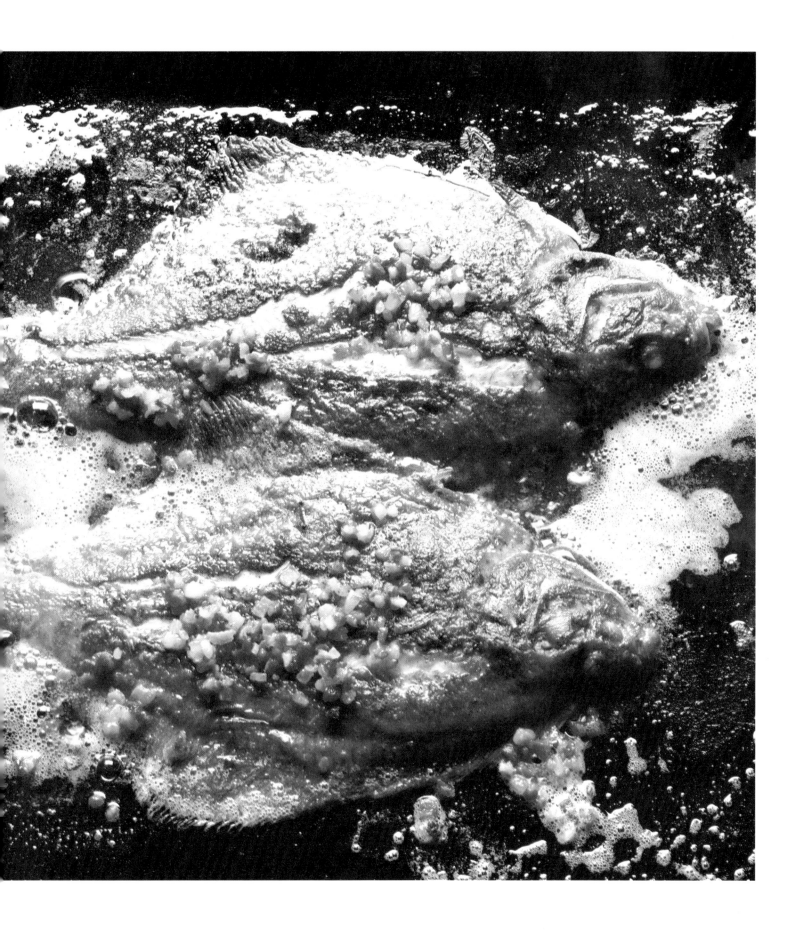

The trout septet

Since Schubert set it to music the trout has been regarded quite simply as the German romantic fish. Trout – one can hear the rippling stream, the creaking of the millwheel and see the beautiful miller's wife at her stove. Of course things are not now so picturesque – our trout come from farms or the supermarket freezer. This has had no effect on their popularity, however. A sure indication of this is that the trout, more than any other fish, has been subjected to all the subtle variations on the art of cooking fish – and each has proved more delicious than the other.

Trout in lettuce

Wrap the prepared fish in lettuce leaves (or spring cabbage or spinach) which have first been soaked for a few minutes in hot water. There are two ways in which it can be cooked:
1. In a smoking oven.
2. Baked in the oven in an ovenproof dish (see step-by-step photographs pages 166–7).

Blue trout

Bring 1 litre/2 pints water, 300 ml/½ pint vinegar, juice of 1 lemon, soup vegetables and ½ teaspoon salt to the boil. Cook the trout covered in the liquid for 8–10 minutes. Do not allow it to boil.
Important: For blue trout use fresh-caught fish. This is the only guarantee that the slimy layer covering the fish is undamaged and that the trout will be really 'blue' when cooked. For the same reason the fish should only be rinsed very quickly under cold running water.

Trout in foil

Cooking in foil is a very easy method which needs no fat.

Pack the trout with sliced spring onions, herbs (e.g. basil, tarragon and dill), crushed garlic and seasoning then wrap firmly in aluminium foil. Cook in a hot (220C, 425F, gas 7) for 20–25 minutes.

Grilled trout
Clean the fish and slit the sides several times. Stuff with herbs (e.g. dill, tarragon and thyme). Oil the grill rack and cook for 10 minutes.

Grilling is much easier with a fish basket or on a piece of greased foil.

Almond trout
Dip the cleaned fish first in flaked almonds, then in flour. Fry in butter for 10 minutes.

Trout meunière
Dip the prepared trout in flour and fry in hot butter over a moderate heat for 10 minutes. Serve with brown butter, lemon slices and parsley.

Salted trout
Cover the fish both sides with a mixture of 1 teaspoon coarsely milled black pepper, 2 teaspoons freshly chopped dill, 3 teaspoons sugar and 4 teaspoons coarse salt. Leave in the refrigerator for 2–3 days. Then thoroughly clean off all the seasoning.
Tip: This fish can be served with a special Scandinavian mustard sauce available ready-made from good delicatessens.

Poultry: a world of flavour

The idea of being able to eat chicken occasionally has been a dream for many centuries. The French king Henry IV decreed that it was his ambition that every family in his kingdom would be able to have chicken on their tables once a week. It is only in the twentieth century that this dream was realised. Chicken dishes have always been popular – for poultry is one of the most appealing of meals throughout the world. One has only to think of the thousands of poultry recipes created, for example, by the Chinese – among them being the famous Peking Duck.

Trussing chickens

It is of course easiest to cook any type of poultry in portions. This is one way of getting round the problem which besets any bird cooked whole, that is that the breast cooks much quicker than the legs. Nevertheless roast poultry is much more attractive if brought whole to the table – especially if you have guests. To cook poultry whole it should first be trussed. For heaven's sake don't be put off by this! It is no more difficult than sewing on a button.

What you should know about chicken

The most popular type of poultry is chicken. It is cheap enough to be available to all, yet extremely rich in protein and, with its low fat content, easily digestible. It is extremely good as part of a diet. Whole chickens and portions are universally available both fresh and frozen.

Chickens are usually sold oven-ready, i.e. plucked and cleaned. Edible giblets come cleaned and separately packed, either inside the chicken or sold separately.

Preparation: trussing

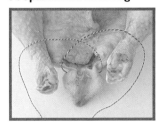

1. Take the string under the parson's nose and cross it over the legs.

2. Take each string around one leg and then cross the strings over one another.

3. Tie the ends firmly.

4. Bring the string between the breasts and the legs.

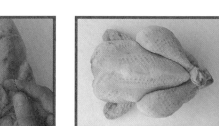

5. Turn the chicken onto the breast.

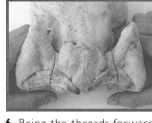

6. Bring the threads forward over the wings.

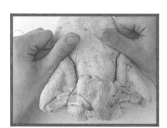

7. Take the strings round the wings and pull tight.

8. Knot the string.

9. Cut off any excess string.

10. The oven-ready chicken.

Trussing

To prevent chickens from becoming too dry and losing their shape during roasting, they should be trussed.

There are several methods of trussing. One of the simplest ways of keeping a chicken in shape is shown in the step-by-step photographs on the left. A chicken is used here but the same method applies for any type of poultry.

When trussing your bird make sure that your string (cooking thread) is twice as long as the chicken.

Roasting

Before roasting wash the chicken, drain thoroughly and pat dry. The drier it is, the better it will brown and crisp up.

Young poultry has tender flesh with thin fibres and is especially good for frying, roasting or grilling.

It cooks quicker than older, tougher poultry which should be casseroled or boiled.

Cooking: in the oven

1. Rub the chicken with salt.

2. Set the heat at its highest setting.

3. Place the roasting tin on the hot element and heat 2 tablespoons oil.

4. Brown the chicken all over.

5. Set the oven at hot (220C, 425F, gas 7).

6. Place the chicken in the hot oven in its roasting tin and roast for 15 minutes.

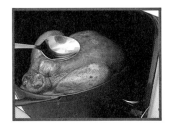

7. Baste the chicken from time to time with the roasting juices.

8. Reduce the oven to moderately hot (200C, 400F, gas 6).

9. Roast for a further 30 minutes.

10. Take the roasting tin out of the oven.

11. Remove the chicken from the tin and keep warm.

12. Dilute the roasting juices with liquid (water or wine) and bring to the boil.

13. Strain the gravy and spoon off any fat.

14. Reduce the gravy slightly and season to taste.

15. Thicken with soured cream, double cream or a little cornflour.

Tips for frozen poultry

Frozen poultry should be stored in a refrigerator and will freeze for eight to ten months.

If you intend roasting frozen poultry it is best to defrost it slowly in the refrigerator.

Thawing time: 4–7 hours. Remove the wrapping and wash thoroughly to prevent the risk of salmonella poisoning.

If you are boiling poultry (in soups, stews or casseroles) it can be added to the liquid semi-frozen, but you will need to increase the overall cooking time.

Frozen poultry, once defrosted, is cooked in exactly the same way as fresh poultry.

When buying frozen poultry make sure that the package contains no liquid or large ice crystals because that suggests that the poultry may have been defrosted and re-frozen.

Boiling chicken: A recipe for boiling chicken to make soup is included on page 147.

The whole poultry family

The basic methods of trussing and roasting (see pages 182–3) apply of course to any type of poultry, with slight variations in some instances. Understandably, different rules apply for fatty goose than for lean pheasant which easily becomes dry. There follows a list of things you should watch out for.

Barding

Game birds, whose meat is extremely lean, need to be covered in bacon to prevent the tender breasts becoming too dry. This is known as barding. The bacon, which should be tied in place with thread, is removed shortly before the end of the cooking time to allow the bird to brown and crisp up. (The photograph shows a barded pheasant.)

Tips for a crisp skin

1. Before roasting, chicken can be rubbed with a mixture of oil and paprika, or with cream and paprika.
2. An alternative is a mixture of honey, oil and lemon juice.
3. Goose automatically crisps up as the fat under the skin gradually seeps through. Near the end of the cooking time scoop off the excess fat and keep to use as goose dripping (e.g. for red cabbage).
4. Duck, usually served with a sweet fruity sauce, will be crisp if basted frequently with the sauce during roasting.

Sauces for poultry

The juices produced as the poultry roasts can be diluted and made into a sauce.

You will find suitable recipes in the sauce chapter (see pages 210–11). The roasts chapter (see pages 234–5) provides several suggestions on improving gravies.

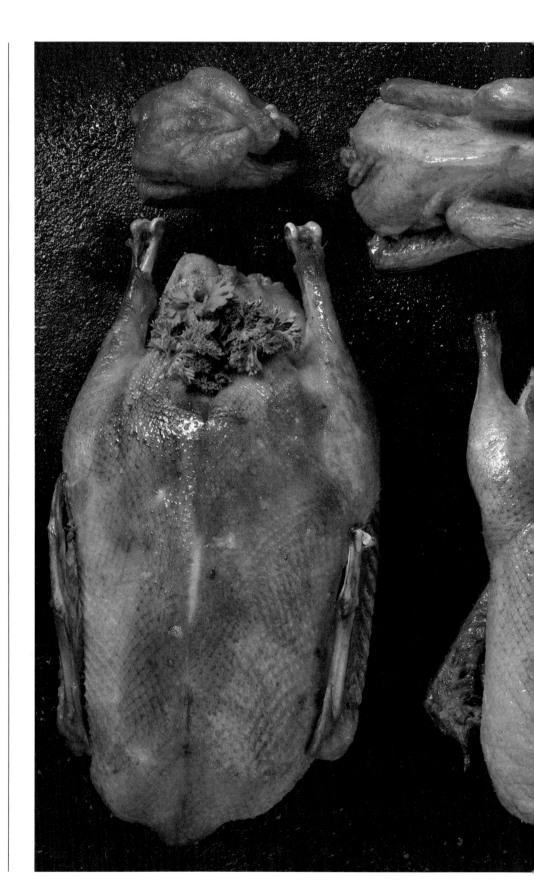

Poussin or Cornish hen

(illustrated top left). Oven-ready weight: 225–350 g/8–12 oz. Roasting time: 20–30 minutes.

Broiler or spring chicken

6–7 weeks old. Oven-ready weight: 800 g–1.25 kg/1¾–2½ lb. Roasting time: about 30 minutes.

Roasting chicken

(illustrated bottom right). 8–9 weeks old. Oven-ready weight: 1 kg/2¼ lb minimum. Roasting time: about 45 minutes.

Boiling fowl

A bird of about 2 years old, generally one that has been laying. Only suitable for boiling! Oven-ready weight: about 2 kg/ 4¼ lb. Cooking time: 2–3 hours.

Guinea-fowl

(illustrated centre top). The flesh of young guinea-fowl has a gamey flavour similar to pheasant. Roasting time: about 40 minutes.

Duckling

Oven-ready weight: about 1.75 kg/4 lb. Roasting time: 1 hour.

Duck

(illustrated centre bottom). Above 1 year old. Oven-ready weight: about 2.5 kg/ 5½ lb. Roasting time: 1½ hours.

Young fattened goose

About 10 weeks old. Oven-ready weight: about 3 kg/6½ lb. Roasting time: 1¾–2 hours.

Goose

(illustrated far left). Above 1 year old. Oven-ready weight: about 4.5 kg/10 lb. Roasting time: 2½–3 hours.

Young turkey

20–24 weeks old. Oven-ready weight: 4–7 kg/9–15 lb. Roasting time: 3–4 hours.

Turkey

Over 1 year old. Oven-ready weight: up to 12 kg/26 lb. Roasting time: 4½–5 hours.

Pheasant

(illustrated top right). Young birds have grey legs and short, stumpy spurs. Older birds have darker legs and longer spurs. Pheasants are now farmed as well as being shot as game. Oven-ready weight: about 1 kg/2¼ lb. Roasting time: 30–45 minutes.

Quail

(illustrated centre right). Farmed game-bird. Oven-ready weight: about 100 g/ 4 oz. Roasting time: about 20 minutes.

Oranges and other fruits

Duck à l'orange is one of the dishes that has made haute cuisine so famous. It is a dish that we could not ignore since it is one of the most delicious poultry dishes ever created. It is also a good example of the way in which the flavour of poultry can be changed over and over again using either exotic or local ingredients.

Duck à l'orange

(illustrated right)

1 young oven-ready duck (about 2 kg/4¼ lb)
3–4 tablespoons oil
600 ml/1 pint orange juice
2–3 tablespoons orange liqueur
1 tablespoon honey
100 g/4 oz butter
1 orange
basil and orange slices to garnish

1. Roast the duck for about 1 hour as shown in the step-by-step photographs on page 183.
2. After 30 minutes drain off the excess fat, add the orange juice, liqueur and honey. Baste the duck every 10 minutes so that the meat can absorb the flavour and the skin becomes brown and crisp.
3. At the end of the cooking time take the duck out of the oven and keep warm.
4. Strain the sauce and reduce by half until syrupy.
5. Add the butter and whisk in. Do not on any account allow the sauce to boil from this point onwards.
6. Season to taste.
7. Thinly peel 1 orange (avoid peeling any of the pith as this is bitter) and add the peel to the sauce.
8. Garnish the duck with basil and orange slices. Pour on a little of the sauce and serve the rest separately.

Variations

Basic recipe omitting oranges, orange juice and liqueur.
1. *With fig and port sauce*
Made with fresh figs and 600 ml/1 pint port.
2. *With honey and sherry*
Add 4 tablespoons honey and 300 ml/½ pint dry sherry. Season with soy sauce and double cream.
3. *With juniper berries*
Add 150 g/5 oz juniper berries, 3 tablespoons brandy and 150 ml/¼ pint red wine to the duck.

4. *With peaches*
Add 3 peeled peaches and 600 ml/1 pint peach juice. Season with the juice of a lemon.

Choosing side-dishes

Poultry with its fine flavour naturally calls for the finest side-dishes. With highly flavoured, fatty meat serve any strongly flavoured vegetable. One exception is chicken which seems to go with any type of vegetable or seasoning, be it truffle or peperoni, vinegar or honey.

The following list recommends side-dishes for the various types of poultry:

Goose
Red cabbage, fried apple, potato croquettes, chestnuts, raisins.

Duck
Carrots, mushrooms, young peas, small onions, rice, potato straws. potato gratin, duchesse potatoes, turnip, fried apple wedges.

Chicken
Carrots, celeriac, pearl onions, artichoke hearts, boiled potatoes, pulao rice, risotto, green peppers (see also: garnishes pages 190–1).

Pheasant
Sauerkraut, potato purée, grapes, chanterelles, cèpes, mushrooms.

Quail
Spinach, Savoy cabbage, carrots, celery, leeks, potato gratin.

Good things inside

Nature could not have made chickens easier for cooks to deal with. She has supplied the ideal cavity for a stuffing. All you have to do is sew up the opening when you have finished. Stuffings have several advantages. First they keep the poultry in shape. Secondly they prevent lean meat drying out if the stuffing contains plenty of fat. Thirdly fatty poultry (such as goose) can give a dry stuffing an excellent flavour. Fourthly the flavours and seasonings of the meat and stuffing intermingle for added flavour. As you can see you have a wide field to experiment in here!

Fruit stuffing

(illustrated right below) The simplest way of stuffing poultry is by using whole fruit, e.g. apples, oranges (peeled), grapes. Of course there is no reason why you shouldn't cut the fruit up first.

Dried-fruit stuffing

(illustrated right centre) Another popular stuffing is made with dried fruit which should be soaked, stoned and peeled where appropriate. Use dates, apricots, prunes, figs, apple rings, mixed with boiled rice, peanuts, cashews, pistachios, walnuts or hazelnuts.

Liver and vegetable stuffing

(illustrated right above) Savoury stuffings made with meat, herbs and vegetables, as well as giblets, are amongst the most popular. To make the stuffing the separate ingredients should be fried briefly. Try crumbled white bread with strips of liver, finely chopped onion, crushed garlic, mushrooms, spring onions and ham, bound with egg, generously seasoned and mixed with herbs.

Stuffing variations

1. Plain fried cubes of bread.
2. Bunch of herbs.
3. Spring onions.
4. Plums and peaches with fresh stem ginger.
5. Mixed minced meat.
6. Almond and raisin gingerbread stuffing (shelled almonds, raisins and gingerbread soaked in water or alcohol).
Tips: For stuffed poultry increase the roasting time by about one third.
  Never stuff poultry over-full as the stuffing expands as it cooks and will escape.

Carving and serving poultry

There are several ways of cutting up poultry.

It is important to have the right tools for the job: a large carving fork and a narrow, flexible, sharp knife which will cut the meat cleanly off the carcass.

An easy way to carve poultry is as follows. Hold the bird steady with the fork and with the knife cut through the skin between the legs and breast. Bend the leg outwards and cut through the joint to remove the leg. Cut along both sides of the breast bone, gently loosen the breasts from the carcass and carve into slices.

Finally remove the stuffing from the inside of the bird, place on a hot plate and surround with the chicken.

This method of carving can be used for any type of poultry.

Six gourmet garnishes

There could scarcely be a more economical delicacy than boned chicken breasts bought from a good supplier. You need do no more than fry them quickly in butter and serve with a wine and cream sauce – the effect is mouth-watering. When making these recipes take care not to overcook the chicken breasts, or they will become a bit dry and tough and lose their flavour.

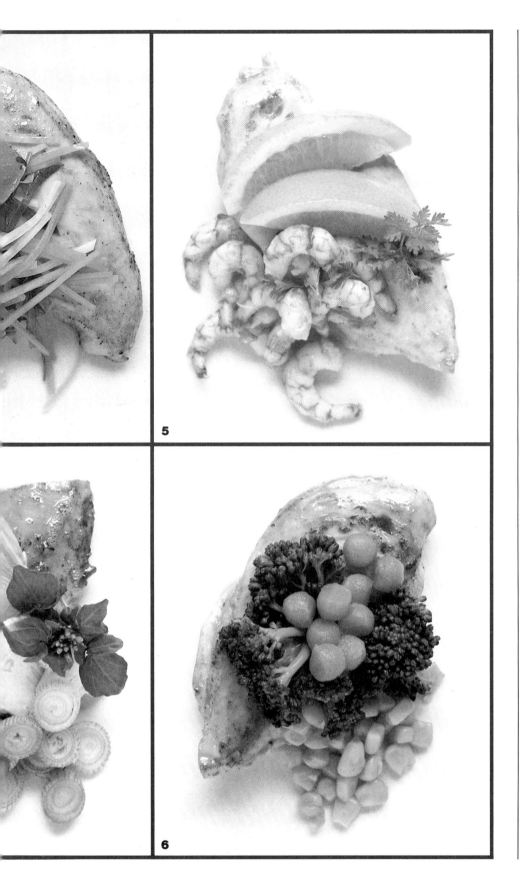

5

6

Basic recipe for boned chicken breast

Heat some butter over a moderate heat. Season the breasts with salt and freshly ground pepper. Fry on both sides for a total of 10 minutes maximum.

The following ingredients are for 1 chicken breast in each case.

1. Melt 1 tablespoon sugar in a little butter and lightly brown 3–4 canned chestnuts. In separate pans warm 2 tablespoons peeled grapes in a little butter and heat up 1 tablespoon cranberry sauce.

Arrange these ingredients over the chicken breast and garnish with marjoram leaves.

2. Peel and slice a banana, dip the slices first in beaten egg and then in 1–2 tablespoons desiccated coconut. Deep fry in oil. Warm 2 tablespoons curry sauce (see page 257). Fry 1 apricot in butter. Arrange all the ingredients over the chicken breast, sprinkle with desiccated coconut and garnish with cocktail cherries and mint leaves.

3. Cut 1 carrot and 1 leek into very fine strips. Braise in butter for 3–4 minutes. Arrange over the meat with basil leaves to garnish.

4. Cut 2 canned artichoke hearts in half, heat in butter with a sliced mushroom and spring onions, season to taste, arrange on the chicken and garnish with cress.

5. Warm 50 g/2 oz peeled prawns in butter for about 2 minutes, season to taste and arrange over the chicken with chervil and lemon wedges.

6. Warm 2 tablespoons cooked sweet corn in butter. Sprinkle 3–4 cooked broccoli rosettes with butter and arrange on the chicken with 2 tablespoons braised carrots.

Six crispy coatings

Coated chicken drumsticks are ideal to serve at informal buffet parties, garden parties or children's birthdays. The best thing about them is that they can be eaten so easily in the fingers. Make sure you have plenty of paper serviettes handy for holding the chicken and for cleaning up afterwards. One more tip: coated chicken looks extremely attractive if you combine several varieties on one plate. Your guests will find it difficult to choose if you follow these recipes.

1. With paprika

Sprinkle the chicken leg with salt and coat generously in sweet paprika. Set the oven at moderately hot (200 C, 400 F, gas 6) and roast on a rack for 20–30 minutes.

2. With peanuts

Crush the peanuts using the blade of a broad knife. Season the chicken leg with salt, dip in beaten egg and then in the peanuts. Roast on a rack in a moderately hot oven (200 C, 400 F, gas 6) for 20–30 minutes.

3. With apricot jam

Season the leg with salt and seal both sides in oil. Cover in apricot jam. Set the oven at moderately hot (200 C, 400 F, gas 6) and roast on a rack for 15–20 minutes.

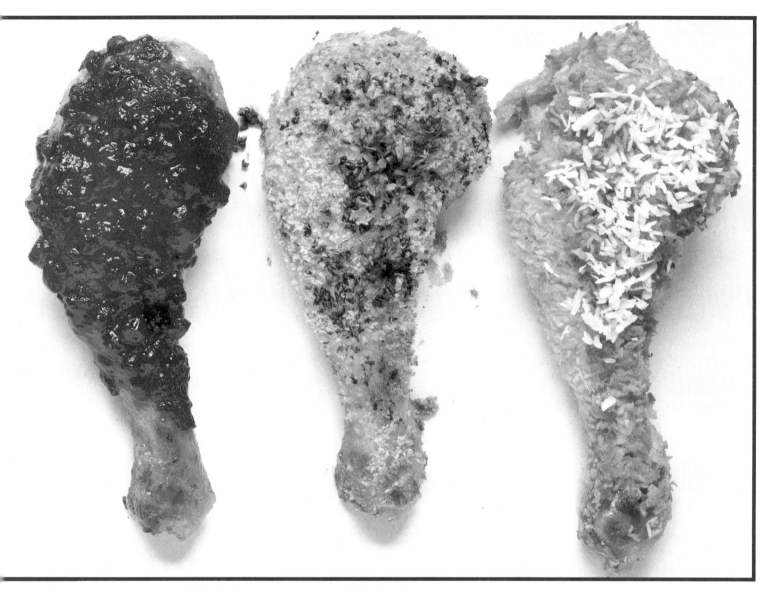

4. With cranberry sauce

Season the drumstick with salt. Seal both sides in hot oil and coat in cranberry sauce. Set the oven at moderately hot (200 C, 400 F, gas 6) and roast on a rack for 15–20 minutes.

5. With parsley panade

Season the leg with salt, dip in flour and beaten egg and then in breadcrumbs mixed with chopped parsley. Set the oven at moderately hot (200 C, 400 F, gas 6) and roast on a rack for 20–30 minutes.

6. With desiccated coconut

Season the leg with salt, dip in beaten egg and desiccated coconut and press the coconut on. Set the oven at moderately hot (200 C, 400 F, gas 6) and roast on a rack for 20–30 minutes.

Coq au vin

2 medium-sized chickens
2 tablespoons vegetable oil
2 onions, diced
4 carrots
3 tablespoons flour
600 ml/ 1 pint red wine
1 bay leaf
salt and pepper
20–30 pickling (button) onions
1 tablespoon butter
1 tablespoon sugar
50 g/ 2 oz bacon
225 g/ 8 oz mushrooms
2 tablespoons chopped parsley to garnish

1. Divide the chickens into portions.
2. Fry in the oil over a high heat to give plenty of juice.
3. Add the onion and 1 coarsely chopped carrot and brown for 3 minutes. Sprinkle with the flour then add the wine. Add the bay leaf, season with a little salt and cook over a moderate heat for 20 minutes.
4. Cut the remaining carrots into sticks and fry with the small onions in butter and oil for 2 minutes on the highest setting. Season with salt, pepper and sugar. Add 4 tablespoons water and braise for 4 minutes.
5. In a frying pan fry the diced bacon and mushrooms for 2 minutes.
6. After 20 minutes remove the chicken from the pan and strain the sauce, pressing the vegetables through a sieve with the back of a spoon. Season to taste and return to the pan with the chicken.
7. Add the braised onions and carrots, diced bacon and the mushrooms and simmer gently for 15 minutes over a moderate heat. Sprinkle with parsley before serving.

Sweet and sour duck

1 oven-ready duck
1 litre/ 2 pints orange juice
salt and pepper
3–4 tablespoons cornflour
600 ml/ 1 pint vegetable oil
For the sauce:
1 spring onion
a small piece of root ginger
300 ml/ $\frac{1}{2}$ pint dry sherry
2 tablespoons sugar
2 tablespoons wine vinegar
8 tablespoons soy sauce

1. Cut the duck into bite-sized pieces.
2. Simmer in the orange juice over a moderate heat in a covered pan for 15–20 minutes.
3. Remove the duck from the pan, drain, wipe dry and season to taste.
4. Dip each piece of duck in cornflour.
5. Fry in the hot oil until brown and crisp.
6. To make the sauce thinly slice the spring onion and ginger.
7. Heat 2 tablespoons oil in a frying pan over a moderate heat and fry the ginger. Add the spring onion and fry for a further 2 minutes.
8. Add the sherry, sugar, vinegar and soy sauce and bring to the boil.
9. Continue boiling until the sugar has dissolved.
10. Arrange the pieces of duck on a bed of rice and pour on the sauce.

Variation: Instead of sherry, use the same quantity of the orange juice in which the duck was cooked.

Poulard niçoise

1 oven-ready chicken
8 tablespoons olive oil
2–3 large onions
2 red peppers
450 g/ 1 lb tomatos, peeled
2 cloves garlic, crushed
salt and pepper
1 courgette
1 aubergine
1 tablespoon flour
1 tablespoon chopped parsley or basil

1. Cut the chicken into portions.
2. Heat 2 tablespoons oil in a heavy frying pan.
3. Fry the chicken portions until golden brown all over.
4. Slice the onions.
5. Cut the peppers into long thin strips.
6. Fry the onion and peppers in 2 tablespoons oil over a low heat for 3–4 minutes.
7. Add the chopped tomatoes and garlic and cook for a further 3 minutes.
8. Add the above vegetables to the chicken, season to taste, cover the pan and braise for 30–45 minutes, adding a little water if necessary to prevent it burning.
9. Slice the courgette and aubergine, sprinkle with flour and fry in 4 tablespoons olive oil until golden brown.
10. Arrange the chicken with its vegetables on a hot plate.
11. Garnish with the courgette and aubergine and sprinkle with chopped herbs.

Chicken curry

1 oven-ready chicken

salt and pepper

4 tablespoons vegetable oil

2–3 onions

2–3 apples

1–2 teaspoons concentrated tomato purée

600 ml/1 pint coconut milk (or chicken stock)

2–3 tablespoons curry powder

1 tablespoon flour

1. Cut the chicken into portions and season to taste.
2. Seal in the hot oil over a moderate to high heat.
3. Remove the chicken from the pan.
4. Dice the onions, cut the apples into small pieces and fry in the oil from the chicken.
5. Stir in the tomato purée, dilute with coconut milk or stock and return the chicken to the pan.
6. Sprinkle with the curry powder and flour and stir in.
7. Simmer the chicken curry over a low heat for 25–30 minutes until the chicken is cooked through. Serve with rice.
Tip: Serve with mango chutney, small pickled onions, diced egg and pineapple.

Chicken pie

1 (212-g/7½-oz) packet frozen puff pastry

2 oven-ready spring chickens

salt and pepper

6 slices uncooked ham

2 thin veal schnitzels

2 shallots, finely chopped

1 tablespoon chopped parsley

300 ml/½ pint dry white wine

1 egg

1. Thaw the pastry at room temperature.
2. Cut the chickens into small portions.
3. Season with salt and pepper.
4. Line a pie dish (shallow ovenproof dish) with the ham.
5. Dice the veal and sprinkle over the ham.
6. Sprinkle with the shallots and parsley and season to taste.
7. Cover with the chicken pieces and pour in the wine.
8. Roll out the puff pastry.
9. Moisten the rim of the pie dish with water.
10. Cut a thin strip of pastry and press firmly around the rim of the dish.
11. Cover the dish with pastry and press the edges firmly together.
12. Beat the egg with 1 tablespoon water and brush over the pie.
13. Bake in a moderately hot oven (200 C, 400 F, gas 6) for about 1 hour. If the piecrust browns too quickly cover it with aluminium foil.

Chicken fricassee

1 oven-ready boiling fowl

1 tablespoon butter

1 tablespoon flour

1 litre/2 pints water

1 bunch soup vegetables (carrot, leek and celeriac)

salt and pepper

225 g/8 oz fresh asparagus, peeled

225 g/8 oz mushrooms, quartered

2–3 artichoke hearts, quartered

2 egg yolks

150 ml/¼ pint single cream

1 lemon

chopped parsley and lemon wedges to garnish

1. Cut the chicken into portions and seal in the butter over a moderate heat.
2. Sprinkle with flour and pour on the water.
3. Add the soup vegetables. Season with ¼ teaspoon salt and simmer for 1 hour over a low to moderate heat (stirring frequently to prevent burning).
4. Remove the soup vegetables and chicken from the pan.
5. Remove the chicken meat from the bones, cut into pieces, remove the skin and return to the sauce.
6. Cut up the asparagus, add to the sauce and cook for 15 minutes.
7. Add the mushrooms and artichoke hearts and bring back to the boil. Remove from the heat.
8. Thoroughly stir in the egg yolks and cream, do not boil beyond this point.
9. Season with the juice of 1 lemon and salt and pepper.
10. Serve with chopped parsley and lemon wedges.

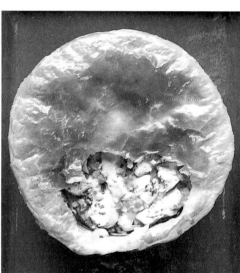

Steaks:
the sheer joy
of meat

The smell of a piece of meat, quick-fried, still has connections with a Stone Age campfire: even though it comes from the kitchen of a first-class restaurant or a modern steakhouse. The steak has become part of everyday twentieth-century mythology: satisfying without being fattening, rich in protein, the food of sportsmen, and always a magnificent way of satisfying one's appetite.

The basics of good meat

If a steak is to be a success it is not enough to know a few good recipes. There are things you should be aware of that many cookery books take for granted. Before the question of the right pan or the correct preparation even arises, there are things you should know when buying the meat. Here are some guidelines.

Buying

1. Find a butcher you can trust. The steaks he sells should never be bright red, attractive as this may be. Red steak is too fresh and will shrink in the pan.
2. Steak should be hung for about two weeks in the coldroom until it is a dull brownish-red in colour. Beef which is flecked with fat is also excellent.
3. Get the butcher to cut steaks of uniform thickness – at least 3–4 cm/1–1¾ in. Those who know about steak buy them at least 5 cm/2 in thick.
4. Fillet steak is the most tender and most expensive cut of meat. For cheaper, less tender cuts buy rump or topside steaks (see also page 217).

Frying pans

For frying steaks a dark, heavy pan (e.g. cast-iron) is ideal. These retain and distribute the heat better than shiny pans. Non-stick pans are not suitable for the classic method of cooking steak.

The base of the pan should be completely flat, so that it absorbs heat evenly. Where possible the diameter of the base should just fit on the cooking element.

Fats

Steaks are always fried at a high temperature and so require fat that contains as little water as possible.

Vegetable fat, vegetable oil and clarified butter are all suitable.

Neither salted butter nor margarine should be used as these contain a fair proportion of water and can spit and burn at high temperatures.

1. Get out ingredients and utensils.

2. Cut fillet steaks 4–5 cm/1¾–2 in thick. Do not flatten them.

3. Set the heat at the highest setting.

4. Place the pan on top and add 2–3 tablespoons oil.

5. The oil is hot when a wet wooden skewer hisses in it.

6. Lower the fillet steaks into the hot pan on a spatula.

7. Brown the first side for 1 minute.

8. Turn the steaks.

9. Brown the second side for 1 minute.

10. Reduce the heat to medium.

11. Turn the steaks.

12. Fry the steaks for a further 1 minute each side (2 minutes in all).

13. Add 1 tablespoon butter and reduce the heat even more.

14. Hold the pan at an angle and spoon the butter evenly over the steaks.

15. Again fry the steaks on each side (2 minutes in all).

16. Test whether the steak is cooked: it should give slightly when pressed.

17. Season the steaks to taste.

18. Take the steaks out of the pan, wrap in foil and put the pan to one side.

19. Leave the steaks in the foil for about 2 minutes.

20. Fry again for 30 seconds per side. The steak is now medium cooked.

Ten steak rules for beginners

1. Trim the steak before frying to remove any gristle or small irregularities.
2. For rump steak make cuts in the fat. Cook the steak with the fat and remove it on the plate.
3. Never flatten steaks or coat them in breadcrumbs!
4. Cooking time depends on thickness. As a basic rule: increase or decrease the time by 1 minute per centimetre/half inch.
5. Begin frying over a high heat to seal the meat and prevent the juice escaping.
6. Continue cooking at a lower temperature otherwise the steak will be dry and the outside tough.
7. Even famous cooks use their finger to test if steak is cooked. Use this method yourself. Medium steak feels like a child's ball when you press it and returns to its shape when you take your finger away.
8. If you want to cook several steaks with different cooking times in *one* pan, start with the medium steaks and add rare ones after 2–3 minutes. Both will then be ready at the same time.
9. While the steak is wrapped in foil you can add spirits to the cooking juice (whisky, brandy, cherry brandy, etc.) and flame it.
10. For a quick meal serve steaks on croûtons. Fry slices of white bread in butter and rub with a cut clove of garlic. Top with the steak and serve!

The four classic types

It is at one and the same time both extremely easy and extremely difficult to fry a steak which is really worthy of the name. You certainly need sensitive fingers, for every stove heats differently, every pan absorbs heat differently and no two pieces of meat are the same. But never fear; there a few set rules you can keep to.

Raw – bleu

The steak has a thin, brown crust, but is still raw inside. Cooking time for a 225 g/ 8 oz steak: about 1 minute per side.

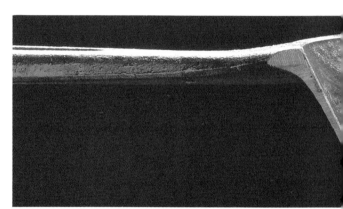

Rare – saignant

The steak has a brown crust. Inside it is pink and at the centre still raw and bloody. Cooking time for 225 g/8 oz steak: about 2 minutes per side.

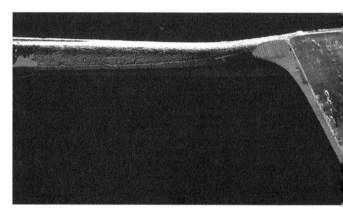

Medium – à point

The steak has a brown crust and is pink right through. Cooking time for a 225 g/ 8 oz steak: about 3–4 minutes per side.

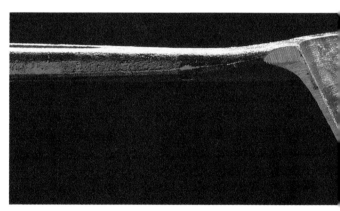

Well-done – biencuit

The steak is completely cooked throughout. This method is not recommended – it is a waste of beautiful meat. Cooking time for a 225 g/8 oz steak: about 5 minutes per side.

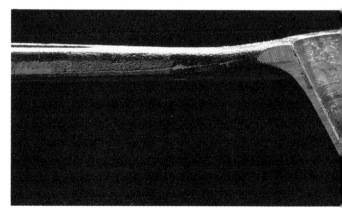

Sixteen unusual variations

While steak seems to be served with chips and mushrooms as a matter of course, this should not prevent you trying a few original variations. You can use the examples given here as a source of inspiration and encouragement.

Recipes for four steaks
(illustrated from left to right)

With tomato

Peel, halve and deseed 1 tomato and cut into wedges. Pluck the leaves off a sprig of parsley and fry in 2–3 tablespoons hot vegetable oil, turning occasionally. Season with a little salt. Toss the tomato wedges in 1 tablespoon melted butter and arrange on the steaks with the parsley.

With onion

Slice 4 onions. Mix together 1 tablespoon flour and 1 tablespoon paprika. Coat the onion rings and fry in 3–4 tablespoons hot oil. Top the steaks with the onion rings.

With herb butter

Spread 100 g/4 oz herb butter (see page 114) on 4 slices lemon and place on the steaks, garnishing with chervil leaves.

With bacon

Fry 4 rashers bacon on both sides in 1–2 tablespoons hot vegetable oil and place on top of the steaks with watercress.

With beef marrow

Bring 2–3 marrow bones to the boil in water and boil for 1–2 minutes. When cool press out the marrow and cut into slices. Bring the juice in which the steak has cooked to the boil with 150 ml/$\frac{1}{4}$ pint red wine and use to warm through the marrow. Place on the steaks and sprinkle with chopped chives.

With green peppercorns

Warm 8 tablespoons bottled green peppercorns in the frying juices and spoon onto the steaks. Garnish with watercress.

With sweet corn and red pepper

Cut 1 red pepper into thin strips and blanch. Braise with 2 tablespoons sweet corn for 2 minutes.

With asparagus

Cut 350 g/12 oz blanched asparagus into pieces and toss in 2 tablespoons hot butter. Sprinkle with finely chopped parsley.

With artichokes

Quickly braise 4 artichoke hearts in 2 tablespoons melted butter and 4 tablespoons peas in 1 tablespoon melted butter. Fill the artichoke hearts with peas.

With pears and cheese

Spread 100 g/4 oz Roquefort on 4 pear halves. Brown in a moderately hot oven (200 C, 400 F, gas 6) for 4 minutes.

With anchovy fillets

Arrange 16 anchovy fillets on the steaks and garnish with stuffed green olives.

With mixed pickles

Drain 1 small jar mixed pickles and place on the steaks with chervil leaves.

With palm hearts

Cut 2 palm hearts into quarters and braise in 1 tablespoon melted butter with the juice of $\frac{1}{2}$ lemon. Arrange on the steaks with a halved slice lemon and a sprig of lemon balm.

With celery

Cut 2 sticks of celery into small pieces and braise in a little water and 1 tablespoon butter.

With mango

Peel 1 mango and cut into wedges. Quickly braise in 1 tablespoon melted butter and arrange on the steaks with chervil leaves.

With bean sprouts and mushrooms

Slice 225 g/8 oz mushrooms. Mix with 100 g/4 oz bean sprouts, 2 tablespoons vegetable oil and seasoning then spoon onto the steaks. Garnish with fresh thyme.

Tips for advanced cooks

There are incredibly simple but highly effective ways of dressing up steak. You can soak it overnight (or longer) in olive oil to make it extra tender. Before frying you can press it into freshly crushed white or black peppercorns to give peppered steak. You can add a clove of garlic to the final frying fat. But there are other tricks you can use – a few of which are listed here . . .

Marinating

(illustrated right)
For marinating good quality herb oil, olive oil or walnut oil should be used; together with seasoning, herbs, chillies, garlic, soy sauce, lemon juice, brandy or wine.

4 tablespoons herb or olive oil
3 tablespoons brandy
1 tablespoon soy sauce
2 tablespoons fresh mixed herbs
1 tablespoon dried herbs
1–2 cloves garlic, crushed
coarsely ground pepper
chilli powder to taste

Mix all the ingredients together and soak the steaks in the marinade for several hours, turning frequently, to allow the flavour to soak into the meat. Before frying pat the steaks dry and remove the herbs otherwise these will burn during frying.

Barding

The steaks are surrounded by fatty bacon secured in place with cooking thread. The fat prevents the lean meat becoming dry during frying.

Trussing

Irregular pieces of steak are tied round with cooking twine to give a good rounded shape. The twine should be removed before serving.

Frying juices

The frying juices can be diluted with water, wine or a little brandy or whisky. Bring to the boil and pour over the steaks. The gravy can be thickened with a little double or soured cream if preferred.

Flaming

To flame, the frying juices are mixed with a high-percentage alcohol and then lit. The steaks are served flaming from the pan.

Sauces

(illustrated left)
There are a wide variety of manufactured sauces: Grill sauce, steak sauce, barbecue sauce, chilli sauce or soy sauce.

You can improve any of these or make them hotter with seasonings such as sambal oelek, chilli powder, pepper or herbs.

Grilling

Grilling is a method of cooking steaks with very little fat. On a barbecue you can give added flavour by burning thyme, rosemary, juniper or myrtle twigs on the charcoal.

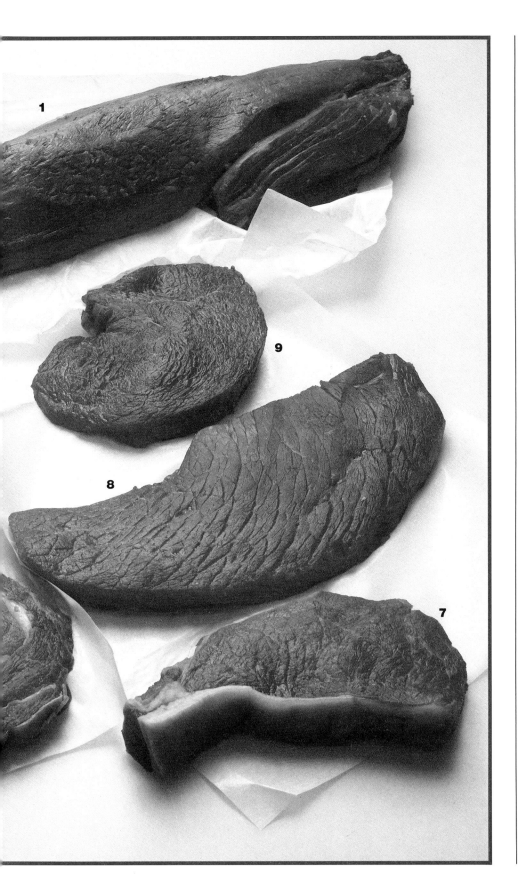

The art of cutting steaks

There are many different ways of cutting meat. It tends to vary not only from country to country but also, sometimes, from region to region. Below are listed some of the different cuts of meat used in Europe and in America.

European-style

The beef fillet (1) is cut into several pieces:

Châteaubriand (2), double fillet piece from the thick end of the fillet, cooked in one piece, about 450 g/1 lb.

Fillet steak (3) from the middle of the fillet.

Tournedos (4), smaller fillets from the thin end.

Filet mignon (5), small steaks from the tip of the fillet.

Fillet tips (6) used for goulash, etc.

Entrecôte, top part of the rib, about 5 cm/2 in thick, about 450 g/1 lb.

Rumpsteak (7), about 2.5 cm/1 in thick with edging of fat, cut from the rump, about 2.5 cm/1 in thick, about 150 g/5 oz.

Buttock steak (8), cut from the thigh, about 2.5 cm/1 in thick, about 225–75 g/ 8–10 oz.

Top-side steak (9), about 2.5 cm/1 in thick, about 150 g/5 oz.

American-style

T-bone steak (10), cut containing both fillet and sirloin steak separated by a T-shaped bone, about 450–575 g/1–1¼ lb.

Porterhouse steak, similar to T-bone, but with more of the sirloin and often twice as thick, about 575 g–1 kg/1¼–2¼ lb.

Prime rib (11), cut of top-rib with bone and fat.

Rib eye (12) similar to prime rib, but more streaked with fat.

Various alternatives

Admittedly classic steak comes from beef and nothing else. But for a long time lamb and veal, game, pork and liver have been cooked in the same way. The range is wide: from the delicately tender to the spicy and filling. As in other chapters, we hope the examples included here will prompt you to develop your own ideas.

Game

Game steaks are brownish-red in colour and more strongly flavoured than other types of meat.

Game steaks are cut 2.5–4 cm/1–1½ in thick and fried in butter over a moderate heat. The cooked meat should be pink but not bloody.

Serve with:
Cranberries in pear halves
Canned chestnuts (boiled)
Apple cooked in white wine
Wild mushrooms (fried in butter)
Brussels sprouts
Red cabbage
Croquette potatoes
Spätzle

Illustrated above:
Venison steak with chestnuts, pears and cranberries, garnished with fresh thyme sprigs.

Lamb

Lamb fillets are very small and thin. They are fried whole, allowing 2 fillets per person. Cooking time is extremely short (about 2–3 minutes).
Lamb chops are cut from the ribs. The rim of fat can be removed or slits cut in it. Lamb chops should be fried quickly (4–6 minutes) in a little fat over a moderate heat. The meat should be pinkish on the inside.
Serve with:
Mint jelly (ready-bought)
Green beans
Tomato quarters (quick-braised)
Potato straws (see page 119).

Illustrated above:
Lamb chops garnished with mint jelly and a sprig of fresh mint.

Pork

Pork fillet is smaller than beef fillet and can either be fried whole or in slices (medallions). Pork fillet should be fried in butter over a moderate heat until still pink at the centre.
Pork schnitzel is made like Wiener Schnitzel.
Pork chops (on the bone) or sparerib cutlets (without bone) are dipped in flour and fried in oil or margarine over a moderate heat for 10 minutes. Chops can also be fried in breadcrumbs (see page 26).

Illustrated above:
Pork chop with braised peppers and a sprig of parsley.

Veal

Veal steaks are cut into pieces 2.5–4 cm/1–1½ in thick, but can also be fried whole. Fry in butter over a moderate heat for about 6 minutes until still juicy in the centre.

Veal rib steaks are larger than fillets. They can be fried in butter over a moderate heat either on the bone or boned like beef steaks.

Wiener Schnitzel Cut steaks 1 cm/½ in thick and flatten evenly with a wooden steak hammer. First coat in flour, then in beaten egg yolk and finally gently beat in a thin covering of breadcrumbs. Fry in plenty of butter over a moderate heat for about 4 minutes. After frying season with salt. Garnish with lemon slices, rolled anchovy fillets and capers.

Uncoated veal schnitzel should not be beaten, but should be cut very thin and fried over a moderate to high heat for 2–3 minutes.

Illustrated above:
Wiener Schnitzel garnished with lemon slices, anchovy fillets and capers.

Liver

Calf's liver is the best and most expensive. Pig's and ox liver easily dry out when fried and have more veins. Cut the liver into slices 1 cm/½ in thick, coat in flour and fry quickly (about 3–4 minutes) over a moderate heat. It should be pink and juicy at the centre. If liver is overcooked it becomes hard and dry. Always season with salt after frying.

Illustrated above:
Calf's liver with apple slices and onion rings fried in butter.

Zurich-style veal stew

450 g/1 lb veal
1 tablespoon oil
1 onion, finely chopped
1 tablespoon flour
4 tablespoons dry white wine
300 ml/½ pint double cream
1 tablespoon butter
salt and pepper
1 tablespoon chopped parsley to garnish

Slice the veal and then cut into strips. Heat the oil in a frying pan and seal the meat over a high heat for about 1 minute. Take the meat out of the pan and keep hot. Reduce the heat to moderate, tip the onion into the pan and fry for 2 minutes. Sprinkle in the flour, stir into the onions and then stir in the wine. Add the cream and simmer for about 2 minutes. Return the meat to the pan, add the butter and warm through. Season to taste and serve sprinkled with parsley.

Italian escalopes

Anyone who has ever eaten a tender, delicately seasoned veal escalope, cut extremely thin in Tuscany or Rome, in Piedmont or Lombardy, has only to think back for his or her mouth to begin to water. Why not copy the Italians? You will find the basic recipe here, and once you have mastered it, it will not be long before you are making your own special escalopes.

Basic recipe for scaloppine al Marsala

Small veal escalopes with Marsala

4 tablespoons oil

8 small thin veal escalopes

300 ml/½ pint Marsala (sweet dessert wine)

juice of 1 lemon

salt and freshly ground black pepper

2 tablespoons butter

1. Heat the oil in a large frying pan.
2. Fry the escalopes over a moderate heat for 2–3 minutes until golden brown on each side.
3. When fried, remove the meat from the pan and keep hot.
4. Using the frying juices and Marsala make a sauce. Pour the Marsala into the hot pan, bring to the boil and reduce slightly, stirring in the frying juices from the bottom of the pan.
5. Stir in the lemon juice.
6. Season to taste.
7. Whisk the butter into the sauce.
8. Pour the sauce over the escalopes.

Veal escalopes with ham and sage

'Saltimbocca alla Romana'

8 small thin veal escalopes

8 slices Parma ham

8–16 fresh sage leaves

3 tablespoons oil

½ cup dry white wine

2 tablespoons butter

salt and freshly ground black pepper

1. Cover each escalope with a slice of ham, fold over, secure with a cocktail stick and top with 1–2 sage leaves.
2. Heat the oil in a frying pan and fry the escalopes for 3–4 minutes each side until golden brown.
3. Take the escalopes out of the pan and keep hot.

4. Stir the white wine into the frying juices and reduce slightly.
5. Whisk the butter into the sauce and season to taste.
6. Pour the sauce over the escalopes.

Veal escalopes with tarragon sauce

8 small thin veal escalopes

3 tablespoons oil

salt and freshly ground black pepper

½ cup dry white wine

300 ml/½ pint double cream

2 tablespoons butter

2 tablespoons finely chopped tarragon

1. Fry the escalopes in the oil over a moderate heat for 2–3 minutes until golden brown.

2. Season to taste, remove from the pan and keep hot.
3. Stir the white wine into the frying juices, add the cream and reduce slightly.
4. After 30 seconds stir the butter into the sauce and simmer for a few minutes more.
5. Add the tarragon to the sauce and adjust the seasoning.
6. Pour the sauce over the escalopes.

Veal escalopes with lemon

8 small thin veal escalopes

juice of 1 lemon

3 tablespoons oil

salt and freshly ground black pepper

150 ml/¼ pint dry white wine

2 tablespoons butter

lemon slices and lemon balm to garnish

1. Sprinkle the escalopes with the juice of ½ lemon.
2. Heat the oil in a frying pan and fry the escalopes for 2–3 minutes until golden brown.
3. Season to taste, remove the veal from the pan and keep hot.
4. Stir the juice of ½ lemon and the wine into the frying juices and reduce slightly.
5. Stir the butter into the sauce and adjust the seasoning.
6. Garnish with lemon slices and lemon balm.

Money-saving tip:
It is not essential to use expensive veal fillet for these recipes. Veal from the leg, from which schnitzel are usually cut, will do just as well. Get your butcher to cut the meat as thin as possible (about 5 mm/¼ in thick). All you have to do is to cut the slices in half and you have your escalopes ready to cook.

Minced meat: meat for shaping

Freshly minced meat combined with every imaginable seasoning, onion and – for those who like it – garlic, makes a really appetising meal. Rissoles, meat balls, meat loaves and stuffed cabbage or peppers form just part of the large array of dishes that can be prepared from minced meat. From abroad one can remember such tasty delights as ćevapčići, dolmades and lasagne, not forgetting the hamburger. There are hundreds of different ways of garnishing or serving the latter, a few of which are shown in this chapter. Mince may be the meat of everyday cooking but the pleasure it can bring makes it a feast.

The different kinds and the basic recipe

Anyone new to minced meat needs to begin with a brief lesson on the different types available, otherwise they will be thoroughly confused when they get to the butcher's. In addition there is one basic recipe with which you need to become familiar, for this will provide the basis for creative and enjoyable cooking with minced meat.

What you should know about minced meat

Basic rule: Never use anything but fresh meat. Minced meat provides an ideal breeding ground for bacteria (salmonella) even at refrigerator temperature.

Always buy freshly minced meat – all butchers are obliged to mince meat for you if asked. If you buy frozen or pre-packed mince take note of the sell-by date.

Mince is sold in the following types:
1. *Mince* is uncooked boned meat, beef and/or pork, with no additives and with a certain fat content.
2. Ground beef or *tatare*, is uncooked, minced lean beef. It should contain no fat, gristle or additives and is very finely minced.
3. *Hamburger mince* is ground beef with salt, onion or other ingredients and seasoning added.

Basic recipe

1 bread roll
225 g/8 oz minced beef
225 g/8 oz minced pork
2 onions, finely chopped
1 egg
½ teaspoon salt
pepper
2 tablespoons vegetable oil or margarine for frying

Tip: The bread roll can be replaced with breadcrumbs, or white or wholemeal bread.

1. Get the ingredients ready.

2. Soften the roll in 300 ml/½ pint warm water.

3. Place the minced meat, the onion and the egg in a bowl.

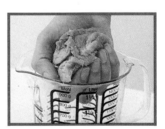

4. Squeeze the excess moisture from the roll.

5. Add the roll to the minced meat (this makes the mixture lighter).

6. Season with ½ teaspoon salt and a little pepper.

7. Mix all the ingredients thoroughly together.

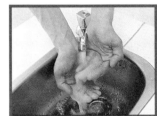

8. Wet your hands to prevent the mixture sticking.

9. Using wet hands shape the mixture into eight rissoles.

10. Put the rissoles to one side until ready to cook.

Cooking methods

Minced meat can either be cooked in the frying pan, in the oven, under the grill or on a barbecue.

Frying

Use the frying pan to cook hamburgers, meat balls and minced meat for sauces.

Roasting

Meat loaves and minced meat pies are cooked in the oven.

Grilling or barbecuing

Minced meat in any of its smaller forms can be cooked either on or under a grill.

To grill minced meat cover the grill rack with aluminium foil to prevent the meat becoming too brown or falling apart.

Cooking fat

Since minced meat is not fried over a particularly high heat, butter, clarified butter, margarine and possibly pork dripping are all suitable for frying the various minced meat dishes.

1. Set the heat at moderate.

2. Heat half the margarine in a hot frying pan.

3. Slide a hamburger into the pan using a palette knife.

4. Add the remaining three hamburgers.

5. Fry the first side for 4 minutes.

6. Turn the hamburgers.

7. Press into shape using a palette knife or spatula.

8. Fry for a further 4 minutes.

9. Transfer from the pan to a baking tray.

10. Fry the remaining four hamburgers in the same way.

Other minced meat mixtures

Of course mince dishes can be made with other types of meat or combinations of types.

Veal has an excellent delicate flavour and should be only lightly seasoned.

Lamb is strongly flavoured and can be mixed with a variety of herbs and seasonings, including the more exotic.

Good combinations: lamb and beef, pork and lamb, veal and beef.

Minced meat hot and cold

Many minced dishes are extremely popular for parties, picnics and barbecues. They can be made several days in advance and frozen. When you need them all you need to do is defrost them and warm them up in the oven. They are just as good served cold.

Since the eyes play an important part in the eating process, for special occasions minced meat dishes should look as well as taste good. You can improve the appearance of meatballs, rissoles or hamburgers by dipping them in various coatings.

Ideal for coating are: sesame seeds, grated coconut, chopped pine nuts, flaked almonds or chopped walnuts.

Twelve appetising ideas

A hamburger on its own can be an enjoyable experience – eaten, in a sesame bun, with the fingers with a choice of toppings in a hamburger restaurant. But at home you and your family will probably welcome more variety and originality from the standard choice. Nothing could be simpler! There are a dozen ideas included here and more in the steak chapter (see pages 202–3) if you need them. Eventually when you have tried all of these you will be able to think up a few of your own . . .

From oranges to horseradish

1. Orange wedges and tarragon leaves.
2. Sliced mushrooms and radishes marinated in vinegar, oil and seasoning. Garnished with watercress.
3. Onion rings and parsley sprigs.
4. Strips of red and green pepper.
5. Garnished with pickled beetroot and burnet or parsley.
6. Place hamburger on a slice of pineapple, top with 1 slice cheese and brown.
7. Garnish with sliced tomato and basil leaves.
8. Shredded white cabbage marinated in salt, pepper, sugar, vinegar and oil for 24 hours.
9. Top with fried egg sprinkled with paprika.
10. Garnish with sliced pickled cucumber and dill.
11. Top with 1 tablespoon ketchup and chives.
12. Shredded fresh horseradish and parsley.

'Big Mac' and other burgers

The decline in western eating habits has produced an excellent alternative to hot dogs or fish and chips in the area of quick food. There is nothing essentially bad about the hamburger – the trouble is that it is often badly made with dry meat, limp lettuce and tasteless rolls. Yet the hamburger has limitless possibilities.

Basic hamburger recipe

(illustrated right)

Makes 4

450 g/ 1 lb minced beef
1 onion, finely chopped
1 egg
salt and pepper
2 tablespoons oil
4 white sesame-seed rolls
4 lettuce leaves
2 tomatoes, sliced
2 gherkins, sliced
4 slices cheese
4 teaspoons mayonnaise
4 teaspoons ketchup

1. Fry four flat, round beefburgers as shown in the step-by-step photographs on pages 214–15 using the first five ingredients.
2. Halve the rolls. Cover each bottom half with 1 lettuce leaf, a slice of gherkin, a beefburger, tomato slices, cheese and 1 teaspoon each mayonnaise and ketchup.

Top with the other half of the roll.

Double-decker

Make the beefburgers using
the basic recipe on page 214

Salad ingredients:

2 onions

4 tomatoes

½ cucumber

4–5 tablespoons oil

3 tablespoons vinegar

pinch of sugar

salt and generous pinch

pepper

I. Dice the onions, chop the
tomatoes into small pieces
and slice the cucumber
paper-thin.
2. Beat together the oil,
vinegar, sugar, salt and
pepper.
3. Add the cucumber,
tomato and onion, mix
thoroughly and marinate for
1–2 hours.
4. Fry the beefburgers as
shown in the basic recipe.
5. Make up the hamburgers
with the following layers:
roll, salad, beefburger,
salad, beefburger, roll.

Variations:
The following five variations
show how versatile
hamburgers can be:
I. Poppy-seed roll,
ketchup, onion rings,
beefburger, Iceberg lettuce,
poppy-seed roll.
2. Milk roll, ketchup,
mayonnaise, cucumber, red
onion, beefburger, lettuce,
milk roll.
3. Roll, ketchup,
beefburger, tomato, roll.
4. Roll, cheese slice,
pineapple slice, beefburger,
roll.
5. Roll, fried bacon,
beefburger, chopped onion,
roll.

The simplest form of variation

Mince – in addition to its other advantages – is primarily a malleable mixture. It can be kneaded, mixed, shaped, and this makes it the ideal starting point for imaginative cooking. It is no wonder that the regional cooking of many countries have used it to make tasty and interesting dishes (see also pages 226–7). Regardless of whether you prefer ćevapčići or minced meat, one thing is sure – it is excellent in recipes and even better in your own variations.

Minced meat ring

Fill the ring mould with the minced meat mixture (see basic recipe) and bake in a moderately hot oven (200 C, 400 F, gas 6) for 40 minutes. Finally turn out of the mould.

Stuffed cabbage

Blanch Savoy cabbage leaves in boiling water for 2–3 minutes then drain thoroughly. Roll the minced meat securely in the cabbage leaves. Quick-fry in hot fat and add a little water. Braise over a moderate heat for 20 minutes.

Minced meat rolls

Shape the minced meat mixture into a long roll and cut into 10-cm/4-in lengths (see ćevapčići, page 226).

Meat balls

With wet hands shape the mixture into small balls. These can be fried or cooked in liquid. Serve as a main course or on skewers as a starter.

Minced meat cake

Press the minced meat mixture into a round ovenproof dish and bake in a moderately hot oven (200 C, 400 F, gas 6) for 40 minutes.

Rissoles

Shape the mixture into fairly large balls.

Imitation chops

Shape the minced meat mixture into a cutlet shape.

Puff pastry packets

Defrost 1 (368-g/13-oz) packet frozen puff pastry and cut into 7.5-cm/3-in squares. Top with the minced meat mixture. Brush the edges with egg yolk and fold together. Bake in a hot oven (220 C, 425 F, gas 7) for 15–20 minutes until golden brown.

Minced meat

Season ground beef to taste and quickly fry in hot butter, stirring continuously.

Foil-baked meatloaf

Make the minced meat following the basic recipe on page 214, shape into a loaf and wrap in aluminium foil. Bake in a moderately hot oven (200 C, 400 F, gas 6) for 35–40 minutes.

Seasoning — the tastiest variation

It all comes down to flavour, and mince is a field wide open for experiment if you want to ring the changes with seasonings or additional ingredients. At a basic level fresh meat, with its relatively neutral taste, really only requires salt. Whatever else you sprinkle, grate, mill or mix in is entirely up to you. Basic rule number 1: never use too many different seasonings — they will cancel one another out. Basic rule number 2: never use too much of one seasoning — most do not develop fully in flavour until cooked.

Mixtures

For flavouring a minced meat mixture use herbs, seasonings, fruit, vegetables and nuts. The quantities of extra ingredients are for 450 g/1 lb minced meat (see basic recipe on page 214). It is important to work the extra ingredients thoroughly into the mince. When shaping the mixture it is advisable to stick to the variations on the preceding page.

Arabian mixture

Additional ingredients:

1 small green pepper, diced

2–3 tablespoons dried fruit, chopped

2 tablespoons pine nuts

2 tablespoons pistachio nuts

pinch of allspice

$\frac{1}{4}$ teaspoon saffron powder

1 tablespoon chopped mint

serve with rice and yogurt

Northern mixture

Additional ingredients:

2 tablespoons chopped beetroot

2 tablespoons diced carrot

3 tablespoons leek rings

1 tablespoon capers

1 teaspoon chopped anchovy

1 tablespoon soured cream

2 tablespoons chopped parsley

South American mixture

Additional ingredients:

1 tomato, peeled and diced

2 tablespoons sweet corn

1 tablespoon chopped olives

1 green chilli, finely chopped

$\frac{1}{2}$ apple, diced

1 clove garlic, crushed

1–2 tablespoons raisins

2 tablespoons chopped almonds

Indian mixture

Additional ingredients:

1 slice pineapple, finely chopped

2 apricots

1 hot red chilli, chopped

1 tablespoon sweet paprika

1 tablespoon curry powder

generous pinch of ground caraway

1 teaspoon green peppercorns

a little grated nutmeg

Stuffed tomatoes

8 beef tomatoes

450 g/1 lb minced meat mixture (see basic recipe, page 214)

2 tablespoons olive oil

Cut a lid from the tomatoes and, using a spoon, scrape out the flesh. Fill the tomatoes with the minced meat mixture and replace the lids. Arrange the tomatoes in a greased ovenproof dish and bake in a hot oven (220C, 425F, gas 7) for 30 minutes. Smaller stuffed tomatoes can be baked on a baking tray and served directly from it.

Stuffed kohlrabi

4–6 kohlrabi

150 ml/¼ pint double cream

salt and pepper

450 g/1 lb minced meat mixture (see basic recipe, page 214)

thyme sprigs to garnish

Peel the kohlrabi and cut out the inside. Dice the flesh from the kohlrabi and place in an ovenproof dish with the cream. Season to taste. Drop the whole kohlrabi into boiling salted water and pre-cook for 10 minutes. Stuff the kohlrabi with the minced meat mixture and bake in a moderately hot oven (200C, 400F, gas 6) for 30–45 minutes (depending on size) until completely cooked. Garnish with sprigs of thyme.

Stuffed peppers

4–6 green peppers

450 g/ 1 lb minced meat mixture (see basic recipe, page 214)

6 small tomatoes

2 tablespoons olive oil

salt and pepper

Cut a lid off each pepper and remove the seeds. Stuff the peppers with the minced meat mixture and replace the lids. Peel and quarter the tomatoes. Grease an ovenproof dish with the oil, arrange the peppers and tomatoes in the dish and season to taste. Bake in a moderately hot oven (200C, 400F, gas 6) for 45 minutes.

Crumbly fillings for vegetables

The combination of minced meat and vegetables has become something of a classic. One only has to think of stuffed cabbage! When it is made well it can be a real feast. Yet there are other combinations which are less well known but just as good. The basic recipe is the same in each case, with seasoned minced meat used as a filling for hollowed out vegetables. During cooking the flavours of the mince and vegetables combine deliciously.

Stuffed vegetables

Many types of vegetables are excellent for stuffing with minced meat. The starting point in each case is the basic minced meat mixture recipe (see page 214). You can vary the flavour by adding herbs such as thyme, basil or oregano, or seasonings such as paprika or curry powder, and of course garlic or rice.

Tip: All stuffed vegetables can be sprinkled with cheese and browned.

Other vegetables suitable for stuffing

aubergines
courgettes
Spanish onions
cucumber
large mushroom caps

Stuff the chosen vegetable with minced meat mixture and either bake in the oven or braise in a covered pan.

Don't forget to add liquid to the pan as it evaporates!

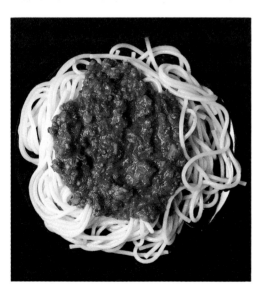

Meatloaf

675 g/ 1½ lb mixed minced
meat (e.g. beef and pork)
2 eggs
2 onions
1 bread roll
1 clove garlic, crushed
4 tablespoons chopped
chives
2 tablespoons chopped
parsley
2 carrots, finely chopped
2 tablespoons oil
3 hard-boiled eggs

1. Make the minced meat
mixture with the
ingredients listed, finishing
with the herbs and carrots
(see page 214).
2. Tip half the mixture into
a greased loaf tin. Press the
shelled hard-boiled eggs
into the mixture and cover
with the remaining minced
meat mixture. Press gently
down into the tin.
3. Set the oven at moderate
(180C, 350F, gas 4), place
the tin in the heated oven
and bake for 45 minutes.

Stuffed cabbage

1 kg/2 lb white cabbage
450 g/ 1 lb minced meat
5 onions
3 tablespoons chopped
parsley
salt and pepper
3 tablespoons butter
300 ml/½ pint water
100 g/4 oz bacon

1. Separate the cabbage
leaves and blanch in boiling
water for 2 minutes. Drain.
2. Mix the minced meat
thoroughly with 2 chopped
onions, parsley and
seasoning.
3. Wrap the minced meat
mixture in the blanched
cabbage leaves and secure
with kitchen thread.
4. Heat the butter. Fry the
cabbage rolls gently.
5. Add the water, cover the
pan and cook over a
moderate heat for 30
minutes.
6. Dice the bacon and the
remaining onions. Fry in a
frying pan and serve with
the stuffed cabbage.

Variation: Mix 2 tablespoons
rice into the minced meat.

Bolognese sauce

75 g/3 oz bacon, diced
1–2 onions, finely chopped
1 medium carrot, diced
1 piece celeriac (about 1 cup
when chopped)
4 tablespoons butter
350 g/ 12 oz minced meat
(half beef, half pork)
2 tablespoons concentrated
tomato purée
½ cup meat stock
1 cup red wine
pepper
freshly grated nutmeg
1 bay leaf
150 ml/¼ pint double cream

1. Fry the bacon until crisp,
add the onion, carrot and
celeriac and fry over a
moderate heat for about 2
minutes.
2. Add the butter and
minced meat and stir well.
3. Add the tomato purée,
stock, red wine and
seasoning and simmer over
a low heat in the open pan
for about 1 hour.
4. Remove the bay leaf.
Adjust the seasoning of
pepper and nutmeg and
thicken with the cream.

Ćevapčići

cloves garlic

*50 g / 1 lb mixed minced
meat*

00 g / 4 oz minced lamb

lt and pepper

*onions, coarsely chopped,
serve*

Finely chop the garlic.
mix all the ingredients
together to make a minced
meat mixture and shape
to fingers about 10 cm/4 in
ong.

Grill on an oiled rack for
pout 10 minutes, or fry in a
ying pan.

Serve with coarsely
hopped onion.

Königsberg
meatballs

For the meatballs:

*50 g / 12 oz mixed minced
eat*

00 g / 4 oz minced veal

slices white bread

onion, chopped

anchovy fillets

*tablespoons chopped
arsley*

tablespoon double cream

lt and pepper

For the stock:

litre / 2 pints water

teaspoon salt

bay leaf

cloves

onion

For the sauce:

5 g / 1 oz butter

0 g / 1½ oz flour

*00 ml / 1 pint stock in which
he meatballs were cooked*

lt and pepper

tablespoons lemon juice

—2 tablespoons capers

tablespoons soured cream

egg yolk

1. Make the minced meat
mixture using the
ingredients listed. With wet
hands shape the mixture into
four or six large meatballs.
2. Bring the salted water to
the boil and then reduce the
heat to moderate. Stick the
bay leaf and cloves into the
onion and drop into the
water. With the water off
the boil, gently lower the
meatballs into the pan and
cook gently for 15–20
minutes until cooked. Once
the meatballs rise to the
surface they need to cook
for another 5 minutes or
they will be raw at the
centre. Lift the meatballs
out of the stock.
3. Over a moderate heat
melt the butter, sprinkle on
the flour and cook until
golden. Remove the pan
from the heat and gradually
whisk in the liquid (after
removing the onion from
the stock). Make sure there
are no lumps, but strain the
sauce to remove them if
necessary.

Bring the sauce back to
the boil and add the
seasoning, lemon juice,
capers and soured cream.
Thicken with the egg yolk.
Do not allow the sauce to
boil from here on or the
egg will curdle.

Lumpia
Shanghai

*35–40 small sheets rice
paper (from cookery or
food shops)*

100 g / 4 oz peeled prawns

350 g / 12 oz bean sprouts

1 clove garlic

1 onion

*225 g / 8 oz mixed minced
meat*

salt and pepper

*about 600 ml / 1 pint oil for
frying*

1. Place the rice paper
between damp cloths for 15
minutes to make it easier to
roll up.
2. Very finely chop the
prawns, bean shoots, garlic
and onion and mix well with
the minced meat and
seasoning. Place a little of
the mixture on each sheet
of rice paper. Fold the sides
in and roll up. If you find it
difficult to make the end of
the paper stick, brush it
with a mixture of flour and
water.
3. Pour the oil into a deep
pan and set the heat at
moderate.
4. Fry the lumpia in batches
in the hot oil until golden
brown.

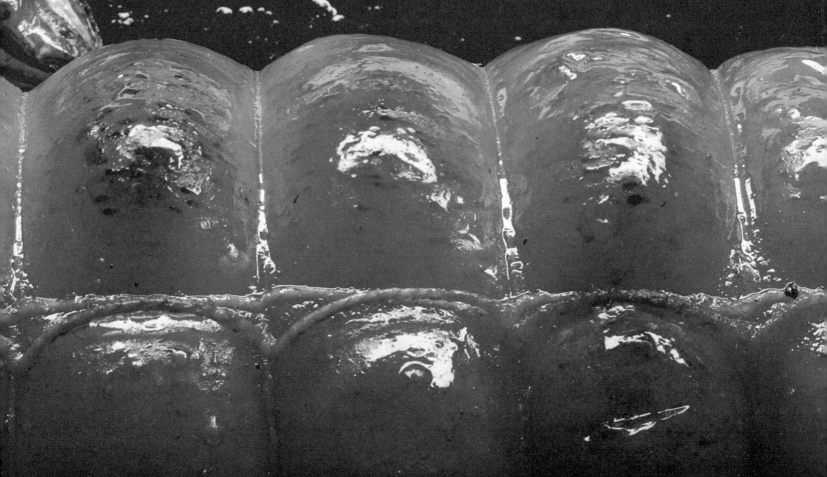

Roasts: delicious meats, crisp and flavoursome

Although vegetarians would disagree, there is nothing that brings people together at the table like a large roast. For hours beforehand the appetising roasting smell draws groups of people into the kitchen. And then there is the unforgettable moment when the crisp brown meat is carved! All your guests are rendered speechless as their mouths water in expectation. But have no fear, they will all find their tongues once more, for nothing brings praise as readily as a successful roast. Nothing is better for a special meal between friends. Entertaining in this way need not be expensive, there are inexpensive cuts of meat which, with a little care, will taste extremely good . . .

Two methods from our grand-mother's day

Our grandmothers were world champions in every aspect of roasting and braising. They knew all the tricks and were familiar with all the disasters that could occur in the oven if you failed to follow the rules. Nothing has changed since those times, so we will show you how roasts were made in the good old days.

Meat for roasting

The remarks about meat and butchers which were included in the steaks chapter (see page 198) also apply here. For a good roast you need good meat. Watch for the following points:

Beef: Should always be well hung (dark red-grey in colour). You don't need to buy the expensive quick-cooking cuts (fillet or rump) as these would be a waste for a pot-roast. You can get inexpensive shoulder and leg cuts for this. Even shin of beef can be delicious.

Pork: For large roasts never buy the watery meat from young fatted pigs. This shrinks during cooking and can be tough if cooked too long. Choose firmer meat with a layer of fat. The fat crisps up during roasting and keeps the meat moist. The crackling forms a delicious crisp crust.

Veal: The same remarks apply here. If the meat looks juicy, it contains too much water. Veal should be dry and greyish in colour. For roasting always buy veal with a little fat on it.

Lamb: Beware of fatty mutton! It will always have a greasy taste. Make sure you ask for lamb specifically, and buy a large piece (e.g. the leg).

Preparation

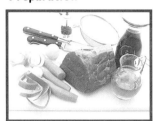

1. Get the prepared ingredients together.

2. Rub the meat with a little salt to bring out the flavour.

3. Put the heat on the highest setting.

4. Add 3 tablespoons vegetable fat or oil to the pan.

5. Place the meat in the pan.

6. Seal the meat all over on a high heat.

7. Reduce the heat to moderate.

8. Add the vegetables.

9. Brown the vegetables with the meat for 2 minutes.

10. Add liquid and seasoning.

Ingredients:

2 kg/4¼ lb topside of beef
3 tablespoons vegetable fat or oil
salt
3 carrots
1 small leek
2 onions
1 piece celeriac
10 peppercorns
1 small bay leaf
300 ml/½ pint liquid (water, stock or red wine)
freshly ground pepper

Pot roasting

(illustrated right)
Prepare the meat as in the step-by-step photographs on the left.
The liquid should come half way up the meat, so you may need more liquid depending on the size of the pan.
Two basic rules:
Thick cuts of meat need longer to cook.
Allow about 10 minutes for each centimetre/half inch.

Braising in the oven

(step-by-step photographs extreme right)
This method is suitable for large pieces of meat (from 1 kg/2¼ lb) and especially for cheaper cuts such as neck, belly, leg, shoulder, collar.

Prepare the meat as in the step-by-step photographs on the left. You do not need much liquid for oven braising.

The high temperature at which the meat cooks gives a delicious roast flavour.

If the meat is not to become dry, buy meat with a covering of fat (or wrap in bacon). For larger roasts increase the cooking time by 30 minutes to 1 hour.

Pot roasting

1. Set the heat at the highest setting.

2. Add the liquid (water, wine or stock) and bring to the boil.

3. Reduce the heat to moderate.

4. Cover the pan.

5. Cook the meat for about 1½ hours.

6. Turn the meat.

7. Cover the pan and simmer for 1 hour until cooked.

8. Remove the meat from the pan and wrap in aluminium foil.

9. Turn up the heat to the highest setting.

10. Boil the liquid in the open pan.

11. Reduce over a high heat for 4 minutes.

12. Strain the gravy.

13. Press the vegetables through the sieve into the gravy.

14. Season the thickened sauce to taste.

15. Stir 1 tablespoon corn-flour or starch with 1 tablespoon water and stir into the sauce.

Oven braising

1. Set the oven at very hot (240C, 475F, gas 9).

2. Place the prepared meat in the middle of the oven.

3. Cook for 30 minutes then reduce to moderately hot (200C, 400F, gas 6).

4. Baste the meat occasionally with the gravy.

5. Cook for 1 hour until tender.

Perennials – veal, beef and pork

Any cook today would find it difficult to say for how long these three super roasts have been developing into what they are today, our staple Sunday food. The fact that a roast made with the same recipe will taste different in different parts of the country is all part of its magic. It would be fair to guess that your favourite roast has its own individual family touch.

Veal kidney roast

(illustrated below left)
Ingredients:

1.5 kg/3¼ lb roasting veal with the kidney

3 tablespoons oil

I onion

300 ml/½ pint liquid (water or white wine)

6 sage leaves

I sprig tarragon

½ teaspoon crushed peppercorns

salt

I. Prepare the veal as in the step-by-step photographs on page 230.
2. Roast in a very hot oven (240C, 475F, gas 9) in the open pan for 15 minutes.
3. Turn the oven down to moderately hot (200C, 400F, gas 6) and roast for a further 1¼ hours until cooked.
4. At the end of the cooking time season the gravy to taste. Serve the gravy as it comes or make into a sauce by adding a little soured cream and white wine.
5. Serve the veal with noodles (see pages 82–3), risotto (see page 104) or Swiss rösti (see page 121).

Larded pot-roasted beef

'Boeuf à la mode'
(illustrated below centre)

1 kg/2¼ lb boned beef topside

50 g/2 oz bacon pieces, for larding

3 tablespoons oil

3 carrots

1 piece celeriac

1 leek

600 ml/1 pint liquid (water, red wine or stock)

3 tablespoons vinegar

10 peppercorns

5 allspice

2 cloves

sprig of thyme or ½ teaspoon dried thyme

salt and pepper

2 tablespoons port

1. Using a larding needle (see page 234) stick strips of bacon into the beef. This makes the meat juicier.
2. Prepare the meat with the vegetables and seasonings as shown in the step-by-step photographs on page 230.
Gourmet tip:
'Boeuf à la mode' has more flavour if you use only red wine for the liquid.
3. Braise the beef in the covered pot for 2½ hours as shown in the step-by-step photographs on page 231. Press the vegetables through a sieve and finally flavour the sauce with port.
4. Serve with boiled potatoes or croquette potatoes (see page 118). It is a good idea to drink the same wine used for cooking with the beef.

Roast pork

(illustrated below right)

1 kb/2¼ lb boned leg of pork

3 tablespoons oil

2 onions

3 carrots

1 bay leaf

2 cloves

sprig of rosemary or ½ teaspoon dried rosemary

1 bottle beer

salt and pepper

1. Prepare the meat and vegetables as shown in the step-by-step photographs on page 230 and add the beer (no wine).

2. Roast the pork in the oven as shown on page 231 for 1½ hours.
3. At the end of the cooking time press the vegetables through a sieve. Defat the gravy and season well.
4. Serve with boiled or fried potatoes (see pages 112–13) and mixed vegetables.

Dressing up your roasts

While a large roast is a pleasure in itself, it offers chefs and amateur cooks a host of possibilities in the way of creative embellishment. As well as exotic expensive ingredients there are many amazingly simple ways of making meat more tasty.

Herbs

Basic rule: cook dried herbs with the meat, add fresh herbs at the end of the cooking time. Many herbs go best with a particular type of meat. Here are included the usual variations.

This is not to say, however, that you shouldn't experiment for yourself.

Beef: thyme, parsley, chives, oregano, marjoram.
Pork: rosemary, parsley, chives, basil, sage.
Veal: tarragon, sage, chervil, basil.
Lamb: thyme, oregano, rosemary, marjoram, mint, *herbes de Provence* (mixed herbs).

Alcohol

Every gravy can be improved by adding alcohol. The idea that alcohol has no place in food would amuse any Frenchman.

In fact the alcoholic content disappears almost completely during cooking to leave only the flavour. For this reason never use cheap wine. And stick to dry wines or your sauces will turn out sweet.

Brandy and Calvados not only add flavour, but also make the meat tender.

The following combinations of meat and alcohol are all excellent:

White wine: Goes with any sort of meat, especially veal and rabbit.
Red wine: Good for beef, lamb and especially game.
Sherry: Mainly with veal.
Lager: Pork.
Beer: Pork and beef.
Brandy: Veal and also rabbit.
Whisky: Especially good with beef.
Calvados: Pork; interesting combination with lamb or beef.

Don't let this basic list limit your imagination. Maybe you will find some other combination even better.

Larding

Lean meat is larded to prevent it becoming dry. For larding use fresh (green) unsmoked bacon. Chill the bacon and cut into thin threads. Use a larding needle to thread the bacon through the meat along the grain. An unusual variation is larding with garlic cut into thin sticks. Make holes in the meat with the needle and push in the garlic.
Tip: Do not make too many incisions for with every hole you make you lose juice!

Improving Gravies

You can improve both the flavour and colour of gravy with a few very simple ingredients.

Double cream:
The easiest way of improving gravy. Cook with the gravy (to thicken it). Makes sauces lighter in colour and milder in flavour.

Butter:
Just before serving whisk chilled butter flakes into the hot gravy. Do not boil after this point. Butter gives the gravy an excellent flavour and makes it light and creamy.

Soured cream or crème fraîche:
Simply stir into the hot gravy. Thickens and adds a slightly sour flavour.

Sugar colouring:
If the gravy is too light in colour use sugar colouring to make it darker. You can buy sugar colouring ready-made, but it is quite easy to make too.

To make it, place 1 table-spoon sugar in a small pan and cook until dark brown over a high heat. Then dilute with $\frac{1}{2}$ cup water or malt beer and add to the gravy. You can make sugar colouring for the store cupboard. Surprisingly it does not sweeten.

Concentrated tomato purée:
Thickens, gives a slightly acid flavour and a strong red colour.

Seasonings

What is true of herbs is equally true of seasonings – better too little than too much. You can always increase the seasoning ultimately – but you can do nothing about over-seasoned food!

Ideally a seasoning should bring out the taste of the roast, never mask it.

Of the seasonings illustrated use cloves, bay leaves and juniper berries sparingly, for even a small quantity adds a lot of flavour.

Stuffings

Many joints can be improved with either sweet or savoury fillings. Two suggestions:

Dried fruit:
Rinse plums, apricots, apples in hot water and soak in hot water for 30 minutes. Cut a slit in boneless shoulder of pork and fill with the drained fruit. Sew up with a needle and cooking twine. Brown the pork and then roast with a little added liquid in a very hot oven (240C, 475F, gas 9) for $1\frac{1}{4}$ hours.

Duxelles:
For this savoury stuffing, mix chopped onion with crumbled white bread, chopped mushrooms and parsley in equal quantities. The onions and mushrooms should first be fried in a little butter and seasoned to taste. An excellent stuffing for beef fillet, which can then be cooked in puff pastry (e.g. Beef Wellington).

Three favourite casseroles

As with stews, every country, every region in fact, has its own speciality casseroles. Many are so typical of the region that you could use them as the basis of maps. But the real crown should go to those housewives who offer their friends and guests something really personal.

Osso buco
(illustrated below)

salt and pepper

4 slices leg of veal on the bone (3–5 cm/$\frac{1}{8}$–$\frac{1}{4}$ in thick)

4 tablespoons flour

4 tablespoons olive oil

2 onions

2 sticks celery

2 carrots

4 small tomatoes

1 clove garlic, crushed

150 ml/$\frac{1}{4}$ pint dry white wine

150 ml/$\frac{1}{4}$ pint water

1 teaspoon oregano

1. Season the veal and coat lightly in flour. Brown both sides in the hot olive oil.
2. Chop the vegetables and brown with the veal.
3. Peel, deseed and chop the tomatoes. Add to the meat with the garlic, wine, water and seasoning to taste.

4. Stir occasionally to prevent the osso buco sticking to the pan.
5. Cook for 1$\frac{1}{2}$ hours in a covered pan.

Rabbit with prunes
(illustrated top right)

4 rabbit portions

4 tablespoons butter

300 ml/$\frac{1}{2}$ pint red wine

150 ml/$\frac{1}{4}$ pint water

400 g/14 oz prunes

salt and pepper

1. Fry the rabbit in the butter over a moderate heat until golden brown.
2. Add the liquid and prunes and season to taste.
3. Cook in a covered pan for 40–45 minutes.
4. You do not need to thicken the sauce as the prunes fall to give the cooking sauce a creamy consistency. Serve with noodles or spätzle (see pages 82–3).

Rhenish marinated beef
(illustrated bottom right)

Before cooking the beef has to be marinated. This makes the texture less dense, makes the meat more tender and the cooking time shorter as well as giving the dish its typical taste.

1 kg/2$\frac{1}{4}$ lb boned topside of beef

For the marinade:

2 onions, chopped

1 carrot, chopped

1 piece celeriac, chopped

300 ml/$\frac{1}{2}$ pint red wine vinegar

300 ml/$\frac{1}{2}$ pint water

1 bay leaf

2 cloves

3 juniper berries

1 teaspoon peppercorns

2 allspice

salt and pepper

Steep the beef in the marinade for 3–5 days. It is essential that the marinade completely covers the beef.
For roasting:

4 tablespoons oil

1 small onion, chopped

2 carrots, chopped

600 ml/1 pint liquid (water or wine)

100 g/4 oz pumpernickel

50 g/2 oz raisins

salt and pepper

1. After marinating dry the beef thoroughly and brown all over in the hot oil.
2. Add the onion and carrot then the liquid.
3. Cover the pan and cook for 2–2$\frac{1}{2}$ hours, turning the meat frequently and adding more liquid as and when necessary.
4. Strain the gravy. Crumble the pumpernickel and simmer in the gravy with the raisins for 5 minutes. If preferred, flavour the gravy with a little of the marinade. Serve with: potato croquettes (see page 118) and apple sauce.

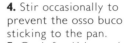

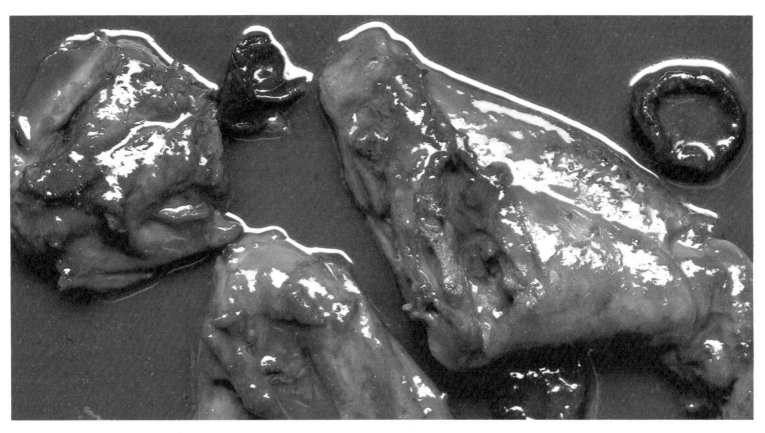

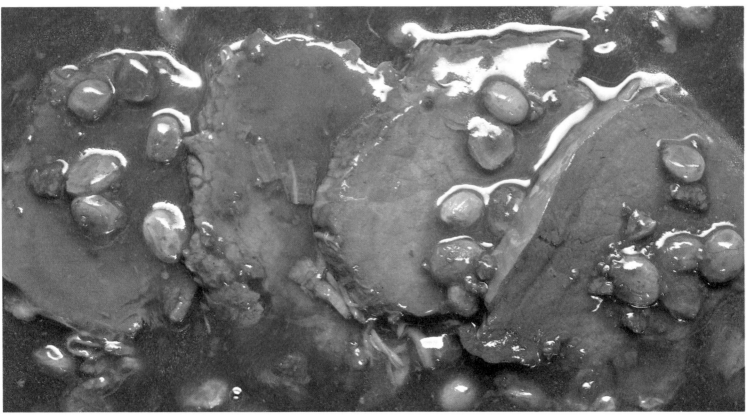

Hungarian goulash

(illustrated right)

575 g/ 1¼ lb braising steak
4 tablespoons olive oil
2 medium tomatoes
350 g/ 12 oz onion
1 clove garlic, crushed
2 tablespoons sweet paprika
salt and pepper
generous pinch of ground
caraway (optional)
1 litre/ 2 pints water
2 red peppers
350 g/ 12 oz potatoes

1. Cube and brown the meat in the hot oil over a high heat.
2. Add the peeled tomatoes and coarsely chopped onion and garlic.
3. Sprinkle with the paprika and fry for a few minutes over a low heat.
4. Add the remaining seasoning and stir in the water.
5. Cover the pan and simmer the goulash over a low heat for 1½–2 hours. Add strips of pepper and cubes of potato 30 minutes before the end of the cooking time. You can improve the flavour of the goulash with a dash of red wine or with cream.

Tempting casseroles from Hungary

We could spend a whole chapter discussing the multitude of sins covered by the term goulash in many a restaurant, but what makes a genuine goulash is a point argued even by Hungarians – and they invented the dish! Between ourselves, every Budapest housewife has her own special recipe. Why not follow their example!

Pork goulash

2 tablespoons pork dripping
575 g / 1¼ lb neck or shoulder
pork, diced
1 tablespoon flour
100 g / 4 oz bacon, diced
225 g / 8 oz onion, chopped
salt and pepper
600 ml / 1 pint water
225 g / 8 oz mushrooms
1 tablespoon soured cream

1. Heat the dripping in a
large pan and brown the
meat.
2. Sprinkle with the flour
and add the bacon and
onion.
3. Season to taste and stir in
the water.
4. Simmer over a low heat
for 1–1½ hours.
5. Add the cleaned,
quartered mushrooms 10
minutes before the end of
the cooking time. Stir in the
soured cream.

Variation:
You can vary pork goulash
by adding meatballs (see
pages 214–15), green
peppers or peas and stirring
in 2 tablespoons rice 20
minutes before the end of
the cooking time.

Goulash

An inexpensive meat dish which can be
varied in a host of ways by adding
peppers, onion, tomatoes, sweet corn,
mushrooms and seasonings such as
ground caraway, lemon rind, paprika,
chilli, bay leaves and star aniseed.

An authentic Hungarian goulash should
be made entirely with beef, but it is just
as good made with pork (e.g. neck or leg)
or a mixture of pork, beef and offal (e.g.
ox heart or kidney).

Mexican pepper pot

Add chillies, sweet corn and red kidney
beans. Make as Hungarian goulash but
omit the potatoes.

Italian casserole

Same recipe as Hungarian goulash but
omitting the potato and ground caraway.
Add aubergines, courgettes, fennel or
artichoke hearts and season with thyme,
rosemary and sage.

Rolled meat for braising

The concept is as simple as it is delicious: stuffing meat by slicing, rolling and securing in place. Meat rolls offer the most variety of all casserole dishes. And they are one of the least expensive. You don't need the best meat, and a good butcher will cut the meat nice and thin for you.

Basic recipe for beef rolls

A classic meat roll is made with beef. Flatten the beef with the ball of your hand and season. Arrange the filling on the beef to leave a narrow border all round. Roll up the meat and secure with a wooden cocktail stick. Alternatively you can tie them with kitchen string or use a special clamp. Brown the rolls in hot fat (2 tablespoons oil). As with pot roasted joints (see pages 230–1) you can add vegetables (e.g. leeks and carrots). This improves the flavour of the gravy and makes it thicker. Half-cover with liquid (water and red wine). Cover the pan and simmer for $1\frac{1}{2}$–2 hours. Stir soured cream into the gravy and season to taste. (For other ways of improving the sauce see pages 234–5).

Tip:
Beef rolls are excellent cooked in a pressure cooker, and take only 15 minutes to cook.

Rolled veal

Brown in butter over a moderate heat. Half-cover with water and possibly white wine, cover the pan and cook over a moderate heat for 10–15 minutes. Thicken the sauce with double cream and/or butter (see page 235).

Filling 1

(per roll)

2 pieces of bacon
1 teaspoon prepared mustard
1 small onion, sliced
1 gherkin, sliced
salt and pepper

Filling 2

(per roll)

1 slice boiled ham
1 tablespoon cream cheese
2 mushrooms, sliced
leek rings
salt and pepper
sprigs of thyme

Filling 3

(per roll)

1 slice uncooked ham
1 slice Swiss cheese
1 tablespoon spinach, blanched
1 small clove garlic, sliced
salt and pepper
2 sage leaves

Filling 4

(per roll)

2 tablespoons sauerkraut
$\frac{1}{4}$ red pepper, cut into strips
salt and pepper
sprigs of parsley

Large roasts

Over the centuries artists have delighted in representing feasts and groaning tables with large roasts as the centre-point: for example legs of lamb or saddles of venison. Cooks have played their part in turning these dishes into showpieces, all of which is quite superfluous. You will realise this if you serve a roast for a special occasion. The effect can be compared only with that of serving a whole fish (see page 170), although the smell is even more tempting . . .

Cooking test

To check that the meat is cooked, stick a long thin knife or metal skewer into the thickest part of the joint. Leave it in for a few seconds. If the point of the knife feels cold when you take it out the meat is still raw at the centre. You can buy meat thermometers which measure the temperature inside the joint more precisely.

Descriptions of the various grades of cooking are given in the steak chapter (see page 200).

Basic recipe for herby leg of lamb

(illustrated right)
Serves 4–6

4 tablespoons fresh chopped herbs, or 2 tablespoons dried (thyme, rosemary, basil, parsley)
8 tablespoons olive oil
1 (2-kg/$4\frac{1}{4}$-lb) leg of lamb
4 cloves garlic, unpeeled
6 tomatoes
300 ml/$\frac{1}{2}$ pint water or white wine
salt and pepper

1. Stir the herbs into half the olive oil and spread over the lamb. Leave to stand for 4 hours at room temperature to allow the flavour to penetrate.
2. Pour the remaining oil into a shallow roasting tin, and place the lamb and unpeeled garlic in the tin.
3. Place in a hot oven (230C, 450F, gas 8) and allow 15 minutes per 450 g/ 1 lb weight. For a 2 kg/$4\frac{1}{4}$ lb leg this would be $2\frac{1}{4}$ hours, and the meat would be still pink inside. If you prefer your meat well done allow 20 minutes per 450 g/1 lb.
4. Baste the lamb from time to time with the herby oil.

5. Place the tomatoes in the roasting tin 15 minutes before the end of the cooking time and add the liquid (water or white wine) to dilute the roasting juices.
6. Take the lamb out of the oven, wrap in aluminium foil and leave to stand for 10 minutes.
7. Meanwhile transfer the tomatoes to a warm plate and serve the gravy with the lamb.
8. Serve with: herby potatoes, small thyme potatoes tossed in butter, fried potatoes or simply French bread. Green beans are also excellent with lamb.

Saddle of lamb

Saddle of lamb is cooked in almost exactly the same way as a leg. Place fat side undermost in a roasting tin. Set the oven at hot (220C, 425F, gas 7) and place the lamb in the heated oven. After 10 minutes turn the lamb over and reduce the oven to moderate (180C, 350F, gas 4). Roast for a further 20–30 minutes.

Roast beef

Large pieces of beef can be cooked in the same way as leg of lamb. In this case the garlic is optional. For medium-cooked roast beef allow 15 minutes per 450g/1 lb in a hot oven (220C, 425F, gas 7). If you prefer beef well done, increase the cooking time accordingly. When the temperature inside the meat reaches 65C/150F (on a roasting thermometer) then it is done to a turn.

Saddle of venison

Set the oven at hot (220C, 425F, gas 7). Season the meat and brown in the hot oven for 10 minutes. Reduce the oven to moderate (180C, 350F, gas 4) and roast until cooked. Allow 8 minutes per 450g/ 1 lb, including the browning time. Don't forget to baste the meat frequently with butter as it soon dries out. Dilute the roasting juices with red wine, strain the gravy and stir in a little cranberry or redcurrant jelly to thicken.

Traditionally saddle of venison is served with spätzle (see page 83) or croquette potatoes (see page 118).

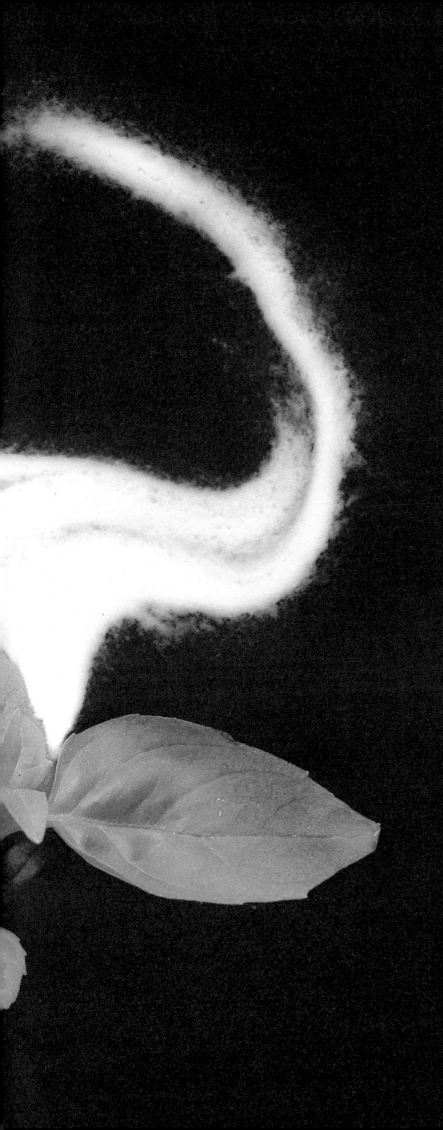

Sauces:
the height
of enjoyment

If one reads only a few of the numerous stories and legends which surround sauces one soon comes to believe that there is some magic and mystery here. The devotion with which great masters like Carême and Escoffier spent years thinking up and perfecting sauces was something akin to a cult, and had a unique outcome. 'French chefs owe their reputation to sauces', said Michel Guérard, the superstar of nouvelle cuisine. And he went on, 'The sauce chef is their magician!' It needs clever fingers, a dash of imagination, a pinch of daring, a touch of recklessness, together with a whole arsenal of useful rules, tricks and secrets.

The five main techniques

If you want to make your way in the wonderful world of sauces, you must first master the five techniques shown here. When you have done this, there will open up before you a culinary landscape of unlimited possibilities. Many famous sauces are no more than variations on one of these basic methods. Once you have developed a real interest in cooking it is only natural that you will want to invent your own sauces. You will soon discover for yourself the curious and exciting fact that the same sauce tastes different every time.

Roux

Roux is made by heating butter or margarine, adding flour and cooking until it stops forming bubbles.

For a brown roux, the flour is stirred until brown in colour.

Basic dark sauce

Brown roux diluted with stock or water.

White sauces

Roux diluted with a variety of liquids such as water, milk, coconut milk, vegetable stock (cauliflower or asparagus water), fish or meat stock, and then made into tasty light sauces.

Béchamel sauce

Béchamel sauce is a white sauce made with milk (see step-by-step photographs for basic white sauce, right).

In the classic béchamel sauce recipe, I small onion and a little thyme is fried with the butter (photograph 1). The finished sauce is seasoned with a little nutmeg. Basic béchamel sauce can be improved by adding cream, crème fraîche (or soured cream), butter or wine, or varied by adding grated horseradish or onion, or chopped mushrooms.

Beurre blanc

White butter sauce
Ingredients:

5 shallots

300 ml/½ pint dry white wine

100 g/4 oz cold butter

salt and pepper

(see page 250)

Hollandaise sauce

Ingredients:

225 g/8 oz butter

2 egg yolks

4 tablespoons white wine

juice of ½ lemon

salt and white pepper

(see pages 254–5)

Béchamel sauce

Basic white sauce
Ingredients:

25 g/1 oz butter

25 g/1 oz flour

300 ml/½ pint milk

salt and white pepper

(see page 254)

Cream sauce

Ingredients:

150 ml/¼ pint dry white wine

600 ml/1 pint double cream

1 tablespoon butter

salt and white pepper

(see page 259)

Gravy

Ingredients:

150 ml/¼ pint dry white or red wine

300 ml/½ pint double cream

1 tablespoon butter

salt and pepper

(see page 260)

1. Finely chop the shallots and tip into a pan.

2. Add the dry white wine.

1. Melt the butter over a moderate heat.

2. Boil, and spoon off the scum.

1. Melt the butter over a moderate heat.

2. Sprinkle on the flour.

1. Pour the wine into a pan.

2. Reduce by half over a moderate heat.

1. Dilute the roasting gravy with the wine.

2. Reduce.

246

 **3.** Bring the wine and shallots to the boil over a high heat.

 **4.** Evaporate off almost all the wine so that just the base of the pan is still moist.

 **5.** Add the cold butter in pieces.

 **6.** Whisk in and season to taste.

 **3.** Tip the egg yolks and white wine into a metal bowl.

 **4.** Whisk over a pan of hot water (see page 37) until frothy.

 **5.** Whisking continuously, add the butter a few drops at a time.

 **6.** Season with the lemon juice, salt and pepper.

 **3.** Whisk over the heat until the mixture has no bubbles.

 **4.** Gradually whisk in the cold milk.

 **5.** Whisk vigorously, bring to the boil and season.

 **6.** Strain the sauce through a fine sieve.

 **3.** Add the double cream.

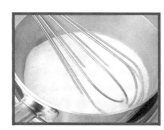 **4.** Whisk over a moderate heat to reduce by half.

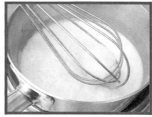 **5.** Add the butter and whisk in thoroughly.

 **6.** Season to taste.

 **3.** Pour in the double cream.

 **4.** Whisk and reduce by half.

 **5.** Off the heat stir in the butter. Do not boil beyond this stage.

 **6.** Season to taste.

Useful aids from the supermarket

Even professional chefs in large restaurants find it impossible to make all the ingredients for the many different sauces. How much more true this is of the amateur cook! Since the early days of the first stock or bouillon cube, the food industry has made enormous advances with ready-made products.

Instant products

If you are in a hurry you can tip powder into a pan, add water, bring to the boil – and the sauce is made. In instant form you can buy: light and dark gravies, mushroom, onion, tomato or red wine sauce. These sauces can of course never replace home-made ones, so only use them when absolutely unavoidable! More acceptable short cuts are provided, on the other hand, by stock cubes (chicken, beef, fish and vegetable) when you have no stock available (see page 260).

Dressings

There is a wide choice of ready-made salad dressings, usually with a mayonnaise, cream or yogurt base. You can also buy marinades which combine vinegar, oil and seasoning.

Nevertheless there is nothing simpler or more individual than making a classic dressing yourself.

Main types of oil:
Olive oil (best is the first pressing – virgin oil)
Walnut oil
Hazelnut oil
Grapeseed oil
Vegetable oil
In addition there are special oils containing herbs, but these are really intended for flavouring grills.

Main types of vinegar:
Sherry vinegar
Red wine vinegar
White wine vinegar
Aceto Balsamico (special Italian vinegar), matured in old wooden casks to give it its wonderful flavour.
In addition there are several herb vinegars (e.g. tarragon), lemon, raspberry, garlic vinegar, etc.

Ready-bought sauces

Often it is a question of time that prevents you whipping up your own mayonnaise. Sometimes, as with chutney or Cumberland sauce, the sauce may be too complicated or time consuming for you to make it yourself. In either case it is always possible to give bottled sauces a personal note by adding seasonings, herbs or other ingredients. Let us take mayonnaise as an example.
Mayonnaise can be turned into aioli by adding garlic (see page 149) or used as a basis for Thousand Island dressing (see page 141). Even *remoulade* is just a variation on mayonnaise – with gherkins, capers, anchovies and herbs added. And if you find mayonnaise too heavy try folding in whipped cream to give *mayonnaise Chantilly*. To serve with salted trout or salmon (see page 178) simply stir in hot mustard, a pinch of sugar and finely chopped dill.
Other bottled cold sauces:
Pesto (oil, pine nuts, basil, pecorino cheese, etc.) with pasta dishes.

Mint sauce (mint leaves, vinegar, sugar) with lamb.

Cumberland sauce (redcurrant jelly, orange rind, mustard) with game, cold meats or pies.

Chutney (ginger, mango, cucumber, apple, garlic, peppers) with grills.

Sweet sauces (chocolate, strawberry, nougat, etc.) with desserts.

Sauces for grills

The children at least would be upset if there were no ketchup! This bottled tomato sauce is almost a classic and its worldwide success has made it the basis of many variations (e.g. curry ketchup). Other sauces to serve with grills, beefburgers and fondues, as well as with pasta and chips are:

Chilli sauce
Pepper sauce
Ginger sauce
Barbecue sauce

Seasonings

Those new to cooking who are afraid that, despite detailed instructions, they will season marinated beef or goulash wrongly, can also find an answer to their problems in a range of ready-mixed seasonings.

You can buy seasoning mixtures which are not intended for one particular dish, the best-known of these is probably *herbes de Provence*, a herb mixture from the south of France which includes lavender and thyme and is sold in earthenware jars. This is excellent for grilled fish and savoury meat dishes. Both the *herbes* and other mixtures (e.g. Italian) can be used for salads after softening for 10 minutes in vinegar.

Liquid seasonings

This type of seasoning should be used in the same way as medicines – a few drops at a time. Most are so concentrated that using too much can ruin a whole meal. But in small quantities they can work real miracles.

The main ones are:
Tabasco (made from chillies and very hot) – for exotic dishes but also for *sauce à l'Américaine* and some cocktails.

Soy sauce (usually slightly salty, made from fermented soya shoots) – universal sauce with any Far Eastern dish and other rice, pastry, meat and poultry dishes. The world's oldest sauce.

Worcestershire sauce (sweet and sharp, made from a secret recipe) – with dark soups, Irish stew, kidneys, casseroles and Béarnaise sauce.

Other liquid seasonings: onion and garlic, Herbadox (herb flavour), Angostura Bitters (for cocktails) and the most universal of all seasonings, Maggi.

Seven methods of thickening sauces

1. Roux
This was once the main method used but is unpopular in modern cooking mainly because brown roux is fairly indigestible. See page 246 for method of preparation.

2. Cornflour or cornstarch
Another traditional method: dissolve 1 teaspoon cornflour in cold water and bring to the boil once in the sauce. Do not continue to boil or it will become thin again! Instant sauce thickeners are sprinkled directly into the boiling liquid.

3. Flour and butter
A method which combines all the advantages of flour as a thickener with the elegance of modern cooking techniques. Flour and butter (beurre manié) is made by working equal quantities of flour and butter into a ball. This is stirred into the sauce and boiled until the sauce is velvety.

4. Egg yolk
Not all sauces can be thickened with fresh egg yolks. They taste best in white sauces intended for poultry or fish. With the sauce off the heat, whisk in 1 egg yolk with 1 tablespoon cold water. Do not boil any more!

5. Butter
Thickening with butter is quite a difficult professional method. Chilled flaked butter is whisked into a much reduced sauce off the heat until the sauce begins to thicken. Excellent with fillet steak.

6. Cream or soured cream
The most popular method of binding for nouvelle cuisine. Tastes best without lengthy boiling. Crème fraîche can be used instead of soured cream. Double cream is even better for thickening sauces.

7. Purée
Avant-garde nouvelle cuisine chefs sometimes thicken sauces with finely puréed vegetables previously cooked with the stock. Excellent for those who are watching their waistlines.

The favourite of nouvelle cuisine

Cooking, like other areas, has become part of our everyday culture. Sometimes it is impossible to explain why old-fashioned ideas, apparently almost forgotten, come back into favour. Beurre blanc, white butter sauce, is a case in point. Nouvelle cuisine chefs have fitted it admirably into their concept of easily digestible menus, serving these quick sauces with blanched vegetables. Give it a try in either its red or white variation and you will be won over to it.

Beurre blanc

A fine sauce made with very few ingredients which is quick to make. Nevertheless things can go wrong if the liquid is not reduced sufficiently or if the butter is not whisked in quickly enough. Beurre blanc is excellent for dishes which produce no sauce of their own during cooking. Its flavour harmonises with almost any food as various seasonings can be added.

What to serve with beurre blanc

Natural beurre blanc (see illustration left) can be served with the following dishes:
1. With poached fish, e.g. sole, plaice, cod or salmon (see pages 168–9).
2. With white meat, e.g. veal, pork or poultry.
3. With fine vegetables, e.g. carrots, mangetout, peas, beans, cauliflower, spring onions and especially asparagus.

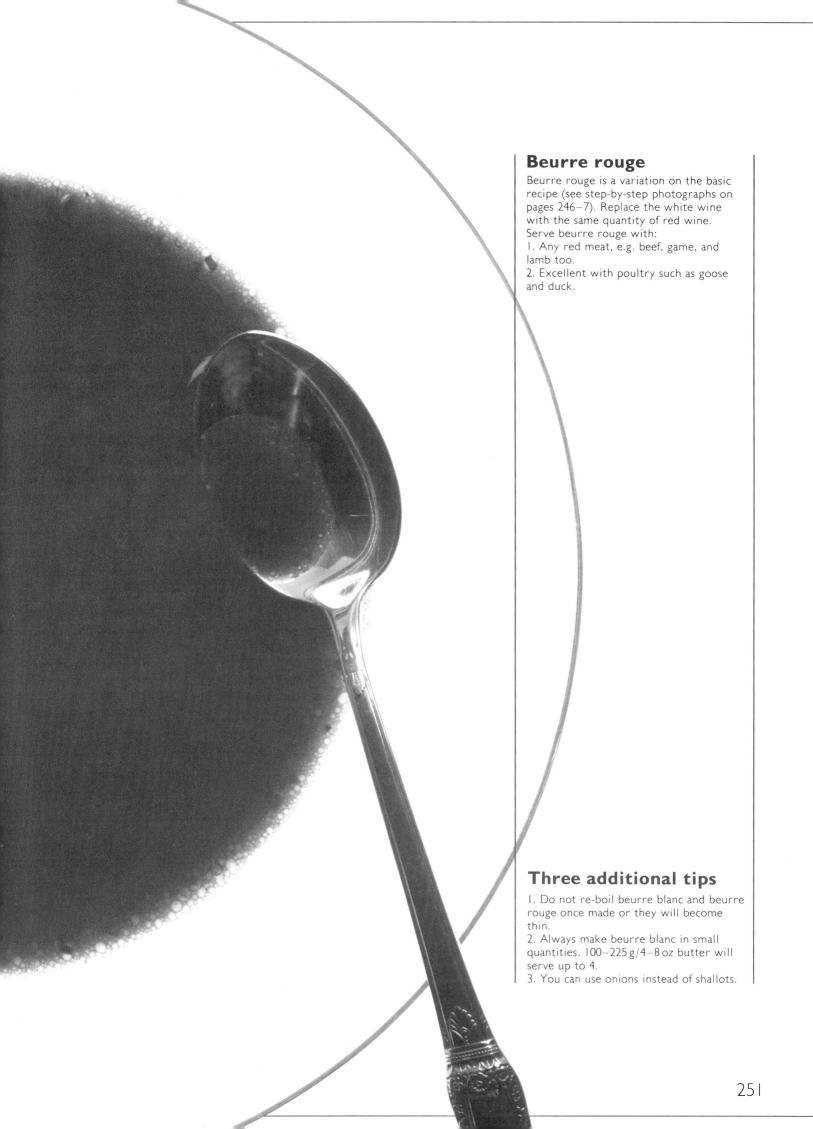

Beurre rouge

Beurre rouge is a variation on the basic recipe (see step-by-step photographs on pages 246–7). Replace the white wine with the same quantity of red wine. Serve beurre rouge with:
1. Any red meat, e.g. beef, game, and lamb too.
2. Excellent with poultry such as goose and duck.

Three additional tips

1. Do not re-boil beurre blanc and beurre rouge once made or they will become thin.
2. Always make beurre blanc in small quantities. 100–225 g/4–8 oz butter will serve up to 4.
3. You can use onions instead of shallots.

Juicy and full of flavour

Hot butters formed part of the basic equipment of our grandmothers' cooking. They have several great advantages. First they are easy to make, even for beginners. Secondly the basic recipe allows for a host of variations. Last but not least, butters are delicious with vegetables, fish and meat. There are also the cold butters (see page 114).

Basic recipe for clarified butter

100 g/4 oz butter
salt

1. Quickly boil the butter in a saucepan.
2. Using a skimmer take off the foam. This gives clarified butter.
3. Season with a little salt.

Five variations

1. Quickly brown clarified butter over a moderate heat.
2. Hard-boiled, finely chopped eggs.
3. Chopped capers, parsley and vinegar.
4. Chopped walnuts.
5. Finely chopped anchovies.

1. Tarragon butter

Add 1 tablespoon finely chopped tarragon to the clarified butter. Serve with boiled fish (illustrated below with halibut).

2. Herb and wine butter

Whisk in 1 tablespoon chopped herbs (parsley, chives, basil, thyme) with 2 tablespoons white wine. Serve with grilled or fried meat and vegetables.

5. Hazelnut butter

Crush 1 tablespoon hazelnuts with a rolling pin and fry quickly in the clarified butter. Serve with any sweetish vegetable such as broccoli (illustrated above), mangetout, carrots or with fried veal.

6. Breadcrumb butter

Fry 3 tablespoons bread-crumbs in the clarified butter. If the mixture is too thick add a little more butter. Serve with cauliflower (illustrated above), dumplings or pasta.

3. Garlic butter

Thinly slice 1 clove garlic
and stir into the clarified
butter. Serve with prawns
(illustrated below) or pasta.

4. Butter sauce

Serve clarified buter with
fine vegetables such as
asparagus (illustrated
below), mangetout, or with
fish or shellfish.

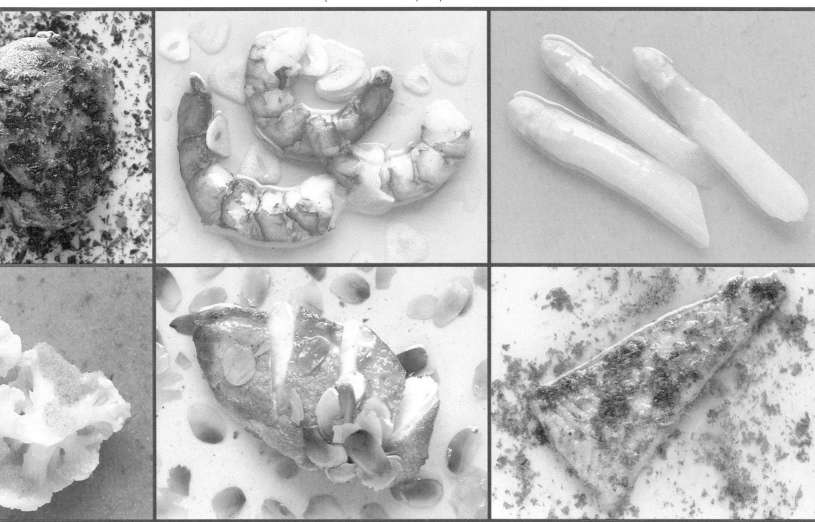

7. Almond
butter

Brown 2 tablespoons flaked
almonds in clarified butter
over a moderate heat and
serve with poultry
(illustrated above) or other
white meats.

8. Parsley and
lemon butter

Whisk 1 tablespoon
chopped parsley and the
juice of half a lemon into
the butter. Serve with fried
fish (illustrated above) or
vegetables.

Hollandaise sauce and variations upon the theme

Anyone with any experience of cooking will have heard the most awful stories about this, the most wonderful of all French sauces. To the complete beginner hollandaise sauce must appear like a culinary wall of death, which only the chosen few can master. Admittedly it is quite difficult the first time, but this is the price we have to pay when we tackle anything new. It is important to learn and master the basic technique and finer judgement will come naturally given time. Hollandaise sauce is a basis for several variations, which have also become world-famous.

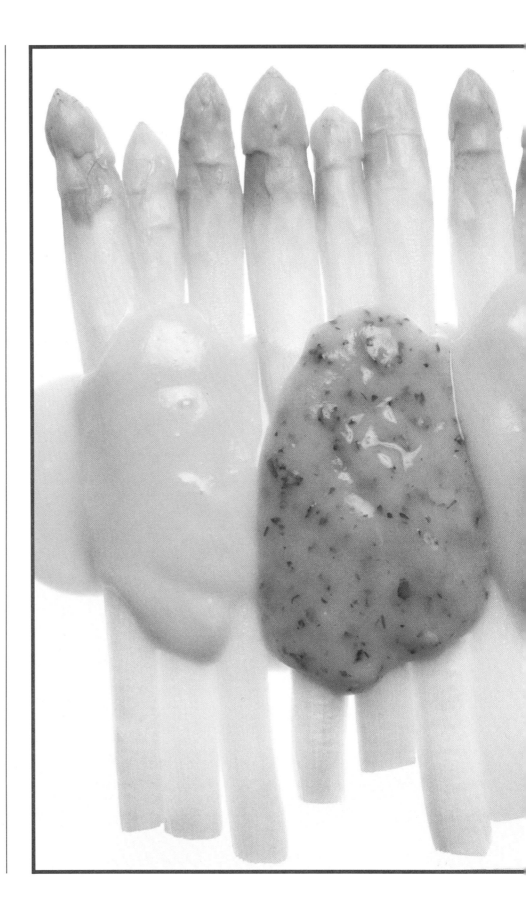

Hollandaise sauce

Classic method:
The basic cooking method (see page 246) shows the easy way to make this sauce. Authentic hollandaise sauce is made by the reducing method: reduce 300 ml/$\frac{1}{2}$ pint dry white wine and 3 tablespoons vinegar with 1 chopped shallot, 10 peppercorns and 1 teaspoon chopped tarragon to leave only 3 tablespoons liquid. Strain and use in place of the white wine.

Béarnaise sauce

Mix 2 tablespoons chopped chervil and tarragon with the basic hollandaise sauce. Season with a few dashes of Worcestershire sauce.
   Serve with any grilled or fried meat.

Maltese sauce

Mix the basic hollandaise sauce with the juice of a blood orange and grated orange rind.
   Served mainly with asparagus and artichokes.

Mousseline sauce

Mix 150 ml/$\frac{1}{4}$ pint whipped cream with the basic hollandaise sauce. Serve with boiled fish or fine vegetables.

Choron sauce

Stir 2–3 tablespoons concentrated tomato purée into the basic hollandaise sauce. Serve with any fried meat or fish.

Six points to watch

1. If the butter sauce is too hot it may curdle.
2. If the butter is stirred in too quickly it may curdle.
3. If the sauce does curdle stir in a few drops very cold water, stirring outwards from the centre.
4. If this does not solve the problem beat an egg yolk with 2 tablespoons cold water in a basin and gradually add to the curdled sauce.
5. Butter sauces can be kept warm in hot water, but only for a limited time.
6. Once cold the butter sauce cannot be reheated.

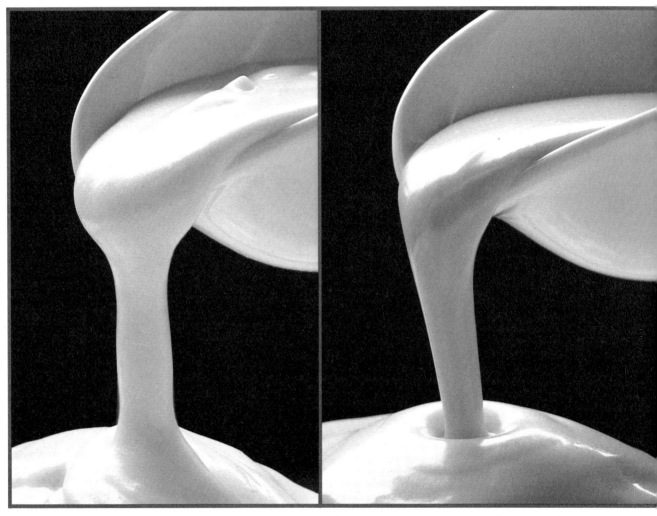

A nostalgia for white sauce

The fact that béchamel sauce has come to be regarded as 'pasty' is due almost entirely to those miserable chefs and ignorant amateur cooks whose lumpy, tasteless sauces have ruined a masterpiece of old-school cooking. It is of course true that béchamel sauce is not exactly slimming, but this is equally true of other dishes which have maintained their popularity. Have a try at our basic recipe (see pages 246–7) and maybe you will be converted.

Cheese sauce

Mornay sauce
Flavour the basic white sauce (see pages 246–7) with I tablespoon grated Gruyère, Parmesan or other strongly flavoured cheese and add an egg yolk to make the sauce more velvety (see page 155). Delicious with pasta or vegetables and also suitable for browning under the grill.

Mustard sauce

With the basic white sauce (see pages 246–7) mix I tablespoon medium-hot prepared mustard and I tablespoon butter. Serve with fried or poached fish, hard-boiled eggs or minced meat.

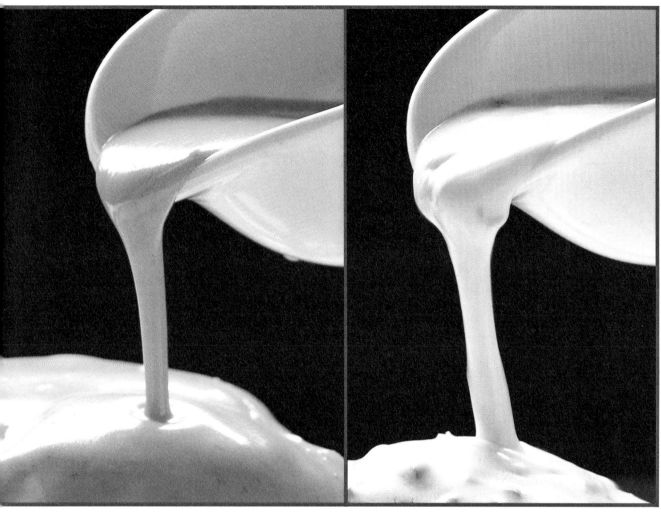

Curry sauce

Replace the milk in the basic white sauce recipe with coconut milk (see page 171). Flavour with 1 tablespoon curry powder, 1 tablespoon apple purée and 2 tablespoons sweetened cream.

Delicious with poultry, boiled fish, mince, rice, hard-boiled or poached eggs.

Curry sauce can be varied by adding fresh ginger, mango chutney and sugar.

Chive sauce

Stir 2 tablespoons chopped chives, a little lemon juice and 1 tablespoon soured cream into the basic white sauce. Serve with boiled fish, pasta or boiled meat.

Three tips

1. Any white sauce can be made smoother by adding cream, soured cream, butter or egg yolk to it.
2. To prevent lumps, always add cold liquid to the roux and whisk in thoroughly.
3. White sauce can be made in advance, stored and reheated.

Variations on cream sauce

These sauces are fun to make; nothing can go wrong! They are also very easy to make and give extremely impressive results. Cream sauces have taken over from béchamel in popularity. They are not too thick, and are very tasty. The basic method is extremely simple, with cream and wine reduced to give the sauce a little body.

Tomato sauce

Peel, deseed and purée 2 tomatoes and add to the cream sauce, or alternatively simply stir in 1 tablespoon concentrated tomato purée. Flavour with brandy or add 1 teaspoon chopped basil.

Serve with pasta or grilled white meat.

Herb sauce

Into the basic cream sauce (see pages 246–7) stir 2 tablespoons finely chopped fresh herbs (e.g. chervil, basil, thyme, chives, parsley) and season with freshly milled pepper.

Serve with fish, pasta, poached eggs or poultry.

Roquefort sauce

Mix 50 g/2 oz crumbled blue cheese with the cream sauce.

This tasty cheese sauce is delicious with ravioli, tortellini, noodles or fried meat.

Four tricks for cream sauces

1. Cream easily boils over, so stir frequently and use a deep pan.
2. Do not over-reduce the sauce or it will separate.
3. Replace part of the cream with soured cream or crème fraîche for a thicker, slightly sour flavour.
4. For a really light, airy sauce fold in whipped cream just before serving.

Saffron cream sauce

Add 1 generous pinch ground saffron strands or saffron powder when making the cream sauce.

This gives the sauce a good yellow colour and a slight saffron flavour. Delicious with fine fish.

Sorrel sauce

Sort, wash, coarsely chop and purée 50 g/2 oz fresh sorrel. Stir into the finished sauce and season with lemon juice and white pepper.

Serve with prawns, scampi, fried veal or eggs.

Seven further variations

Basic cream sauce recipe plus:
1. 2 tablespoons chopped chanterelles.
2. 2 tablespoons chopped cèpes.
3. 1 tablespoon chopped tarragon.
4. 2 tablespoons red wine.
5. 1 tablespoon grated Gruyère cheese.
6. Greatly reduce 300 ml/$\frac{1}{2}$ pint fresh orange juice and use in place of the wine in the basic recipe.
7. Use beetroot juice or puréed beetroot to give the cream sauce an unusual colour and flavour.

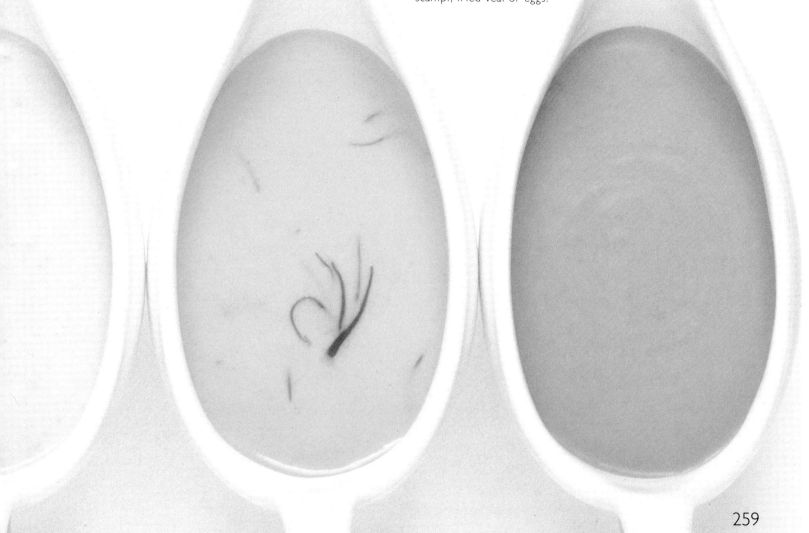

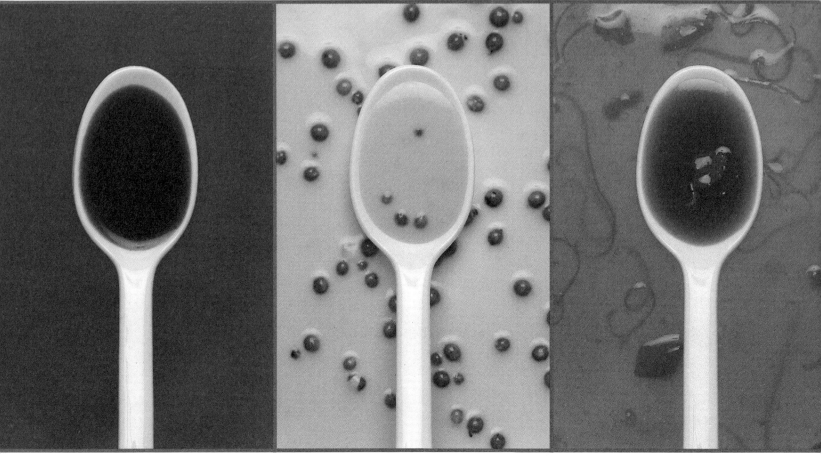

The simplest way

Finally, after so many complicated sauces we come to the easiest, but by no means the least tasty. Gravies are made from the roasting juices from the meat. The adding of liquid and the subsequent reduction can, of course, be combined with the cream sauce method and this gives the best gravy of all. This is an area where you can find your own method.

Red wine sauce with beef

Dilute the roasting juices with red wine, reduce and stir in 1 tablespoon butter.

Green pepper sauce with pork

Dilute the roasting juices with 2–3 tablespoons Calvados. Add 150 ml/ ¼ pint single cream and 2 teaspoons green peppercorns.

Orange sauce with poultry

Add 300 ml/½ pint orange juice to the roasting juices and reduce by half. Flavour with 1 teaspoon marmalade and bind with 1 tablespoon butter.

White wine sauce with veal

Dilute the roasting juices with 150 ml/¼ pint dry white wine and thicken with 2–3 tablespoons crème fraîche or soured cream.

Cranberry sauce with game

Dilute the roasting juices with 150 ml/¼ pint port. Stir in 1 tablespoon cranberries and 1 tablespoon butter.

Sherry and mint sauce with lamb

Dilute with 150 ml/¼ pint dry sherry. Add 1 teaspoon chopped mint, 1 tablespoon peeled, chopped tomato and 1 chopped clove of garlic. Bind with 1 tablespoon butter.
Tip: Further suggestions can be found on pages 210–11 and 234–5.

Tricks you should know

1. Always start by pouring the hot fat out of the roasting tin or pan. It is indigestible and makes the gravy bitter.
2. Do not add too much liquid (basic rule: 1 steak = 150 ml/¼ pint). You can always add more if necessary.
3. Always season gravy after reducing, for reducing makes the flavour of the seasoning much stronger.
4. Spirits should be boiled off or flamed otherwise the cream will curdle.

What is a 'fond'?

Professional chefs use fonds to prepare or increase the flavour of sauces. The term fonds covers meat stock, concentrated stock, chicken, game or fish stock and the basic great sauces.

To make fonds, brown bones, gristle, sinews and other meat offcuts in fat in the oven. Add carrot, onion, leek and celeriac. Stir in water or wine. Transfer all the ingredients to a saucepan, add sufficient water to cover and simmer for 4–5 hours, removing scum and fat from time to time.

Strain and then reduce the liquid for several hours to give a syrupy consistency (*glacé*).

Fonds can be made from beef, veal, game or poultry and bones.

For fish stock see page 174.

Desserts: finales with finesse

As contented guests sit around the table feeling comfortably full it is time for the grand finale – dessert. This is the great conclusion to a good meal and should appeal to all the senses at once – through colour and shape, smell and flavour. You can give your imagination free range here. When the can-can was all the rage in Paris actual mountains of coloured meringue were carried in from which emerged a scantily clad female. Whether you could achieve a similar effect with apple purée is doubtful to say the least! But between these two extremes there are a hundred ways of pleasing anybody with a sweet tooth.

Five sweets to start you off

Of course there are many other ways of entering the popular realm of desserts, but most are so complicated to describe and to make that you would be sure to lose your way. There is good reason why the cooking of sweet pastries has produced a highly regarded specialist – the pâtissier. With the five methods shown here you will be well on the way! Especially if you buy the ice cream to go with them. Ice cream available in supermarkets or other shops is now of very good quality.

Seven rules for gelatine

1. Gelatine is a setting agent obtained from animals. It is available in leaf or powder form in white or red.
2. Soften leaf gelatine for about 10 minutes in cold water and squeeze out before using. Powdered gelatine is stronger. Follow the manufacturer's instructions.
3. Always dissolve in hot liquid.
4. If the milk and egg mixture becomes too solid before you have added the cream, repeat the process. Warm the mixture in a pan of hot water, stirring continuously and again leave to cool.
5. You can tell when the mixture is beginning to set because a whisk will leave stripes behind as you draw it through the mixture.
6. The amount of gelatine you use will determine how long it takes to set and how solid it becomes.
7. If you do not intend turning the dessert out you will need only 7–9 leaves or $15 \, g/\frac{1}{2}$ oz powdered gelatine for the basic recipe. If you want to turn the dessert out use 10–12 leaves or $20 \, g/\frac{3}{4}$ oz powdered gelatine.

Compote

450 g/1 lb apricots
300 ml/$\frac{1}{2}$ pint white wine
3 tablespoons sugar
1 stick cinnamon
(see also pages 266–7)

1. Blanch the apricots for 2–3 minutes in boiling water depending on ripeness.

2. Peel using a small knife.

Fruit purée

450 g/1 lb strawberries
1 tablespoon icing sugar
(see also page 268)

1. Wash and hull the strawberries.

2. Using a spoon, press the strawberries through a fine sieve.

Sorbet

oranges to make 1 litre/
2 pints juice
2–3 tablespoons icing sugar
to taste
(see also pages 270–1)

1. Halve the oranges, squeeze the juice and sweeten with the sugar.

2. Place in the freezer for at least 3 hours.

Chocolate mousse

175 g/6 oz plain chocolate
3 eggs
600 ml/1 pint double cream
2–3 tablespoons liqueur or
rum to taste (optional)
(see also page 269)

1. Break up the chocolate and melt in a basin over hot water.

2. Whisk the eggs over hot water until frothy and add the liqueur if used.

Bavarian cream

1 vanilla pod
600 ml/1 pint milk
4 egg yolks
175 g/6 oz sugar
8 leaves gelatine, soaked or
20 g/$\frac{3}{4}$ oz powdered gelatine
600 ml/1 pint double cream
(see also pages 272–3)

1. Slit the vanilla pod and bring to the boil in the milk.

2. In a large bowl whisk the egg yolks with the sugar.

 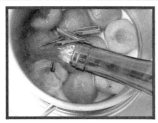  

3. Halve and stone the apricots.

4. Place in a pan with the wine and cinnamon.

5. Sprinkle on the sugar.

6. Boil over a moderate heat for 3 minutes (or more depending on the fruit used).

3. Add the icing sugar to taste.

4. Stir thoroughly into the fruit purée.

   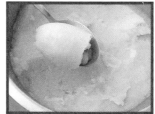

3. Remove from the freezer and defrost for 2 minutes.

4. Break up using a blunt knife.

5. Blend until the sorbet is smooth then re-freeze.

6. Divide into small portions using a spoon or ice-cream scoop.

 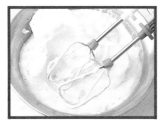 

3. Remove the bowl from the water and stir the chocolate into the eggs.

4. Whip the cream until stiff.

5. Fold a third of the cream into the chocolate mixture and then the remainder.

  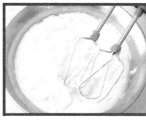 

3. Gradually add the hot milk then remove the vanilla pod.

4. Add the squeezed out leaf gelatine (or dissolved powdered gelatine) and whisk over ice until cold.

5. Whip the cream until stiff.

6. Fold into the mixture when it begins to set.

Apricot compote

Cook the fruit with water (or white wine), a cinnamon stick and sugar as shown in the step-by-step photographs. Flavour the compote with 1 teaspoon apricot jam.

Blackberry compote

Simmer the fruit with juice and sugar over a low heat for 5 minutes.

Pear compote
Cover small peeled pears
with 300 ml/½ pint red wine
and 300 ml/½ pint water.
Add 1 teaspoon black-
currant jelly and simmer
over a low heat for 45
minutes.

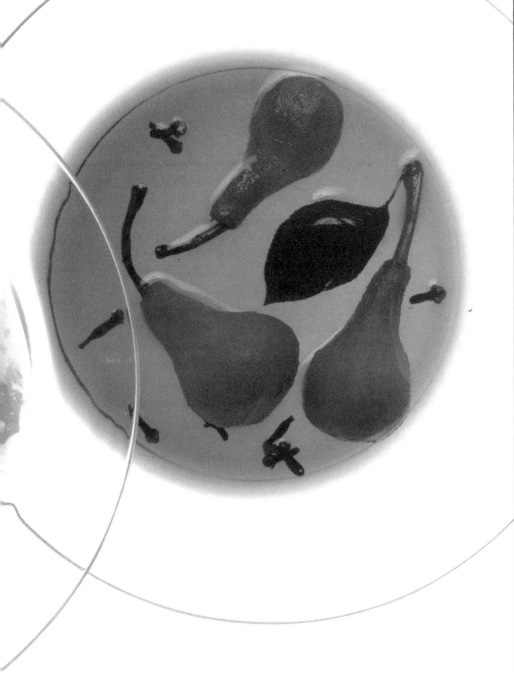

Fine fruits

Compote is like potatoes; both can be
extremely uninteresting unless prepared
with some care. Yet both can give a lot of
pleasure if a little imagination goes into
them. With compote it is important to
remember that the fruit should retain its
shape, colour and flavour as far as
possible.

Three tips

1. Sprinkle peeled apples and pears with
lemon juice to prevent them going
brown.
2. Compote can also be made with dried
fruit which should first be soaked for 2
hours in warm water.
3. Good combinations:
Plums with Armagnac, apples with
Calvados, pears with pear liqueur, yellow
plums with apricot liqueur, peaches with
Cointreau, raisins with rum.

Adding flavour

(For basic recipe see pages 264–5)
Cook the fruit in red or white wine,
port, sherry, fruit juice or water
according to taste. Flavourings such as
cinnamon, vanilla, cloves, lemon or
orange rind, or ginger, can be used to
vary the flavour. Compote can be served
with ice cream, cream, Bavarian cream,
crème fraîche, yogurt or on its own.

Popular compotes

Fruits suitable for compote include
strawberries, rhubarb, yellow plums,
peaches, plums, apples, figs, morello
cherries, pumpkin, mangoes, gooseberries
and grapes.

A play on colour

Purées make the fruitiest sauces you could require for your desserts. Add no liquid if you want to keep the full flavour of the fruit. Purées not only taste delicious they also make desserts look extremely attractive. Emphasise colour contrasts. Combine several purées together or with ice cream, cream or yogurt. Let colours run subtly into one another. In other words, give free rein to your imagination!

Basic rules

Always pass fruit through a very fine sieve to remove pips and fibres. This gives a very fine fruit pulp. It is a good idea to first purée the fruit using a blender or food processor.

Fruit soups

(For basic recipe see pages 264–5.)
It is easy to turn fruit purées into fruit soups by adding yogurt, milk, fruit juice, crème fraîche, fresh fruit and decorating with a sprig of mint or lemon balm.

Popular purées

The following fruits are excellent for purées: strawberries, raspberries, blackberries, blueberries, cranberries, red and blackcurrants, mangoes, kiwis, apricots, papayas and passion fruit.

Illustrated far right top: Chocolate mousse with kiwi purée, raspberries and grated chocolate.

Illustrated far right centre: Vanilla ice cream with apricot purée and praline.

Illustrated far right bottom: Kiwi and strawberry fruit salad with blackberry purée and mint leaves.

Illustrated right: Mango, raspberry, strawberry and kiwi purées.

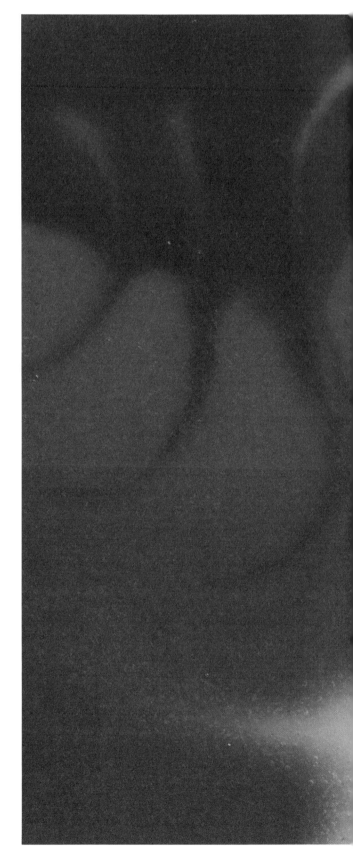

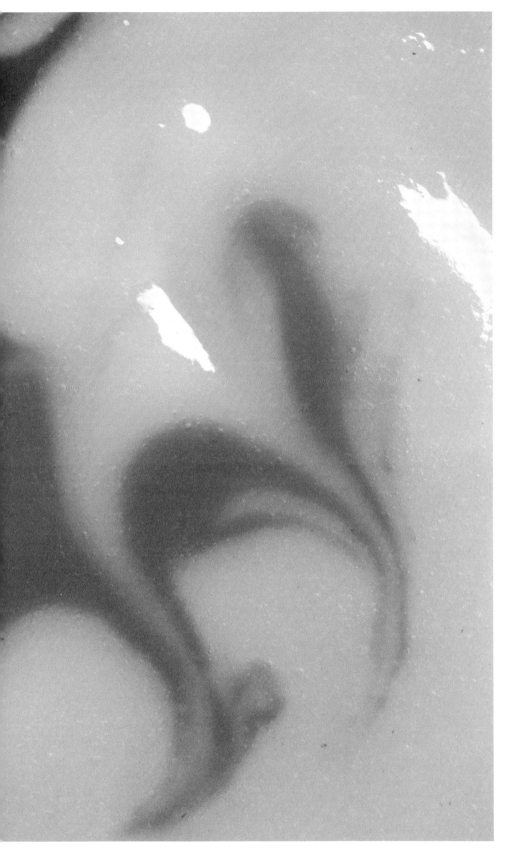

Ice makes its comeback

The ice referred to rather derogatively at the turn of the century as 'water ice' has made a glittering comeback with nouvelle cuisine under the more stylish name of 'sorbet'. Sorbets are no longer merely desserts, they have suddenly become extremely versatile. They are served, for instance, to clear the palate before the main course, or as a stylish cocktail to eat with a spoon, served in champagne or a sparkling or white wine. Young inventive chefs have created sorbets from beetroot, persimmons or yogurt. What can you come up with?

Fruits for sorbet

Any fruit that can be made into a purée is suitable for sorbet. Apple sorbet, for example, is made from pulped or ready-cooked apples.

Basic rules

Freeze fruit juices or purées, sweetened or unsweetened, in the freezer for at least 3 hours. You can, of course, use an ice cream or sorbet maker.

The sorbet should have a soft, smooth consistency. A sorbet made from 450 g/1 lb fruit or 600 ml/1 pint liquid will serve 4.
(For basic recipe see pages 264–5.)

Adding flavour

You can give sorbet an interesting flavour by adding champagne, sparkling wine or white wine to the fruit purée before freezing. Do not allow the alcohol to mask the flavour of the fruit, however.

What is sorbet?

The name comes from the Arabic (sherbet) and originally meant an iced fruit-juice drink. French chefs, and nouvelle cuisine chefs in particular, turned this into a water ice (without milk or cream). This was flavoured with fruit or vegetable concentrates and usually had alcohol added. It is also possible to make sorbets purely with alcohol (e.g. champagne). Sorbets should be of the consistency of snow and should begin to melt slowly after serving. It is easiest to make sorbet in a sorbet maker. If the sorbet becomes too hard it can be crushed and served as 'granita'!

Lime sorbet

Using lime juice, make a sorbet and season to taste with sugar and mint.

Strawberry sorbet

Make a purée with 450 g/ 1 lb strawberries and mix with 300 ml/$\frac{1}{2}$ pint sparkling wine. Freeze to make a sorbet.

Apricot sorbet

Purée 450 g/ 1 lb apricots as shown in the step-by-step photographs on pages 264– 5. Add sugar and 300 ml/$\frac{1}{2}$ pint sparkling wine. Freeze to make a sorbet. Serve in portions decorated with lemon balm.

Five useful tips

1. The sorbet will be smoother if you stir it frequently during freezing.
2. Sorbet should always be fluffed up before serving. This is easiest with a blender or fork.
3. Decorate with lemon balm, basil or mint.
4. As well as in glasses, you can serve sorbet in empty orange, lemon and melon skins. To prevent sorbet melting too quickly, frost skins or glasses in the freezer for 1 hour before use.
5. You can buy quite inexpensive sorbet makers which make really professional sorbets.

Redcurrant sorbet

Make a redcurrant purée as shown in the step-by-step photographs on pages 264–5 and then make into a sorbet. Serve in frosted glasses and decorate with whole redcurrants.

Coffee granita

Sweeten strong coffee with sugar and place in the freezer. Stir frequently as it freezes to prevent the liquid freezing into a solid block. The granita should resemble coarsely crushed ice. It can also be made with tea or fruit juice.

The crème de la crème

Despite its name, Bavarian cream is not a Bavarian but a French invention. It is a dessert fit for a king. It has a kind of noble power to it, but more importantly, after more than two hundred years of cooking and thousands of similar creams, Bavarian cream remains the real 'classic'. This fact speaks for itself. No pâtissier has so far been able to produce anything better from the same ingredients. Here are variations on the basic recipe given on pages 264–5.

Bilberry cream

(below left)
1. Purée 350 g/12 oz bilberries.
2. Add to the basic mixture (see page 264–5).
3. Transfer to glasses and decorate with a few bilberries and fresh lemon balm.
Note: blueberries can be used instead of the bilberries.

Mocha cream

(below second from left)
1. Dissolve 3 tablespoons instant coffee in hot milk.
2. Continue as in the step-by-step photographs on pages 264–5.
3. Decorate with grated chocolate and icing sugar.

Pistachio cream

(below centre)
1. Chop 5 tablespoons pistachio nuts.
2. Stir the pistachios and 2 tablespoons orange liqueur into the cooled milk and egg mixture (see pages 264–5) and finally fold in the cream.
3. Decorate with a whirl of cream, orange rind, cocktail cherries and wafers.

Raspberry cream

(below second from right)
1. Purée 450 g/1 lb raspberries.
2. Add 275 g/10 oz to the milk and egg mixture (see pages 264–5) and fold in the cream.
3. Pipe the cream into glasses using a fluted nozzle.
4. Top with the remaining raspberry purée and decorate with 1 whole raspberry.

Mango cream

(below right)
1. Peel 1 mango, cut off the flesh and, keeping a few slices to one side, purée the remainder.
2. Stir into the milk and egg mixture (see pages 264–5) and fold in the cream.
3. Transfer to glasses and decorate with mango slices and praline.

Adding flavour

(For basic recipe see pages 264–5.)
Mix the basic mixture with chopped toasted hazelnuts, almonds, walnuts, candied fruit or various liqueurs, melted chocolate or nougat.
  Bavarian cream is very attractive mixed or decorated with fruit purée. Decorate with slices and leaves of fruit.

273

Thirty ideas for decorating

If necessary a steak or sole can be served with no garnish at all – but the same would be a real sin with desserts. The finale to the meal should be colourful and impressive. Desserts must appeal to the eye before they begin to make your mouth water. The ways of decorating and beautifying desserts are completely boundless. There are almost too many methods to choose from: powdering and sprinkling, pouring and piping, and even gratining. Include inedible decorations too, such as fruit leaves. For fruit purées or sorbets keep a few whole fruit to add to the decoration.

1. grated chocolate
2. natural yogurt
3. jam
4. icing sugar
5. whole almonds, blanched or unpeeled

6. lime slices
7. coffee beans
8. brown sugar
9. sponge fingers
10. praline

11. hundreds and thousands
12. candied fruit
13. strips of orange rind
14. cocoa powder
15. dessicated coconut

16. almond macaroons
17. almond slivers
18. walnuts
19. flaked almonds
20. sliced strawberries

21. chocolate vermicelli
22. violet petals
23. chocolate squares
24. pistachio nuts, chopped or whole
25. crystal sugar

26. lemon balm
27. candied ginger
28. whipped cream
29. instant coffee
30. dates

Tirami su

5 eggs, separated

200 g/7 oz sugar

2 tablespoons hot water

450 g/1 lb Mascarpone

(Italian cream cheese) or

curd cheese

14–16 sponge fingers

1. Beat the egg yolks with 150 g/5 oz sugar and water for 5 minutes until frothy.
2. Squeeze out the Mascarpone in a muslin bag.
3. Mix the egg yolk mixture with the cream or curd cheese and transfer half the mixture into a rectangular mould.
4. Arrange the biscuits side by side, just touching, over the mixture.
5. Cover with the remaining mixture and chill for at least 4 hours in the refrigerator.
6. Cut round the edge with a knife and turn out onto a plate.
7. Whisk the egg whites until stiff then whisk in the remaining sugar.
8. Spread the meringue over the dessert and serve, or brown lightly under the grill for 4 minutes.
Tip:
The sponge fingers can be sprinkled with cold coffee or liqueur before use.

Crème caramel

3 eggs

3 egg yolks

600 ml/1 pint milk

pith from 1 vanilla pod

6 tablespoons sugar

pinch of salt

butter to grease the moulds

3 tablespoons water

1. Beat together the eggs, egg yolks, milk, vanilla, half the sugar and salt.
2. Butter the moulds.
3. Place the remaining sugar in a pan with the water and melt over a moderate heat until golden brown. If the sugar becomes browner in some places, stir with a spoon so that it melts evenly.
4. Pour the caramel into the moulds to cover the base.
5. Pour the milk mixture into the moulds and cover with aluminium foil.
6. Arrange the moulds in a wide pan and add sufficient water to come half way up the moulds.
7. Cover the pan and, on a low heat, cook for 30–35 minutes. Do not allow the water to boil or you will get bubbles in the custard.
8. Lift the moulds out of the pan, leave to cool and turn out.

Red stewed fruit with sago

1 kg/2 lb mixed berries

(raspberries, red and

blackcurrants, blackberries,

strawberries, gooseberries)

300 ml/½ pint orange juice

about 225 g/8 oz sugar

(according to taste)

50 g/2 oz sago

icing sugar to dust

single cream to serve

1. Wash, trim and drain the fruit.
2. Bring to the boil with the orange juice and sugar.
3. Drain in a sieve and catch the juice.
4. Pour the juice into a pan with the sago and simmer gently over a low heat for 15 minutes.
5. Add the fruit, bring back to the boil and remove from the heat.
6. Transfer to a bowl and sprinkle with sugar to prevent a skin forming.
7. Serve with single cream.

Trifle

225 g/8 oz sponge cake
3 tablespoons raspberry jam
50 g/2 oz flaked almonds
3 tablespoons brandy
3 tablespoons sweet sherry
225 g/8 oz raspberries
500 ml/1 pint double cream
1 tablespoon icing sugar
1 vanilla pod

1. Slice enough sponge to cover the base of a ceramic dish or glass bowl.
2. Spread with raspberry jam.
3. Cut up the remaining sponge and sprinkle into the dish.
4. Sprinkle with the flaked almonds, brandy and sherry.
5. Keep 10 raspberries to decorate and arrange the remainder in the dish.
6. Whip the cream until stiff and sweeten with the sugar.
7. Halve the vanilla pod and scrape out the pith. Stir into the cream.
8. Cover the top of the trifle with cream, keeping a little back to decorate.
9. Decorate with piped rosettes of cream and the reserved raspberries.

Cranberry ice cream

4 eggs, separated
225 g/8 oz sugar
2 tablespoons hot water
350 g/12 oz cranberries,
300 ml/½ pint double cream

1. Beat the egg yolks with 175 g/6 oz sugar and the hot water over a pan of hot water for 5 minutes until frothy.
2. Remove from the water and leave to cool.
3. Simmer the cranberries with the remaining sugar over a moderate heat for 2 minutes. Remove from the heat and leave until cold.
4. In separate bowls, whisk the cream and egg whites.
5. Stir two-thirds of the cranberries into the egg yolk mixture.
6. Add the cream and a third of the egg whites.
7. Gently fold in the remaining egg white.
8. Line a loaf tin with aluminium foil, fill with the mixture and freeze for at least 6 hours.
9. Turn the ice cream out of the tin and cut into slices.
10. Serve with the remaining cranberries.

Zabaglione

2 egg yolks
2 tablespoons sugar
4 tablespoons Marsala

Serves 2
1. Place the egg yolks in a metal bowl.
2. Add the sugar and Marsala.
3. Beat with an electric whisk to give a thick but light foam.
4. Place over a pan of hot water and continue whisking until the foam is warm and light.
5. Serve zabaglione immediately before it falls.
Note: The water in the pan should not boil. Keep taking the bowl out of the water to prevent the egg congealing on the sides of the bowl and to distribute the heat evenly.

Index

Index

Contents
Index

Contents Index

Contents Index